A PROVERB IN MIND

The Cognitive Science
of Proverbial Wit and Wisdom

A PROVERB IN MIND

The Cognitive Science
of Proverbial Wit and Wisdom

Richard P. Honeck
University of Cincinnati

LAWRENCE ERLBAUM ASSOCIATES, PUBLISHERS
1997   Mahwah, New Jersey   London

Lawrence Erlbaum Associates, Inc., Publishers
10 Industrial Avenue
Mahwah, NJ 07430

Cover design by Kathryn Houghtaling

Library of Congress Cataloging-in-Publication Data

Honeck, Richard P.
   A proverb in mind : the cognitive science of proverbial
wit and wisdom / Richard P. Honeck
         p. cm
   Includes bibliographical references and index.
   ISBN 0-8058-0231-2 (alk. paper)
   1. Proverbs—History and criticism.   2. Figures of
speech.   3. Cognition.   I. Title.
PN6401.H59 1997
398.9—dc21   97-1891
                                                        CIP

Printed in the United States of America
10 9 8 7 6 5 4 3 2 1

Contents

ઠ૦ ✦ ૦ક

Preface

ॐ ◆ ௸

The proverb is a complex, intriguing, and important verbal entity. As a result, it has been the subject of a vast number of opinions, studies, and analyses. To accommodate this outpouring, seven views of the proverb have been outlined: personal, formal, religious, literary, practical, cultural, and cognitive. Because the goal of this volume is to provide a scientific understanding of proverb comprehension and production, I have drawn largely on scholarship stemming from the formal, cultural, and cognitive views. In particular, the cognitive view provides the leitmotif for this volume. The essence of this view is that there are universal principles that underlie proverb cognition, irrespective of the individuals who use proverbs or the particular situations and cultures in which they are used. To address this emphasis, it has been necessary to draw on much of what cognitive science has to offer regarding minds. The general point is that in the long run an interdisciplinary perspective will provide the best chance of understanding all aspects of proverb functioning.

There is a great deal of theoretical speculation in this volume. The speculation is mainly about proverbs, but I have also attempted to provide a larger perspective by relating the proverb to other forms of figurative language and to intelligence. The reason for this is that it is unsatisfying to treat proverbs in isolation from other language forms and from mental capacity and activity in general. In particular, proverbs have been framed in terms of a building metaphor for intelligence, and intelligence further still in terms of indirectness. Thus, for all forms of figurative language there is an indirect, nonliteral relationship between what is said and both that about which it is said and the intention in saying it. An individual's understanding of indirection would seem to require an ability to generate, build on, and integrate different layers of information. Significantly, this sort of process is apparent in every realm of human information processing, whether perception, memory, or thought.

Regarding proverbs per se, the conceptual base theory of proverb cognition has been extended via the cognitive ideals hypothesis and the DARTS model. The latter is a speculative model about cerebral hemispheric contributions to proverb comprehension. The former holds that proverbs arise from, and are comprehended and used, in part, to satisfy constraints on the universal human urge to view the world in idealistic, perfectionistic terms. The further claim is that, on some level, these ideals are relatively common to humanity. It follows both from this premise and from the premise of cognitive science that principles of great generality are at work in proverb processing.

On the surface, this approach seems to ignore the more prevalent view that proverbs are culturally specific linguistic forms that tap into unique cultural values, or even that proverbs themselves take on different weights and are used in different ways in different cultures. That, however, is not the case. The cognitive ideals hypothesis allows, nay welcomes, this diversity, while nevertheless maintaining that there are basic cognitive processes involved in all proverb usage.

This approach, though, has several consequences that many proverb scholars may find objectionable. In general, it justifies looking at proverbs independently of a given culture, context, or individual. It legitimizes all manner of experimentation with proverbs.

Of course, this sort of methodological reductionism has been the thrust of every science. There is no compelling reason to abandon it while pursuing the proverb. Perhaps my fundamental belief in this endeavor is that proverbs emerge and function to satisfy basic biocognitive urges to codify and comment on the state of the world relative to some ideal. In this case, it would be inconsistent to approach proverbs exclusively from a culturally based perspective. Moreover, a great deal of mental processing occurs in a very short period of time, and this matter is left untouched by the cultural view. In the long run, however, Humpty

Dumpty must be put back together, requiring the synthesis of several views of the proverb.

A few words should be said about the writing style in this volume. I am an experimental psychologist, but I have sometimes adopted less than the standard, impersonal scientific style, for several reasons. First, this style often fails to communicate, yet above all else this must be a writer's primary goal. Second, I want this study to be accessible to non-experts in cognitive science. This includes not only the literate lay reader, but also all those colleagues who are not experimentalists or cognitive scientists. Although cognitive science, cognitive psychology, and experimental psychology have their jargon, I have generally tried to avoid it, preferring to use equivalent terms or to explain terms when they are first introduced. This produces some redundancy of exposition for experts in cognitive science but a more understandable treatise for everyone else. For similar reasons, chapter 1 begins with a treatment of the personal view, which is the view that an individual has about the proverb. Because practically everyone has such a view, and because it sometimes has negative implications for the study of proverbs, the various personal objections to studying proverbs are described and deflated. This effort will seem spurious to some readers, but it serves to introduce some interesting observations about proverbs.

In summary, this volume has been designed with a large audience in mind. In academia, it may be most appropriate in graduate seminars, but informed undergraduates could use it as well. It is my fondest hope that this study will stimulate others to examine the proverb.

The book is therefore dedicated to all those who are interested in proverbs, minds, and cultures.

ACKNOWLEDGMENTS

Many individuals made this book possible. I especially thank the many graduate students who have worked with me during the last 27 years at the University of Cincinnati. Practically all of my discussions about proverbs, psychology, and cognitive science have been with these students. I have learned more from these discussions than they will ever know.

I am also deeply indebted to all the paremiologists who have provided the vast scholarship on the proverb. Most of these scholars are outside my home area of psychology, and this is in keeping with the interdisciplinary spirit of this volume. In this vein, I have profited from the critiques of several people who read the entire manuscript or parts thereof. Wolfgang Mieder provided commentary on the entire volume and suggested numerous non-English-language references as well. Robert Hoffman provided detailed analyses of chapters 1, 2, and 4, as well as suggestions for illustrative material. Comments by George Lakoff and Alan Paivio improved the presentation of the Great Chain Metaphor theory and the Dual-coding theory of proverb comprehension, respectively, in chapter 4. I have also benefited from discussions with Jon Temple and Jeffrey Welge on the cognitive ideals hypothesis. Finally, comments by an anonymous reviewer motivated a thorough copyediting of the book.

Various individuals at the University of Cincinnati provided necessary copying, inter-library loans, and other support services. Shirley Doxsey and Andy Geers were generous in these efforts.

The staff at Lawrence Erlbaum Associates has been unduly patient in waiting for a finished product from me. I owe special thanks to acquisitions editor Judi Amsel for her friendly and professional shepherding of this volume through to completion, and for her comments on the manuscript as well.

Finally, I would like to thank my wife, Joan, for putting up with my incessant discussions and long hours at the computer.

1

Views of the Proverb

⋄

Most adults know some proverbs. Proverbs are an intuitive aspect of their mental functioning. What is less intuitive is how proverbs are used and understood. This volume takes up this challenge. It is not an easy one, however, because proverbs draw on most of the mind's powers. Moreover, a great deal of proverb mind work can be accomplished in a brief moment. Our emphasis, therefore, is on the mental processes that occur in the actual use of proverbs.

Because proverbs are complex, an interdisciplinary perspective is needed to explain how people use and understand them. Enter cognitive science, a discipline dedicated to solving the puzzle of the mind by using concepts that originate within psychology, linguistics, neurology, artificial intelligence, and the philosophy of language and mind. The puzzle has not been completely solved, but good progress has been made. Thus cognitive science provides our best prospect for revealing the secrets of the proverb.

ORGANIZATION AND GOALS

This volume has seven chapters. In this first chapter seven general views of the proverb are delineated, three that have avowed scientific goals and four that do not. The focus is on the cognitive view, the leitmotif for the study. This chapter also serves to acquaint the reader with the proverb. Chapter 2 discusses proverbs in conjunction with five other forms of figurative language: simile, metaphor, oxymoron, idiom, and metonymy. As we look into proverb processing in chapter 3 it is discovered that practically every major issue in the study of mind is raised.

1

Chapter 4 describes both old and new theories of proverb comprehension and examines their ability to explain proverb microcognition (i.e., the memory and thought interactions that occur during proverb use). Chapter 5 travels under, inside, and outside the proverb while trying to understand how it is created, what its internal dynamics are, and how it applies to various events. Because it takes a healthy, reasonably intelligent 7-year-old brain to comprehend a proverb, the topics of brain, mental development, and intelligence are treated together in chapter 6. Speculation on new studies, new theories, and new applications forms the core of chapter 7.

This volume does not intend merely to summarize or integrate prior analyses of the proverb. In practically every chapter, the author has theorized and speculated about a number of matters. In some cases new perspectives or theoretical ideas about proverbs are offered: the various views presented in this chapter, a systematic way of looking at proverbs and other figurative genres, and the cognitive ideals hypothesis about the conceptual basis of proverbs with its implications for many aspects of proverb cognition. A neurological model of proverb comprehension called DARTS is also proffered, along with an overall framework for appreciating the intelligence behind proverb use.

In the meantime we can get more acquainted with the proverb, then take up the seven views about it.

PROVERBS IN ACTION

Adults in practically every culture have been exposed to some proverbs. In English-speaking American culture they include such familiar forms as these: *The grass is always greener on the other side of the fence* and *A rolling stone gathers no moss*, as well as the less familiar, *All clocks are off* and *Once burned, twice shy*. These proverbs are presented here without a context, something that rarely happens in everyday life. Consider therefore the following more ecologically valid cases.

A College Scene

A college student is discussing his situation with his mother. The young man is doing poorly in his courses and having some interpersonal problems as well. He is trying to convince his mother that it would be better if he could drop out of the public university where he is going and enroll in a smaller but more expensive private university. His mother thinks that he is not working at his studies, that his interpersonal problems should be dealt with, and that the family cannot afford to send him to a private university. The discussion continues for a while before she finally says, *The grass is always greener on the other side of the fence* (Mieder, 1993b, provides a larger perspective on this proverb).

By uttering this proverb the young man's mother seems to be telling her son that he needs to reassess his current situation and deal more adequately with the problems it presents rather than move off to a new and presumably less problematic situation. She is also teaching him to think more broadly about the problems that life presents, in that although it is always possible to imagine better circumstances, sometimes one must stick with the present circumstance and work things out.

An African Scene

Penfield and Duru (1988) described a situation in which Chike, a child from a poor family of Igbo society in Nigeria, has become friends with Obi, a child from a wealthy family. Obi spends his family's money freely and carelessly. Chike's uncle, who has become aware of the situation, seeks Chike out and says to him, "I see you are very friendly with Obi. Remember, *If a rat follows the lizard into the rain they both get drenched*" (Penfield & Duru, 1988, p. 121).

Here, Chike's uncle is advising Chike to do something so that he will not be seen with Obi by other members of the community, because Obi (i.e., the lizard who dries off quickly) has resources that Chike (i.e., the rat that cannot dry off quickly) does not. Thus, Chike could be harmed.

A Baseball Scene

It is the big championship game between two Little League teams. The score is tied 7 to 7 in the bottom of the ninth inning. There are two outs and a runner on second base. The batter hits what looks like a routine groundball toward the shortstop, but just as he is about to pick it up, the ball hits a small stone and takes a hop over the shortstop's shoulder. The runner on second base scores the tie-breaking run that wins the championship. The coach of the losing team, who had seen what happened to the ball, turns to an assistant and says, *Great weights hang on small wires.*

Here, the coach has summarized the sad outcome by invoking the general principle that important outcomes in life can sometimes depend on unforeseen, chancy, and seemingly unimportant details. The proverb undoubtedly functions to soften the blow of losing the big game by integrating what happened into the bigger scheme of things, as if to say, "This kind of thing happens once in a while and there isn't much you can do about it. Let's not get too upset."

VIEWS OF THE PROVERB

The history of proverb use is interesting but cloudy. A case could be made that proverbs were invented shortly after the faculty of speech developed. Of course, our only way of knowing when proverbs were first used is through recorded history. The first recorded instances of writing were those of the Sumerians, who settled the Mesopotamian area in present-day Iraq as early as 5,000 BC. The Sumerians used wedge-shaped instruments on wet clay to produce cuneiform writing, which has been dated to about 3,500 BC, at the earliest (Fagan, 1979). Cuneiform had unique phonetic interpretations in the Sumerian language, but the cuneiform symbols were borrowed by the Akkadian people who replaced the Sumerians and used their own pronunciation of the symbols. According to Gordon (1959), the first cuneiform proverb collections were bilingual Akkadian and Sumero-Akkadian. Proverb-like statements also appear in a Babylonian source of about 1,440 BC (Beardslee, 1970). Later uses in the Hebrew and Christian Bibles are well known.

Although the history of proverbs within the species is sketchy, it is clear that the proverb has fascinated the layperson as well as the scholar. Paremiology, the study of proverbs, is practiced by many different kinds of people including cultural anthropologists, psychologists, folklorists, linguists, sociologists, educators, psychiatrists, historians, students of religion, literature buffs, and even lawyers, advertising executives, management consultants, and an occasional proverb afficionado. It should not be surprising that all of this interest in and resulting vast literature on the proverb has yielded different goals, perspectives, assumptions, methodologies, findings, and theoretical conclusions.

The result is that there is no overarching theory of proverbs. Instead, different views have emerged. Seven reasonably distinguishable views regarding the proverb exist:

Personal: The proverb is treated from a subjective viewpoint based purely on personal experience and understanding.

Formal: This is a scientific approach that primarily uses the methods and concepts of linguistics, logic, and semiotics to define, classify and otherwise analyze proverbs.

Religious: Religious teaching and wisdom are examined in texts such as Bibles.

Literary: Proverbs in prose and poetry are analyzed in terms of their literary value and what they tell us about the writer, their times, and so forth.

Practical: The many uses of the proverb in intelligence testing, advertising, psychotherapy, and other areas are examined.

Cultural: This is a scientific approach to the proverb that treats it as a multifunction form of folk literature that arises from and is embedded in a sociocultural context.

Cognitive: This is a scientific approach based on cognitive science that attempts to explain how individuals use and understand proverbs. This view is the foundation for this study.

Each of these views has something unique and positive to contribute to our knowledge of the proverb, but they do not contribute equally to our understanding of proverb cognition. The personal, religious, literary and practical views rarely have scientific goals. The formal, cultural, and cognitive views do, but differ in goals, assumptions, methods, and theoretical products. There has been cross-fertilization between all of the scholarly views, except for the cognitive view, which has remained relatively isolated from the others. On a larger scale, cognitive scientific interest and research on the proverb has lagged behind that of the noncognitive scientific views, and there has been little rapproachment between the two. A major goal of this study is to begin to remedy these deficiencies.

The seven views are now described in detail. Because the formal, cultural, and cognitive views play a much larger role in elucidating proverb cognition, these views are more elaborated. The goal of this endeavor is to provide the flavor of each view rather than a state-of-the-art treatment, and to do this by sampling ideas and research that have flowed from each view.

The Personal View

The personal view might also be called the phenomenological, subjective, or folk view. Most people in all cultures have knowledge of some proverbs, along with various proclivities, attitudes, and tidbits of information about them. As with puns, there are proverb lovers, haters, and apathetics.

The personal view is in most respects an egocentric and nonscientific view, even though it derives from specific cultural experience with proverbs and may entail scientifically valid ideas. It is a starting point for a scientific view, but it sometimes moves off in antiscientific directions.

In its extreme form, the personal view essentially takes the position that personal acquaintance with proverbs confers a complete knowledge of their nature and function. That is, if one can identify and use what the culture considers to be proverbs, then one "knows about" proverbs. The corollary assumption is that there is not much more to be learned about them. This is akin to believing that because one can experience and take into account the effects of gravity then one knows about gravity. On one level such assertions are true, but they are scientifically inadequate. Although personal reactions to proverbs can sometimes be quite positive, they also can be negative. Some of the latter are presented in the following discussion that moves from the less to the more sophisticated objections and provides a reaction to them.

The Romantic Objection

"I hate proverbs. Don't even talk to me about them."

This is a head-in-the-sand objection, emotionally based, and hardly worth debating. Perhaps the objection tells us something about the people who make it. Individuals who voice this objection maybe could, with some effort, be made into proverb lovers.

Moreover, there are several good reasons why people may hate proverbs. Proverbs preach, and people dislike being preached to. Also, proverbs do not say anything fundamentally new, an objection discussed in the section on emotion in chapter 7.

The Aesthetic Objection

"Yes I know what a proverb is. I even use one from time to time, but they seem trite (mundane, commonplace, lowly, hackneyed, gauche, etc.), so what possible theoretical value can they have?"

This frequent objection confuses aesthetics with scientific importance. One could just as well argue that idioms, slang, and other relatively frozen forms of language should also go unstudied because they seem trite as well. Moreover, moving out of the language realm, any form of triteness should be left untouched according to this criterion, including gestures, clothing habits, music, and even lifestyles. Of course, *Familiarity breeds contempt.*

The "Sayings" Objection

"Proverbs are just sayings, like the things my parents told me. What do they have to do with anything?"

This objection is similar to the triteness objection. Its proponents may not have considered either the ramifications of proverbs, or the larger issue of language, who uses it, and why. As for triteness, it overlooks the potential importance of familiar events. The attitude conveyed may say more about someone's view of their parents and authority figures in general than about anything else, proverbs included. On one level, "Energy is the same as mass" is a saying, but it has great theoretical and practical punch.

The Utilitarian Objection

"What earthly value do proverbs have? Study things that have some practical value."

The antiscience lament, this objection. Presumably, Gregor Mendel was just doing gardening when he systematically observed the characteristics of the common pea, and Barbara

McClintock was wasting her time while toying with the genetic properties of corn. Then too, proverbs do have practical value in advertising, psychotherapy, and other aspects of everyday life (see The Practical View section later). In Western countries, proverbs are less esteemed than they are in some non-Western countries where they serve important social and formal-legalistic functions.

The Phenomenological Objection

"I guess I heard or read some proverbs and I just learned them on the spot. They're in my long-term memory and I know what they mean. I don't feel that I do any complex computations when I use them. They're like a mental reflex. It's not clear to me what light they shed on any important psychological issues."

This objection, although it contains some interesting observations and suggests an educable frame of mind, also assumes some false premises. Although what most people call proverbs probably are in long-term memory, can be accessed rapidly, and have meanings that can be quickly assembled, none of these assertions, even when true, argue against the complexity of proverb processing and the need for a scientific analysis. Phenomenology may tell us that some mental events happen quickly and effortlessly, but this has limited bearing on the complexity of these events. Furthermore, cognitive scientists have discovered that just those kinds of mental processes that occur quickly and effortlessly (e.g., recognizing patterns, talking, playing the piano, etc.) have been very resistant to simulation by computer.

The Frequency Objection

"Proverbs are rare. We should spend more time and effort studying things that are commonplace."

If this kind of objection were true and acted on, then many phenomena would never be investigated, including the magnetic monopole, various heavy atomic elements, rare diseases, certain forms of mental retardation including that of savants, and so on. By itself, frequency of occurrence is an invalid criterion for deciding whether to investigate anything. The particulars of the objection are debateable as well, because we would have to settle on what a proverb is and what standard would be used to decide its relative frequency.

The Ambiguity Objection

"Different people produce different interpretations for the same proverb, the height of nonsense!" (After reading about my view of proverbs in an article in Sky Magazine, which is furnished to passengers on the Delta airline, one person called to ask me why anyone would want to investigate proverbs. He had remembered that the proverb, A rolling stone gathers no moss, *had received differing interpretations, and was skeptical about people coming up with not just different interpretations, but apparently contradictory interpretations.)*

This objection affirms that proverbs can be ambiguous but then goes on to imply that, like triteness, impracticality, and rarity, ambiguity obviates their scientific study. To the contrary, ambiguity is part of the fascination of proverbs. Moreover, despite the ambiguity inherent in all proverbs, as in essentially all language, there is probably something resembling a standard, normative interpretation, even when unfamiliar proverbs are presented without context. In general, of course, ambiguity does not block science: it only invites it. To be sure, my phone critic did pick out a particularly ambiguous proverb.

The Consistency Objection

"Some proverbs, such as Look before you leap *and* He who hesitates is lost, *contradict each other, and what are we supposed to make of the contradictions?"*

This objection takes ambiguity a step further. It seems silly that proverbs are not only ambiguous but contradictory as well. This objection, however, is overfocused, and simultaneously fails to recognize the scientific, cognitive, and cultural importance of contradictions.

Culturally, contradictions abound: in business, be competitive but nice; in sex, be aggressive but sensitive; in assessments of others' products, be critical but civil; pursue excellence, but do not crow over your achievements, and so on. Such contradictions are ripe areas for investigation *because* of the contradiction.

Consider the importance of the dilemma that light can be particle-like under some circumstances but wave-like under others. Rather than being an annoyance, incongruities should motivate further inquiry. Furthermore, as mentioned previously, proverbs are not statements whose empirical faithfulness is at stake, but means of construing situations. That is, proverbs are used to say, "For this case, look at it this way because there is some benefit to be gained from looking at it this way." Thus, the contradictoriness of proverbs may well dissolve when the context in which they are used is taken into account. Proverbs do have some truth value in that they are based on ideals, norms, and standards, but these premises are assumed to be true. They are not being tested as such.

The Linguistics Pragmatics Objection

"Well, proverbs are interesting, but they're just things that people use when they want to make a point. Is there anything more to it?"

This objection holds promise: there is an openness to it. A short discussion usually persuades people that making points is not only an important human activity but that proverbs are ideally suited to the task. In the process of explaining this, people learn a lot about how a number of cognitive processes have to occur for any linguistic utterance to make a point. It is nevertheless strange that recognition of a commonplace pragmatic function does not evoke the realization that it requires skill. It as if we were to watch a surgeon move a scalpel around in the brain without appreciating the expertise behind the act. Perhaps the problem is that language is such an intrinsic part of humanity that it is hard to take the bird's perspective and appreciate the expertise involved.

The Linguistic Reductionism Objection

"Proverbs are just metaphors (idioms, aphorisms, old sayings, etc.), so if you study metaphors you don't have to study proverbs. You can kill two birds with one stone (sic!)."

This sophisticated objection could be true, but at present no such conclusion can be drawn. There is good reason to believe that proverbs are not metaphors. For example, proverbs are more likely than metaphors to act as summary devices, occur at the end of discourse, be used by people in authority, be conversationally deviant, and be remembered. In general, there is a clear need to make fine-grained distinctions among the various tropes (kinds of figurative language) and not simply lump them together as metaphors, while simultaneously and without contradiction holding the position that the same general principles apply to their processing and use. (Chapter 2 discusses these matters in some detail.)

All of the preceding expressions of the personal view amount to pessimistic and, in some cases, blatantly antiscientific attitudes about proverbs. Although the personal view can foster such attitudes, it need not. The personal view can be a springboard for a science of proverbs. Indeed, it has been claimed that proverbs act as theories that various investigators have (unconsciously) sought to verify by empirical means. For example, proverbs such as *Birds of a feather flock together*; *Like father, like son*; and *Laugh and the world laughs with you, cry and you cry alone* have been confirmed by empirical work on attractiveness, heritability, and personal preference, respectively. In contrast, some proverbs seemingly have been falsified, such as *Ignorance is bliss*; *A tale never loses in the telling*; and *Familiarity breeds contempt* (Rogers, 1990). Clearly, personal experience with proverbs does not prevent recognition of their personal importance, and it may facilitate a more substantive understanding. Many people, in fact, find proverbs to be very interesting verbal beasts. Otherwise the literature on proverbs would not be so vast.

The Formal View

The formal view is characterized by attempts to describe the linguistic and semantic-logic properties of proverbs. Often the goal is to define the proverb in these terms. In other cases, the goal is to create a proverb typology.

Defining the Proverb. From a linguistic standpoint, a proverb is a phonological, syntactic, semantic, pragmatic, and, some would add, a semiotic (complex sign) entity. There is no question that all proverbs exhibit regularities on one or more of these levels. But then, so do other tropes. Perhaps, then, our starting point should be a discussion of proverb identity, which amounts in part to distinguishing proverbs from other forms. Just the flavor of the issue is provided here. It is taken up again in chapter 2 when proverbs are compared to other tropes.

There is a vast literature that attempts to lay bare the essence of the proverb. In his early modern overview of this literature, Whiting (1932) noted that the proverb was highly valued among the Greeks and Romans. Socrates noted its brevity, philosophical tone, and common usage. Plato used proverbs, but Aristotle was more analytical and provided perhaps a first definition that made antiquity, conciseness, and ease of quotation essential aspects of the proverb (Whiting, 1932).

Somewhat more precise definitions emerged later, including that by Michael Apostolius of Byzantium, who wrote in the 15th century saying, "A proverb is a statement which conceals the clear in the unclear, or which through concrete images indicates intellectual concepts, or which makes clear the truth in furtive fashion" (Whiting, 1932, p. 287). In this same quote, Apostolius mentioned the use of the proverb in everyday speech and its applicability to a range of events, as well as its usefulness, concealing powers, and exhortative uses. Whiting went on to trace definitions of the proverb through various German and English versions, including an early definition that a proverb is "an old said saw," used by Sir Thomas More in 1528. The many later English collectors of proverbs also provided a variety of definitions.

These early attempts could no doubt be content analyzed to provide the elements for a larger definition. Moreover, it is likely that the definition would closely match that rendered by Mieder (1993a), who asked various people to write definitions of the proverb. Using an analysis of 55 definitions, he formulated the following general definition: "A proverb is a short, generally known sentence of the folk which contains wisdom, truth, morals and traditional views in a metaphorical, fixed and memorizable form and which is handed down from generation to generation" (Mieder, 1993a, p. 24). This definition is serviceable but contains components such as "metaphorical" and "fixed" that need further explication. Also, the definition reflects the personal and cultural views of the proverb but leaves out other views.

Norrick (1985) has provided a systematic, feature-based approach to distinguishing proverbs from other forms. The features he mentioned include whether the form is or is not a full propositional statement, used basically in conversations, in common use, spoken, a fixed form, didactic, general, figurative, prosodic/poetic, entertaining, and humorous. In this scheme, proverbs are positive on the first seven dimensions; optional on figurativeness, prosody, and humor; and negative on entertaining. This scheme presumably allows distinctions among proverbs, clichés, Wellerisms (e.g., "So I see, said the blind man as he picked up his hammer and saw"), curses, proverbial phrases (e.g., "Where there's a will there's a way"), riddles, jokes, tales, songs, slogans, and aphorisms (e.g., "When in doubt, tell the truth"). By this approach, clichés such as "The fat is in the fire" and "Farewell and be hanged" are similar to proverbs except that they are not didactic and have optional generality, whereas the proverb is didactic and always general. A proverbial phrase (e.g., "to face the music" or "up the creek") is not a conversationally free form, not didactic, and not generalizable, whereas the proverb is all of these things.

Norrick's (1985) feature-based approach undoubtedly captures some real differences among the genres he considers. However, such an approach fosters dichotomies when there may be continua, and it leaves situation and context out of the picture, factors that will have a heavy impact on the relevance and properties of a particular feature. Depending on the situation, for example, a proverbial phrase such as "face the music" could be a conversationally free form and highly didactic. In general, feature-based approaches tend to emphasize structure at the expense of function, something that simply cannot be done with proverbs.

Silverman-Weinreich's (1978) examination of hundreds of Yiddish proverbs is instructive on this point. She began with the assertion that proverb definition must be function based and that this function is "to point out that a given specific situation or occurrence illustrates an accepted general rule with which the hearer must already be acquainted" (p. 70). To fulfill its function, the proverb takes on characteristic linguistic properties as evidenced by formal markers of some kind. What are these markers?

Silverman-Weinreich (1978) found that, on the phonological level, Yiddish proverbs may use rhyme (e.g., *Man proposes, God disposes*), assonance (e.g., *Frog forgets he had a tail*), consonance (e.g., *There's many a slip twixt cup and lip*), alliteration (e.g., *Let a sleeping lion lie*), and metric patterning, by which there is a balance of stressed and unstressed syllables (e.g., *A nasty tongue is worse than a wicked hand*).

Syntactic patterns are present as well. The typical Yiddish proverb is a self-contained sentence in that it can be interpreted in the absence of context. Personal pronouns and articles that would refer to prior events are lacking. In this sense proverbs are impersonal and timeless, with the occasional use of "one" to be taken in a general way.

Perhaps the most critical aspect of the proverb, not just the Yiddish proverb, is that the grammatical subject of the proverb is "abstract, generic, or symbolic" (Silverman-Weinreich, 1978, p. 72), and the main verb is almost always stated in the present (nonpast) or, less often, the future tense. It is unlikely that proverbs set in the past tense exist, because such usage almost always particularizes an utterance and robs it of its omnitemporal and polysituational potential. Within this constraint, however, there seems to be no limit on the kind of sentence that can be used to frame a proverb. Silverman-Weinreich (1978) illustrated the use of conditional, comparative, imperative, negative, and even interrogative (e.g., *Just because one is angry with the cantor, need one stop saying "amen"?*), and riddle-like (e.g., *A word is like an arrow; both are in a great hurry*) patterns. She also pointed to other grammatical patterns such as the adjective + noun "is better/worse than" adjective + noun pattern as in *A constant penny is better than a rare ruble,* and the ellipsis of the verb pattern as in *Sharply bargained, honestly paid.* Such syntactic variety flies in the face of the oft-heard claim that proverbs are formulaic.

Whereas many proverbs are grammatical, some are not, as demonstrated by verb elliptical proverbs. In some cases, the ungrammaticality is extreme, as for some of the proverbs examined by Norrick (1985): *Sure bind, sure find; Fair in the cradle and fair in the saddle; Who is guilty suspects everybody; Fancy may bolt[sift] bran and think it flour.* Norrick claimed that many ungrammatical proverbs can be considered as cases of radical ellipsis, overextensions of conventional grammatical rules, formulaic, or lexically archaic and requiring special lexical knowledge.

Silverman-Weinreich (1978) found that the Yiddish proverb typically uses one or more semantic markers. These include allegory, by which, when taken literally, a proverb seems irrelevant to its discourse context, metaphor (e.g., *Need is a chain around the neck* and *Policemen catch flies and let hornets go free*), semantic parallelism (e.g., *The tavern won't ruin the good person and the synagogue won't reform the bad person*), irony (e.g., *A luckless person falls on his back and hurts his nose*), paradox (e.g., *All clocks are off*), and other patterns as well.

Silverman-Weinreich (1978) concluded: "Every Yiddish proverb then seems to have at least two grammatical markers (nomic verb and generic or abstract subject), one distinctive semantic feature (metaphor, paradox, sharp or surprising contrasts), and generally at least one phonic device as well (rhyme, assonance, consonance, alliteration, meter)" (p. 80).

The importance of these various markers is underlined in a study by Arora (1984). In this empirical study, 46 Spanish-speaking residents of Los Angeles were provided with 25 statements and asked to indicate whether each statement was either a known proverb, not previously encountered but probably a proverb, or not a proverb. Only 2 of the 25 statements were actual proverbs, however. The remaining statements varied in terms of how many identifying features (markers) they incorporated, including a common structural pattern, rhyme, assonance, metaphor, and even vague meaning. The results indicated that the pseudoproverbs were judged as "probably proverbs" anywhere from 14% to 78% of the time, with overall perceived proverbiality for these items increasing somewhat because some were judged to be actual proverbs. Arora (1984) concluded that many of the pseudoproverbs probably could be used as real proverbs in some context, although she avoided considering such usages as proverbs. Nevertheless, Arora (1984) clearly recognized the proverb currency issue in attempting to define the proverb, stating that, "the hearer's perception of proverbiality may help to understand why it is so very difficult to arrive at an all-inclusive definition of a proverb, and why attempts to analyze the proverb on a cross-cultural or universal basis invariably meet with but limited success" (p. 29). In other words, Arora was on the verge of saying that if a statement is used in such a way that it is perceived as proverbial, then it is a proverb, an opinion that comports more with the cognitive than the cultural view of proverbs.

A more theoretical approach to the linguistics of the proverb was offered by Cram (1994). He began with the assumption that proverbs are word-like and operate as wholes, while also being relatively grammatical and sentential. This presents a problem for Chomskyan transformational grammar in which there is a strict separation between the lexicon and the syntax. Cram's (1994) solution is to place proverbs in the lexicon and to introduce a special loop between the proverb's lexical entry and its syntax. This loop "relates the lexical entry to the phrase structure rules of the syntax" (p. 76). In essence, a proverb is marked as such in the lexicon, along with the usual markers such as noun, verb, and so on. This marking places constraints on how a proverb can be operated on as a syntactic unit.

Cram (1994) also claimed that proverbs have a quotational status in that they are "invoked or cited" rather than used in a propositional way (p. 75). What is being invoked is a culturally based belief. Cram noted in this context that although proverbs may appear to be idioms—some proverbs are idiomatic, such as *Birds of a feather flock together*—they are not idioms, in that most proverbs do not act like idioms, and there is no principled linguistic reason why proverbs must be treated as idioms. In particular, proverbs, but not idioms, are similar to quotations and typically are introduced by tags such as, "Well, you know what they say," "As the saying goes," and so forth. People do not say, "Well, you know what they say, 'She spilled the beans'." Moreover, knowing a proverb does not necessarily mean that one can use it appropriately, as Arewa and Dundes (1964) claimed, because usage requires sensitivity to the speech context, the relationship between the speaker and hearer, appropriateness, and so on. Insofar as proverbs are invoked, they seem like performatives (Austin, 1962), utterances that perform some function such as to marry, promise or ordain. But Cram noted that there are differences as well, in that proverbs, but not performatives, can be referred to elliptically, and illocutionary adverbs (e.g., "hereby") are not allowed along with proverb tags. Cram (1994) argued that the cultural authority of the proverb, its presumption of cultural wisdom, and its wholistic nature make it a "metalinguistic speech act," akin to invoking a rule rather than playing by one.

Cram (1994) also argues that the usual rules of sentence semantics do not apply to proverbs in the sense that different proverbs can be either contradictory or synonymous. For example, *Fools rush in where angels fear to tread* and *Look before you leap* are properly treated as lexical synonymy. Thus, proverbs appear to function as simple assertions whose empirical truth value can be decided, but they, in fact, have more the force of analytic (logically necessary) truths. The reason for this is that proverbs are assumed to be true in some particular context, and these contexts are sought out. According to Cram (1994), "Proverbs are not used to reason about the world but are used as formulae to impose categories and meaning upon events, and their invocation carries the tacit gloss: 'That's just the way things are, and that's all there is to it'. In short, the proverb has the status of a quasi-tautological axiom which is not to be belied" (p. 90). In time, the topics to which proverbs get applied change, and so proverbs become quaint.

Cram's (1994) analysis seems proper in his emphasis on the quotational status of the proverb, its distinction vis-à-vis idioms, and its analytic-like force. The linguistics of the argument is suspect, however, because it leads to undocumented and probably false assertions (e.g., that two proverbs be treated as lexically rather than sententionally synonymous). In general, there is a bias both in the formal and cultural views (see later) to impute a lexicalized (word-like) status to proverbs, as if one could assume without empirical documentation that proverb meanings are stored in memory as wholes that are easily accessed.

In several papers, Norrick (1981, 1994a) elucidated the indirectness of proverbs by setting them in the context of speech act theory (Austin, 1962; Searle, 1969) and conversational implicature (Grice, 1975). In speech act theory, someone can say something (a locutionary act) that performs a different (illocutionary) act and that has some (perlocutionary) effect on someone else. Thus, if a friend hurts her finger, one can say, "That's terrible," a locution, that serves as an illocutionary act of assertion and that may have the perlocutionary effect of our friend recognizing our sympathy. An illocutionary act can be quite distant from the locutionary act, in which case there is an indirect speech act. For example, assuming that George wants to end a conversation with Linda, he might say, "Don't you have an appointment some-

where?" which is literally a question, but has the conveyed meaning of George telling Linda that he wants to stop talking.

For Norrick (1994a), proverbs are "doubly indirect" in that they
act as quotes, a la Cram (1994), that come from the larger culture
rather than the speaker, and their message is not isomorphic with
their literal meaning. Norrick claimed that proverbs are used to
avoid double binds in interpersonal situations because the proverb allows the speaker "to disguise his true feelings, to leave
himself an escape route, to offer his hearer choices and to indicate
real or imagined consensus" (p. 148). Therefore, proverbs are
natural choices for the perlocutionary acts of instructing, consol-
ing, warning, and the like. Norrick also argued that such effects
are intentional and can have either short-term or long-term
effects.

In conclusion, although attempts to define the proverb have
been interesting and highly informative, there is no generally
agreed upon definition. A proverb can be regarded as *A discourse
deviant, relatively concrete, present (nonpast) tense statement that
uses characteristic linguistic markers to arouse cognitive ideals
that serve to categorize topics in order to make a pragmatic point
about them.* This mouthful will not completely satisfy all scholars
including the author of this volume. The problem is that, like any
good definition, it should flow from an adequate theory. Paremiology comes up a bit short on this score. Perhaps Archer Taylor
(1931), one of the century's premier proverb scholars, had this in
mind when he penned the following (what could be called "Taylor's
Curse"):

> The definition of a proverb is too difficult to repay the undertaking;
> and should we fortunately combine in a single definition all the
> essential elements and give each the proper emphasis, we should not
> even then have a touchstone. An incommunicable quality tells us this
> sentence is proverbial and that one is not. Hence, no definition will
> enable us to identify positively a sentence as proverbial. Those who
> do not speak a language can never recognize all its proverbs, and
> similarly much that is truly proverbial escapes us in Elizabethan and
> older English. Let us be content with recognizing that a proverb is a
> saying current among the folk. At least so much of a definition is
> indisputable, and we shall see and weigh the significance of other
> elements later. (p. 3)

Proverb Taxonomies. A second major aspect of the formal view involves the search for a proverb taxonomy. Various classification schemes have been fashioned, based on what their creators believed is the semantics or semantic logic that underlies all proverbs. Because these schemes are rather extensive in some cases, only a brief look at them will be provided.

In his classic text, *The Proverb*, Taylor (1931) included a long chapter on the content of proverbs. The chapter is divided into sections with the following titles: customs and superstitions, historical proverbs, legal proverbs, "blason populaire," weather proverbs, medical proverbs, conventional phrases, and proverbial prophecies. This is a beginning, but content analysis will not get us very far theoretically.

Milner (1969) and Dundes (1975) proposed proverb classification systems based on the assumption that proverbs express semantic oppositions. Milner (1969) asserted that proverbs have a quadripartite structure built on a symmetry of form and content such that a proverb has two halves (major segments), a head and a tail, and each half has two minor segments. Each minor segment can have either a + or a − value. Thus there are 16 possible categories into which a proverb can be thrown. The 16 can be reduced to 4 main categories, A, B, C, and D, in which A has a positive (+) head and positive (+) tail, B is − +, C is + −, and D is − −. For example, *Soon ripe, soon rotten* is designated soon (+), ripe (+), soon (+), rotten (−), in which case the proverb belongs in category C, because only the + + combination yields a plus, whereas all other combinations yield a negative.

There are many criticisms of this approach. Gryzbek (1987) stated that it is too subjective and too focused on the denotative (literal) level. Dundes (1975) opined that the advantage of such classification is unclear, and that the quadripartite assumption is lacking and leads to unfortunate implications (e.g., that proverbs not having this structure actually once had it). It therefore leads to automatic omission of negative cases; it is subjective (as for a "rolling stone" example); and minor segments cannot be defined in isolation from the other segments.

Dundes (1975) offered his own classification, which is based on the notion of semantic oppositions such as one–two, good–bad, before–after, and little–great. His typology postulates oppositional and nonoppositional proverbs. The former include *One swallow does not make a summer*, a case of simple negation; *You can't have your cake and eat it too*, a mutual exclusivity; and *A straight stick is crooked in the water*, which is antithetical in nature. Nonoppositional proverbs include *Money talks, Haste makes waste, A bargain is a bargain*, and *Where there's a will there's a way*. Dundes presented this classification in the context of a comparison between proverbs and riddles. He claimed that riddles are similar to proverbs, although for riddles the answer (referent) is provided, whereas (oppositional) proverbs only pose them. Whatever one thinks of Dundes' scheme, perhaps the major point is one made by Dundes (1975) himself, namely that proverbs are designed to compare and contrast things.

Kuusi (1972) has also proffered a cross-language classification scheme based on the hypothesis of binary opposition: "Every proverb can be interpreted as a selection between two alternative responses" (p. 16). He postulated two superordinate categories: Type Groups 1 and 2. Type Group 1 involves oppositions of the form, one:two (many), as illustrated by the idea that "It is not good to *x* alone; it is good to *x* together." Examples of this include: *Loneliness will wipe you out* (Zulu) and *Where there is no antagonist you cannot quarrel* (Japanese). Another subcategory of Type Group 1 is: One hand (finger, thing) does not perform its task (instead of two hands, etc.). Examples include: *It takes the clap of two hands to make a sound* (Korean) and *One leg cannot dance alone* (Thonga). In total, Type Group 1 includes 15 subcategories. Type Group 2 involves binary oppositions of the form; one part:the whole. Subcategories include: One ingredient (of *x*) does not make (is not) *X*. Examples are: *One tree does not make a forest* (Ashanti) and *One grain fills not a sack* (Portuguese). Another subcategory is: "One member (of a family) suffers, all others (another member) suffer(s)." Examples include: *One finger gashed—all the fingers covered with blood* (Nkundu) and *Pinch the right thigh and the left feels it* (Malay). Kuusi lists six subcategories for Type Group 2.

Kuusi (1972) acknowledged the problems for his own scheme: proverbs that are not easily categorized, proverbs that can only be interpreted with difficulty to have a binary structure, and the problem of coming up with the right generalization as a category description.

Binary opposition undoubtedly occurs in some proverbs, but not all, and perhaps not even in a majority. Hence, opposition is neither necessary nor sufficient as a way of ordering and classifying proverbs, so it cannot be considered a fundamental property of proverbs. The fact that opposition does occur is nevertheless an important insight, one, as contended in this volume, that is derivative of a more basic property of proverbs, namely that proverbs are based on ideals, norms, and standards, whereas opposition, contradiction, and the like are a means of expressing deviation from the ideal (chapter 4 presents this cognitive ideals hypothesis).

A more theoretically oriented approach to proverb classification is that of Permyakov's (1970). Gryzbek (1987), a semiotician, provided a summary of Permyakov's view which is heavily relied on here (see also Zolkovskij, 1978).

Permyakov had proverbs act as both signs and models of particular referent situations. He made proverbs clichés on a denotative level and models on the connotative level. This is here interpreted to mean that the literal meaning of a proverb is a relatively fixed linguistic entity and that the modeling function is accomplished via figurative meaning. Permyakov looked at proverbs in terms of three planes: linguistic, realia, and logico-semiotic. "Realia" is here interpreted to mean the referent or topic for the proverb and "logico-semiotic" to mean the general kinds of situations modeled by proverbs.

It is the logico-semiotic plane that got Permyakov into the classification business, as he distinguished four kinds of higherorder invariants. These invariants are general properties of proverbs in that a set of proverbs share some abstract conceptual structure. This structure, in Gryzbek's (1987) terms, is the p:q in the a:b::p:q::c:d analogy, in which a and b are ideas taken from the literal proverb level, p and q are analogous interpretive ideas, and c and d are ideas about some referent for the proverb. Gryzbek (1987) used Crépeau's (1975) notion that the first part of the analogy generates a "proverb idea" or "une idée générale" (p. 48), a formulation very similar to the idea of a conceptual base (Honeck & Temple, 1994; Honeck, Voegtle, Dorfmueller, & Hoffman, 1980). For example, the same underlying structure is presumably shared by *No fire without smoke, No rose without thorns*, and *No river without bank*, because the first part requires the second part. Permyakov therefore separates meaning from logical classification and, according to Gryzbek, makes thematic matters a fourth and separate plane. Permyakov's system functions like an atomic chart in which there is both order as well as room for new elements. Similarly, for Gryzbek (1987), Permyakov's system "can, retrospectively, subsume all actually realized meanings of a proverb under the model advanced" (p. 62).

Some authors (e.g., Kuusi, 1972) make Permykov's system a "hocus pocus system" in that it requires excessive interpretation, in contrast to Kuusi's system, sometimes called "God's truth system" because it is built presumably from the bottom up on the basis of an a priori reality. Kuusi (1972) found phrases that Permyakov uses to be nearly incomprehensible, phrases such as, "the relation of a thing and its property," or "internal solidity—inconsistency," and other similarly stated bases for classification. Kuusi found it quite difficult to use Permyakov's system to classify proverbs. It seems opaque to the author as well.

Finally, Norrick (1985) analyzed a sample of proverbs from the *Oxford Dictionary of English Proverbs* (Wilson, 1970). He developed a more empirically oriented and less grandiose schematization that categorizes proverbs according to the type of figuration they use. He distinguished five types of figurative proverbs: synecdochic, metaphoric, metonymic, hyperbolic, and paradoxical. Figurative proverbs have figurative meanings (standard proverbial interpretations [SPI] in Norrick's terms) that differ from their literal reading.

Synecdochic proverbs are those in which the literal reading and SPI, "stand in a relation of microcosm to macrocosm" (p. 108). This includes examples such as *The early bird catches the worm*; *Make hay while the sun shines*; and *Fair words break no bones*. In these proverbs, the literal meaning is quite different from the figurative meaning.

In metaphoric proverbs, a nominal becomes metaphoric due to its interaction with another proverb constituent, or the nominal symbolizes some characteristic attribute. An example of the first is, *Favor will as surely perish as life*, and of the second, *Fair play is a jewel*.

Metonymic proverbs are based on associations between something literally named and the thing intended. Examples include

Far from eyes, far from heart; *Fear has a quick ear*; and *The face is no index to the heart.*

Hyperbolic proverbs exaggerate as in *Far shooting never killed bird*; *All is fair in love and war*; and *One father is more than one hundred schoolmasters.*

Paradoxical proverbs are contradictory on the literal level and difficult if not impossible to connect to their SPIs in a principled way. Examples are *Fair is not fair* and *The farthest way about is the nearest way home.*

Arguably, synecdoche is a necessary property of all proverbs, because anything less than a gulf between literal and figurative meaning would make a statement less proverbial. This makes synecdoche a poor choice for classification purposes. As for the other four proverb types, it is clear that many proverbs do not fit because they do not use these poetic devices. These devices are an important aspect of proverb functioning, but a more fundamental aspect of proverbs may be at work (see chapter 4).

In summary, there seem to be serious obstacles to any attempt to define and develop a taxonomy of proverbs. The problem is that proverbs can take on practically any syntactic form, including that of a query, although a standard omnitemporal propositional form is typical. Proverbs do require two words; one-word proverbs are unheard of. But beyond this, it is impossible to say what other properties a proverb must have, structurally speaking. Proverbs do not fit the definition of a classical category in which members belong if and only if they have a set of singly necessary and jointly sufficient properties. Proverbs have characteristic phonological, syntactic, and semantic properties, but that is the end of it. Structural properties provide only the potential for proverb status. What a proverb is has as much to do with its use as with its structure. Yet use is a more ephemeral thing, making it difficult to use for taxonomic purposes.

Similarly, proverbs are hard to classify in theoretically meaningful ways. This is partly because there is no limit to the ideas that can be expressed by proverbs or to the things that proverbs could be about. They are, as Taylor (1931) told us, typically about important episodic human concerns and activities, danger, food, interpersonal relations (especially), how to get things done, weather, how to behave, and so on. Moreover, they often do express oppositions or repeat certain kinds of patterns, such as those described by Kuusi (1972). Oppositions and contrasts can arouse analogical and other mapping strategies for applying and understanding proverbs, but these may be used in any case, when there are no oppositions. From the cognitive viewpoint, however, the nagging question is what the cognitive consequences are of any classification system, a goal addressed later with the cognitive ideals hypothesis (see chapter 4).

The Religious View

Religion is concerned with big issues in life such as how people should conduct themselves, what constitutes good and evil, the place of people in the larger scheme of existence, and questions of afterlife. It is not surprising, therefore, that religious figures have used proverbs to teach about these issues. Every religion has its proverbs, quasi-proverbs, and sayings (Champion, 1945).

Jesus used both the proverb and the closely related story form, the parable. Proverbs occur frequently in the synoptic gospels (those according to Matthew, Mark, and Luke) and include these: *Everyone who exalts himself will be humbled, and he who humbles himself will be exalted*; *Whoever would be great among you must be your servant; Whoever would be first among you must be slave of all*; and perhaps the better known *It is easier for a camel to go through the eye of a needle than for a rich man to enter the kingdom of God* (Perry, 1993, discussed the synoptic tradition).

For Beardslee (1970), the proverbs of the synoptic gospels are overwhelmingly about issues in everyday existence. The gospels have a confrontational or prescriptive tenor that takes the assertive, imperative, and less often, the question form in the proverb itself. The wisdom in these proverbs is augmented through the use of paradox and antithesis, as in *Whoever loses his life will preserve it* and *Many that are first will be last*. The fusing of religion, proverbial wisdom, and an abiding interest in the problems of everyday existence are present in the early Jewish tradition, which continues on into the synoptic gospels.

According to Williams (1981), there are four motifs or themes that characterize the aphoristic teachings of the biblical period: the ethical issues of retribution and divine justice, the proper use of language as an instrument of power, the control and ordering of the self, and faith in the truths of the elders as they pontificate on the first three themes. The biblical book of Proverbs is laced with these themes: *Of no profit are treasures of wickedness, and righteousness delivers from death*; *A person gets pleasure from an apt reply*; *How salutary is a word in season*; and *Hear, my son, the instruction of your father, and forsake not the teaching of your mother*.

Pragmatics theory, the concept of indirect speech acts in particular, has been used to explain how Jesus' proverbs got their meaning. For example, drawing on the work of Norrick (1985), Winton (1990) stated that proverbs can be considered indirect speech acts that distance the speaker from the conveyed message, thereby requiring the hearer to contribute more to the precise meaning of the proverb. The basic premise of this view is that proverbs are often used in situations that are socioemotionally delicate and require some sort of indirect rhetorical strategy.

Winton pursued this idea in the story of the Syrophenician woman (Mark 7:24–30). Jesus enters a house in search of solitude, but a woman finds him and requests his help in healing her daughter of an "unclean spirit." Jesus responds, "Let the children first be filled; for it is not meet to take the children's bread, and to cast it unto the dogs." The woman answers, saying "Yes, Lord; yet the dogs under the table eat of the children's crumbs." Jesus replies, "For this saying go thy way; the devil is gone out of thy daughter." And upon reaching her house the woman finds "the devil gone out."

According to Winton, Jesus has used a proverb to deny the woman's request, although it is clear that it is granted in the end. In any event both speakers have spoken indirectly in a way such that reconstruction of their meaning requires close attention to who the speakers are, what they each want, and how tensions in the situation can be resolved without conflict.

Finally, in analyzing wisdom literature, Perry (1993) emphasized both the form and the message of proverbs. In particular, he hypothesized, a la Milner (1969), that proverbs are typically oppositional, and that a quadripartite logical structure serves as the formula by which proverbs produce their value laden message. For example, the biblical proverb, *A good name is to be chosen rather than great riches* (Proverbs 22:1), presumably decomposes into the (partially implicit) structure of riches and good name, poverty and good name, riches and bad name, and poverty and bad name. Perry argued that full understanding of such proverbs entails understanding the complete fourfold structure, even though it is largely hidden.

Perry's hypothesis is interesting but limited. Some proverbs may well have a quadripartite structure, and an implicit understanding of this structure is probably necessary for complete understanding. But such implicit understanding does not guarantee much about other aspects of understanding. Moreover, most proverbs do not have a quadripartite structure. This structure may simply occur more often for biblical proverbs.

Much that is written about biblical proverbs has the parochial goal of elucidating what the proverbs could have meant or how they fitted into the larger theological realm and helped to spread a religious message. There are exceptions, however. In her discussions of the biblical wisdom tradition, Fontaine (1984) noted the similarity between the functions of biblical proverbs and the use of the Zen koan in the Rinzai Zen literature. Like the proverb, the koan presents a perspective or way of thinking, or not thinking, about experiences. Most koans are put in the form of unanswered questions, such as, "Lift your left hand up; you just may scratch a Buddha's neck; Raise your right hand, when will you be able to avoid feeling a dog's head?" and the infamous "What is the sound of one hand clapping?" The koan attempts to "fatigue the intellectual functions" (Fontaine, 1984, p. 597) so that doubts about normal conceptualization occur and enlightenment or "satori" can be shared with the teacher/master. Wisdom can then take over the life of the individual, a goal that is somewhat similar to the biblical invocation to fear and follow the Lord as a precondition for right thinking. In her analysis of mashal (proverb) performances in the Hebrew Bible, Fontaine (1984) looked at linguistic, folklore, and ethnographic factors. Among other things, she concluded that the proverb was often used to diffuse the potential for hostilities in ambiguous situations.

The Literary View

Proverbs are used in prose, poetry, and song. The reasons vary with the genre. Poetry and song tend to follow certain rhythmic structures, so the poetic and balanced syntactic structure of some proverbs can be appealing. In addition, they pack a great deal of information into a short statement, and poets and song writers often have verbal economy as a goal. For writers of prose and some poetry, the goals may be different, with a shift in focus to the rhetorical, sometimes indirect, distant style that typifies proverbs. Perhaps the fundamental reason why proverbs appear in literary sources is that they pack an emotional and aesthetic punch. (This aspect is discussed in more detail in chapter 7.) This effect can be traced not only to their frequent use of poetic devices, but to their common omnitemporal (timeless) form and their arousal of affect-laden universal ideas about human affairs.

Perhaps the best known user of proverbs among the literati was Shakespeare. (The discussion here draws heavily on Wilson's 1981 study of this topic.) In the 16th century Western Europe was soaked in proverbs, a tradition that continued on into the 17th century. As a keen observer of life, Shakespeare certainly was aware of the many proverbs that were being used. He also created some of his own: *It is better to wear out than rust out*; *They that have nothing need fear to lose nothing*; *Constant dropping will wear the stone*; *The fox barks not when he would steal the lamb*. From Shakespeare's *Henry VI*, we find this comment, quoted in Wilson (1981), on the defeat of the English soldiers by the witchcraft of Joan of Arc:

> A witch by fear, not force, like Hannibal,
> Drives back our troops and conquers as she lists:
> So bees with smoke and doves with noisome stench
> Are from their hives and houses driv'n away. (p. 188)

A fascinating case of proverb use is evident in the poetry of Emily Dickinson. According to Barnes (1979/1994),

> Dickinson's knowledge of proverbs was…fairly extensive; indeed her continued employment of them in letters and poems spanning a period of more than 40 years is sufficient, I think, to warrant consideration of them as a major body of heretofore unrecognized sources, exceeded in the frequency of their appearance only by Shakespeare and the King James Bible. (p. 440)

Her early poems were laced with common proverbs such as *Better late than never* and *After a storm there comes a calm*. Later she parodied and played with proverbs, for example in *Spare the "nay" and spoil the child* and *A pear to the wise is sufficient*.

Barnes interpreted such playfulness as reflecting Dickinson's general skepticism about life. In time, her recitation of simple proverbs gave way to, not only proverb play, but delicate allusion, not always with great imagination. Sometimes the allusions were too subtle, in that she overestimated the reader's familiarity with some proverbs, such as *God tempers the wind to the shorn lamb* in

> How ruthless are the gentle
> How cruel are the kind—
> God broke his contract to his Lamb
> To qualify the Wind (from Barnes, 1994, p. 450)

Barnes went on to argue that Dickinson was so influenced by proverbs that she saw even traditionally nonproverbial literature in proverbial terms. Proverbs came to frame her poetry. And as someone who was weighed down by the tradition of her times, she found in proverbs a form of circumlocution, or "slantness" as Barnes called it, and an outlet for her pessimism by way of finding *No rose without a thorn.*

Finally, one can ask whether there is anything unique about the proverb genre that makes for its use in literature. One hypothesis is that proverbs are detachable from their original context of use, but nevertheless can remind a reader of the social norms they embody (Abrahams & Babcock, 1994). That is, the proverb can retain its general significance in spite of its being resituated in some text. This way, the reader can be led to experience some facets of the original social interactions in which proverbs first appeared. In Abrahams and Babcock's (1994) terms: "The reader is recalled to the common situation of use in talk and the rhetorical motivation that prompted the proverb. Thus, he is given a clue in the complex game of interpreting written signs, a text by which to orient himself" (p. 435). This detachment hypothesis is compatible with the cognitive ideals hypothesis (see chapter 4) that proverbs are designed to arouse universal standards, norms, and ideals irrespective of the pragmatic particulars of their use.

The literary view provides an intriguing look at authors, their concerns and their times. Of course, it also provides more evidence that proverbs have piqued the imagination of individuals who use these facile forms for their own ends.

The Practical View

Proverbs have characteristic properties that make them useful for everyday purposes. They are relatively short, poetic, typically concrete, and used as indirect comments. They have the power and wisdom of many people behind them, and they perform categorization and pragmatic functions. These properties strongly suggest that they can be used to facilitate memory, teach, and persuade. Of course, these properties are precisely why many proverbs develop in cultures in the first place. Their practical uses draw on these same functions. (Hoffman & Honeck, 1987, discussed ecological aspects of proverb use.)

These functions are illustrated by the use of proverbs in treatment for sociopsychological problems such as substance abuse (Rogers, 1989), in psychotherapy (Whaley, 1993), as tests of mental status (Allen & Schuldberg, 1989; Andreason, 1977; Gorham, 1956, 1963; Mieder, 1978), as a way of teaching children to think more abstractly (Feichtl, 1988), as an imagery mnemonic by the elderly (Pratt & Higbee, 1983), as a means of assessing workers' attitudes about work and life (Baumgarten, 1952), and even as tests of a defendant's competency to stand trial (Simon, 1987).

Mieder and Mieder (1977) examined the use of proverbs in advertising, and proclaimed that "one glance at the advertising of any magazine or newspaper shows that proverbs have become the most popular folklore item used by Madison Avenue" (p. 310). These authors point to advertisers' beliefs that messages must be short, inspire trustworthiness, contain the essential message, and be interesting, memorable, and capable of repetition. To this end, advertisers have used proverbs to sell 35-mm cameras (*Good things come in small packages*), trumpet the advantages of banking and saving (*A stitch in time saves nine*), and herald the new McDonald's quarterpounder hamburger (*Man does not live by bread alone*). Of course, advertisers have been inventive in using proverbs by way of twisting, parodying, and alluding to them. For example, Lufthansa airline used *All roads used to lead to Rome* to explain that Frankfurt is the airline's hub. The Coca-Cola Company has used various proverbs, including *Thirst come—thirst served*. Volkswagen announced that it sold more than the famous Beetle with the quasi-proverb, *Different Volks for different folks*.

In addition, advertisers have integrated proverbs with visual illustrations. Four Roses whiskey was advertised with just *In whiskey, this picture is worth a thousand words* and a picture of four roses. Mieder and Mieder (1977) also pointed to cases in which proverbs were used to promote the women's movement: *A woman's place is in the House, the House of Representatives, that is*. They concluded that "Advertising most assuredly has become a new and vital stomping ground of the timeless and adaptable proverb, which of all the folk narrative genres has coped best with the problem of overcoming the dichotomy of tradition and innovation" (p. 319).

The value of proverbs in psychotherapy has been argued by a number of authors (Rogers, 1989; Whaley, 1993). For example, Rogers described the intentional use of proverbs in therapeutic communities designed to end drug abuse. These communities "involve creating a minisociety designed to reinforce particular philosophic and pragmatic positions" (Rogers, 1989, p. 103). In particular, Rogers indicates that there is evidence that if proverbs and other colloquialisms keep abusers in the community, then there is an increased chance that they will remain drug free. He documented the use of proverbs during different stages of an abuser's stay with the community. Upon arrival, proverbs are used that will convey the message that the community has an answer (e.g., *The journey of one thousand miles begins with the first step*). During therapy proverbs become rhetorical and persuasive devices for promoting social bonding and values, and as therapy winds down they serve as reminders for the entire experience. Once out of the group, the client can use the proverbs as reminders so that the treatment regimen can generalize to new situations (e.g., *Only the strong survive*). Curiously, Rogers stated that many mental health practitioners have a negative attitude about slogans and colloquialisms, no doubt reflecting the personal view of proverbs.

Proverbs have many potential everyday uses. They have utility for any situation in which people could benefit from verbal cues to remember to carry out some activity, especially a recurring activity, or to reason about important events, which represent a large number of situations. New applications could arguably be developed for use in dental care, physical therapy, child care, practically any kind of athletic skill, and everyday tasks of all sorts. Many people probably do construct something like proverbs for use in these situations, but the proverb stays wedded to them without attaining cultural status.

Proverbs have been extensively used for mental testing purposes, including their use as subtests in more general tests of intelligence (e.g., Wechsler Adult Intelligence Scale) and in assessing psychopathology (Andreason, 1977). Such testing seemingly has produced relatively uninformative results. However, this topic will be taken up again in chapters 6 and 7.

The Cultural View

The cultural view emphasizes the use of proverbs in sociocultural contexts. The basic premise is that proverbs are cultural linguistic products, created and used in social situations for social purposes. These purposes largely entail the codification of important lessons in the culture.

This premise has numerous theoretical consequences. The first is that the social context becomes enormously powerful. Figurative and other meanings that occur for social interactants are highly constrained if not determined by this context. The meaning of a proverb can be considered only within this context, although a proverb may have a dominant meaning in one context and a somewhat different meaning in another context. It follows that proverbs have little meaning outside some context and, indeed, the abstraction of proverbs from their cultural context of use is typically seen as unnatural, ecologically invalid, and sterile. Rogers (1986) presented the case for this radical contextualist premise.

A second consequence is that proverbs are viewed as having primarily, if not exclusively, social purposes. Private, personal purposes are largely ignored. For that matter, the notion that individuals could create proverbs for their own personal use is hardly ever considered in the cultural view. Of course, were this to happen, and apparently it does, the theoretical issues it presented would be no less interesting than those that arise from social uses.

As a third consequence, the cultural view, of necessity, assumes that all proverbs are familiar to large numbers of people. There can be no unfamiliar proverb. There is an issue of exactly what the terms familiar and unfamiliar mean here, and at what point in its evolution a proverb becomes a proverb. Someone had to create it, and others had to begin using it. Nevertheless, the cultural view seems to rule out unfamiliar or otherwise personal and idiosyncratic proverbs.

The familiarity requirement has a series of other important, psychological consequences. In particular, it leads to the assumption, not only that the literal format of a proverb must be prestored, but that the figurative meaning is prestored as well. This leads to the further assumption that proverb meanings are fixed and automatically accessed—no assembly is necessary. In turn, this tends to foster the conclusion that pragmatics theory is irrelevant to proverb comprehension. If proverb meaning is just there waiting to be accessed in the appropriate context, what possible validity could there be in having to check whether a proverb is appropriate to its context, or in having to go through a series of steps to fashion a contextually appropriate meaning?

The basic premise behind the cultural view is important but inadequate. Each one of its consequences has some validity, but only under specified conditions, whereas various other conditions are left out. Thus, there is good reason and evidence for unfamiliar proverbs, proverbs that are not formulaic, proverbs whose meanings are not prestored and must be constructed, individual and personal reasons for using proverbs, proverbs that retain a figurative meaning that stays relatively constant across contexts, proverbs that can produce consensual interpretations in the absence of background context, proverbs that can produce consensual interpretations across cultures, proverbs (most, it seems) that undergo a series of phases on the road to comprehension, and cases in which proverbs play a dominant role in shaping their own context. Again, proverbs must be accounted for under all circumstances, not just those that are sanctioned by the cultural view.

The cultural view also focuses on questions concerning the particulars of proverbs that occur in a culture: their origin, content/themes, and the history of their diffusion across time and cultures. On a sociopsychological level, there is an intense curiosity about the conditions and prerequisites for the use of proverbs: when are they said, who says them, how their saying is managed, who they are said to, and what the consequences of their saying are.

Research within the cultural view is likely to be carried out by cultural anthropologists, ethnographers, folklorists, some linguists, and an occasional psychologist. The research is distinctly and avowedly nonlaboratory in character, with historical, field study, and naturalistic methodologies taking precedence. The premise and goals of this view lend themselves to nonexperimental methods although they are not necessarily inconsistent with experimental methods. A representative sample of research within the cultural view comes from the following three studies.

In a field study, Briggs (1985) attempted to show that the definition of the proverb pays insufficient attention to the idea that "the rhetorical force of proverb performances emerges from a subtle and complex use of the pragmatic functions of language" (p. 794). Briggs collected data from Spanish speakers living in northern New Mexico. The data were based on tape recordings of Briggs' attempt to elicit proverbs and proverb meanings, descriptions of situations that might elicit these, and open conversations among his respondents. Briggs concluded that a proverb *performance* is accompanied by seven features: ways of tying the proverb to the conversation; provision by the proverb sayer of information about the person, usually an elder, who is responsible for the proverb; the introduction of certain verbs that set up the proverb utterance; the provision of cues by the sayer that the proverb is actually a proverb; the provision of information about the social group ordinarily associated with the proverb; the provision of an interpretation of the proverb that is unique to its specific context of use; and a statement about how the proverb applies to the particular context. A proverb performance is typically ended with a pedagogical attempt to validate the application of the proverb.

Pasamanick (1983) carried out a methodologically similar study with children. In a school setting, children 6 to 9 years old were engaged by the investigator in an open-ended discussion with their peers and the investigator about a small set of proverbs. For example, one discussion focused on the proverb, *Break one link and the whole chain falls apart.* Her analyses of these discussions suggested that these children exhibited a "level of communicative and metaphoric competence with which they are seldom credited" (Pasamanick, 1983, p. 18). The author emphasized the crucial role of situation and peer as well as adult facilitation in fostering this competence. In particular, three processes were deemed to contribute to this competence—a back-and-forth exchange between concrete and abstract modes of thought, various strategies for generating abstractions, and the use of a large body of socially based knowledge for explaining and fitting the proverb meaning.

Finally, Mieder (1993a) traced the Americanization of the originally German proverb, *Don't throw the baby out with the bath water*. This proverb appeared in a German book published in 1512. It then gained some currency during the Reformation, was incorporated into German proverb collections of the mid-1500s, and was later used by many German writers. It was borrowed by the English writer Thomas Carlyle, who used it in a magazine article published in 1849. However, Mieder asserted that it was George Bernard Shaw who, "represents the starting point of its appearance in English language sources of the 20th century" (p. 203).

The cultural view provides valuable information about factors that can facilitate or inhibit proverb understanding in real-life situations, as well as some answers to questions about the social and historical origin along with the circumstance of proverb usage. However, it does not tell us how people can understand and apply proverbs, nor, ultimately, what makes a proverb a proverb. Furthermore, as indicated earlier, its basic premise leads to some empirically undocumented and probably incorrect conclusions. One theory of proverb comprehension, the great chain metaphor theory (Lakoff & Turner, 1989), is built on the cultural premise (see chapter 4).

A case can be made that the predominance of the cultural view and its basic premise stems from a too facile acceptance of the standard social science model (SSSM; Barkow, Cosmides, & Tooby, 1992; Buss, 1995). Because this is a complex and lengthy matter, only its gist will be provided.

The SSSM, as described by Tooby and Cosmides (1992), contains a number of components. It seems to the author that these components and the entire issue can be framed profitably in terms of rationalism and empiricism. Rationalists have traditionally emphasized mind power and nativism. These ideas can be traced at least to Plato and, later, to Descartes and Kant. That is, human behavior is seen as largely controlled by biological and hereditary factors that equip the individual mind with enormous influence over the environment. In contrast, empiricists such as Aristotle, Locke, Hobbes, and Berkeley emphasized environment power and made humans the famous tabula rasa. The environment, especially the social environment, impinges on the senses and produces learning in a mind that contains few if any a priori constraints. Thus, what humans are becomes almost exclusively a matter of social interaction, not of innate human proclivities.

The SSSM arises from the empiricist agenda. Thus, society (the group mind) takes precedence over the individual mind. Cultures predominate over and shape individuals and not vice versa. Societies become emergents that are not reducible to biology or psychology. Genetics is given little role in shaping the mind and little chance therefore of shaping society. Infants differ little, whereas adults differ a great deal. The capacity for culture is provided by content-free, general purpose, domain-general psychological mechanisms of learning.

It seems relatively clear that the SSSM, or something very similar, provides the metatheoretical basis for the cultural view. Insofar as the elements of the SSSM can be questioned or rejected outright, then the cultural view itself can be questioned. It is suggested that just this stance provides a more enlightened, complete, and refreshing direction for research and theory on the proverb.

Basically, the SSSM leaves out universal biological and psychological constraints on social behavior. No one denies the reality of cross-cultural and subcultural differences. It is just that the more fundamental, important, and legion communalities too often get overlooked. This has happened in the case of proverbs. That is a major reason why the cognitive ideals hypothesis has been enunciated (see chapter 4). Briefly, this hypothesis holds that proverbs are generated from universal human knowledge about ideals, standards, and norms, which act as reference points in evaluating events. These reference points are intuitive forms of perfection. Cultures develop idiosyncratic linguistic means of expressing the perfection. Thus, proverbs from other cultures may be hard or impossible for a nonnative to interpret, but once the cultural code is broken, the proverbs can be seen to have a species-wide significance. This means, of course, that if our goal is to explain why a cultural level proverb means what it does, we will have to know something about that culture and its language, but we will also, ultimately, have to know something about the human being. The cognitive view is expressly concerned with those processes and mechanisms that have universal bases. In general, the larger goal is to provide a more balanced rationalist and empiricist approach to proverbs.

The Cognitive View

We finally come to the raison d'être for this volume, the cognitive view. This view attempts to describe the mental structures and processes that subserve proverb learning, comprehension, and use. (Chapter 3 elaborates on this view.) For example, the cognitive view would have us focus on the following issues: the mental background for proverb creation and production, the mental representation of proverbs, the phases in their comprehension, how proverbs categorize events, and the pragmatic functions they perform.

The cognitive view brings proverbs within the general theoretical scope of cognitive science. It follows, therefore, that there is no virtue in having a paremiology or special subdiscipline with its own concepts and theoretical accoutrements devoted exclusively to the study of proverbs. At the same time there is no reason why the study of proverbs cannot or should not inform cognitive science.

Because the cognitive view has proverb cognition fall within the purview of cognitive science, a basic premise emerges for this view and, therefore, for this text. Namely, there is nothing unique about proverbs insofar as their creation, use, and comprehension can be explained by general cognitive principles.

The theoretical implications of the cognitive view are profound. Proverbs are wrested from their sometimes hallowed status as culturally unique linguistic events and are treated instead as *abstract theoretical mental entities*. This means, in turn, that as in any scientific endeavor, investigators are free to perform any sort of study or manipulation, vis-à-vis the entity in question. For proverbs, the implication is that any and all variables that bear on proverb cognition can be changed: the proverbs themselves, who uses and comprehends them, their context of use, and the functions they serve. The cultural view places an imprimatur on methods that leave the proverb and its circumstances unperturbed and therefore ecologically valid. The cognitive view embraces these methods but affirms the necessity of experimental techniques, including laboratory experimentation and field experiments. For example, it now becomes sensible to ask how proverb creation might be examined in the laboratory.

The cultural view, insofar as it sees proverbs as having a privileged status as socioculturally situated events, is inconsistent with the cognitive view. Proverbs occur in cultures; their literal content may be unique to cultures; there may be different interpretations for the same proverb in different cultures; and proverbs may play different roles in different cultures. But the cognitive view rejects the idea that these premises are the proper starting point for a complete and theoretically satisfying understanding of the proverb.

To the contrary, proverbs must be abstracted away from their cultural specifics in order to be understood in their various manifestations and roles in different cultures. The reason for such abstraction is that the goal of science is to develop principles of great generality. That is, the cognitive view assumes the universalist stance that the mental structures and processes of Homo sapiens are explainable on the basis of the same theoretical principles. Although cultural specifics may be interesting and illuminating and should not be ignored, the cognitive view takes these specifics as means to an end and not as an end in itself nor as a starting point. The cognitive view rejects no methodologies or data about proverbs—they all can play a role in forging a general theory of proverbs—but maintains that culture-, individual-, and proverb-specific differences should be encompassed by a general cognitive theory. The contextualism inherent in the cultural view is not inconsistent with the cognitive view. The question is how we are to understand proverb cognition in any circumstance, and not just what some proverb means for particular individuals in some situation in a particular culture.

The cognitive view can be illustrated by three studies. Honeck and Kibler (1984) attempted to confirm some aspects of the conceptual base theory of proverb comprehension (Honeck, Voegtle, Dorfmueller, & Hoffman, 1980; see chapter 4 for details and an update on this theory). Briefly, this theory holds that proverb comprehension occurs in phases that involve getting a literal meaning, recognizing that the literal meaning does not satisfy the communicative context, using the literal meaning and inferences to get a figurative meaning, and then using the figurative meaning for various illustrative purposes. Because proverbs often entail contrasts, the theory stipulates that instantiation involves the analogizing (more generally, a mapping) of figurative meaning components and corresponding components in some context of application (a topic). For example, *Great weights hang on small wires* involves a contrast between "great weights," often interpreted to mean important events, and "small wires," often interpreted to mean seemingly unimportant events. The word "hang" is then interpreted idiomatically to mean "depends on." Thus, a typical interpretation of the proverb is, "The outcome of important events can depend on seemingly unimportant ones." This meaning can then be mapped onto events that are interpreted to have similar meanings, such as a surgeon's knife slipping and the patient suffering, a shortstop tripping on a pebble and missing a ball that drives in the win for the opposing team, or a spacecraft's o-ring failing at a critical moment and dooming its occupants.

Honeck and Kibler created several experimental groups. During a training session, one group saw pictures of literal information mentioned by the proverb; another was instructed to image this information; a third was presented a four-term analogy that related the binary meaning elements in the proverb with those in an abstractly stated interpretation; and a fourth got an analogy plus an appropriate instance of the figurative meaning components of the analogy. By the conceptual base theory, the picture and imagery group participants were induced to develop a literal meaning representation, the analogy group to develop a figurative meaning representation, and the analogy-plus-instance group to develop a more precise figurative meaning.

After the training session, all groups were presented novel positive and negative examples of the figurative meaning of the previously presented proverbs. The participants indicated whether these examples were or were not examples of the old proverbs. The results indicated that the literal groups performed at chance; the analogy-interpretation group was above chance; whereas the analogy-plus-instance group outperformed the analogy group. These results, replicated by Oliver (1991), are consistent with the putative phases and processes postulated by the conceptual base theory.

A basic assumption of both the conceptual base theory and the standard pragmatic model (Grice, 1975; Searle, 1979) is that the comprehension of figurative language runs off in a serial way. That is, a literal meaning is developed, then rejected as inappropriate to the communicative context, and a newer, preferred meaning (the figurative meaning) is constructed, partially by building on aspects of the literal meaning. Those who retain the cultural and formal views tend to reject the serial model, basically because proverbs are seen as highly lexicalized items that have relatively fixed and prestored meanings and because context is given a predominant role in determining meanings. This model has been (indirectly) tested to some extent in experimental studies that have used idioms and metaphors. The conventional wisdom is that the model is inappropriate and that, in context, the meaning of tropes can be directly accessed without having first to get a literal meaning and then reject it (see Gibbs, 1994 for a review and antistandard pragmatic model statement). This issue is taken up in chapter 4, but for now it can be said simply that the issues are complex and that the serial model may rest on firmer ground than the literature suggests. This is certainly the case for proverbs, for which it is clear that the surface or literal aspects of the proverb, constrain possible figurative meanings, but do not determine them. The more familiar a proverb becomes, the more likely it is that the phases of proverb understanding become compressed and that a particular, to some extent prestored, figurative meaning is available. In any event, the methodological issues in investigating this problem are daunting because, if at all possible, an online (as it occurs) measure of processing is highly desirable but difficult to achieve.

The methodology that comes closest to this ideal, vis-à-vis proverbs, was developed by Jon Temple (1993) and the author. In this study, which involved six separate experiments, college students were presented with two short passages on a computer screen. Just one of the passages was an appropriate instance of a proverb, which was presented 35 seconds after the contexts. The major experimental manipulation was that in one condition both of the passages were related in a literal way to their proverb, whereas in the other condition both passages were related in a figurative way, with just one passage being appropriate in each case. A choice reaction-time task was used in which the students had to press a key as quickly as possible in deciding which of the two passages (the top or bottom one on the monitor screen) was appropriate. For example, on a given trial, the students either saw this:

Jane saw a mouse run across the floor. So Jane decided to set a trap in front of the only hole she could see in the wall.

The mouse found a hole near the foundation of the house. Now it had a family and was living happily in the attic.

or this:

Meg lived in the country and didn't have a car, so she had to ride to work with her neighbor Jim. Then Jim moved to the city.

While searching for rare species in the jungle, the biologist caught malaria. He made a speedy trip to the doctor.

Thirty-five seconds later, the students were presented with the following proverb:

A mouse with one hole is quickly caught.

This methodology combines a measure of nearly online processing with one of correctness rather than simply recording reading time or some other time, the validity of which would be debatable. The combination of reaction time, response correctness, and the nature of the verbal materials themselves provides a solid basis for inferring whether literal or figurative processing was occurring, how time consuming it was, and, by implication, what the phases of comprehension might have been. (By the way, the correct choice in both the first and second pairs of sentences is the top one. In the first pair, the top sentence is a less distant inference from the literal meaning of the proverb. Similarly, the top sentence in the second pair is more figuratively related to the proverb than the bottom sentence.)

The results indicated, per expectation, that the reaction times in the figurative condition were longer than those in the literal condition. Moreover, when each experimental condition involved different students, processing mode (literal vs. figurative) contributed more to reaction time than proverb familiarity, whereas when the same students served in both experimental conditions, proverb familiarity was more important.

These results are totally consistent with the standard pragmatic model and with the conceptual base theory. There was no evidence to support the view that literal meaning can be bypassed. Apparently, it had to be computed before figurative meaning. Moreover, the method in this study had some degree of ecological validity because participants had to map the proverb to a foregoing topic, a commonplace in everyday proverb use. (Of course, they also had to make a choice between topics, a less ecological valid situation, but one necessitated by the need to be able to make a valid inference about participants' level of understanding.)

Finally, a study by Nippold, Martin, and Erskine (1988) illustrates the cognitive view as applied to children's understanding of proverbs. In this study, students in grades 4, 6, 8, and 10 read 30 sets of materials. Each set consisted of a setup statement that included the utterance of a proverb and four alternative choices of which one was a correct illustration of the proverb. For example, one set was: "Mother told Sally, *When a wolf shows his teeth, he isn't laughing*." The correct choice was: "The diamond that Sally bought from the friendly salesman turned out to be a fake," whereas an incorrect choice was, for example: "Even though Sally likes her brother Bill, sometimes they fight." The students also were given a reasoning test that involved selecting the correct solution to four-term perceptually based analogies. The results revealed accuracy scores of 67, 77, 83, and 85% across grades 4, 6, 8, and 10, respectively, with all groups performing well above the 25% chance figure. The correlations between performance on the proverb task and the analogies task were .40, .40, .65, and .27, respectively, across the four grades. The authors attributed the age trend on the proverb test to increased exposure to the concept of proverbs or to the proverbs themselves, the vocabulary level of the students (although attempts were made to eliminate this factor by using simple vocabulary), and to an increasing ability to use the literal meaning of the proverbs to construct their figurative meaning. The correlational results were attributed to the idea that both tasks tapped similar analogical reasoning abilities. The authors pointed out that figurative language can be a sensitive indicator of processing problems, as suggested by the observation that language-disabled children have deficits in this realm.

These three studies provide a representative first look at some of the thinking and research that has grown out of the cognitive view. Clearly, the emphasis is on mental microprocesses, but this view does not rule out the relevance of issues, data, or theories that stem from the other views. For example, the more culturally oriented study by Pasamanick (1983) would seem to complement the Nippold et al. (1988) study by way of suggesting factors that could affect proverb understanding both inside and outside the laboratory.

The seven views of the proverb are summarized in Table 1.1.

TABLE 1.1

Summary of the Seven Views of the Proverb

View	Major Goal	Basic Assumption	Primary Disciplines	Main Methods
Cognitive	Explain proverb cognition	Proverbs are theoretical mental entities	Psychology, linguistics	Experiment
Cultural	Describe proverb's cultural functions	Proverb is a culturally familiar form	Cultural anthropology, folklore studies	Ethnography, field studies
Formal	Define proverb, develop taxonomy	Proverb is a unique language form	Linguistics, semiotics	Linguistic analysis
Literary	Describe use of proverbs in prose/poetry	Proverbs have unique poetic properties	Language and literature studies	Literary analysis
Personal	Personal understanding of proverbs	Personal understanding is valid	—	Phenomenology
Practical	Document or implement uses of proverbs	Proverbs have important uses	Varies	Varies
Religious	Describe and interpret proverb use in religious texts	Proverbs provide moral lessons	Religion studies	Historical and text analysis

SUMMARY

Proverbs are interesting, important, and complex. That is why so many different views have evolved to analyze them: the personal, formal, religious, literary, practical, cultural and cognitive views. These views have different goals that have been pursued with different techniques, so they provide us with different information. They are all interesting and worthwhile in their own right. However, the scientific understanding of proverbs is based more on the cognitive, cultural, and formal views. The cultural view uses concepts and techniques that, generally speaking, are not part of cognitive science, but that supplement it in important ways. The formal view provides important information about the linguistic character of proverbs and how they might be classified. In contrast to the cultural and formal views, the cognitive view treats proverbs as a theoretical mental construct and emphasizes the universal microcognitive, pancultural processes that underlie them.

2

The Tangle of Figurative Language

℘ ◆ ℃

There are several forms of figurative language besides the proverb. The major alternatives are metaphor, simile, idiom, metonymy, and oxymoron. Some scholars would include sarcasm, irony, hyperbole, understatement, and rhetorical questions, although these are better treated as linguistic functions than as unique linguistic forms. There are related uses of language such as indirect speech acts. There is also a very long list of figures of speech, many with strange sounding names, like asyndeton, by which conjunctions are omitted between phrases as in "She ate, she talked, she left."

This chapter focuses on the major forms because they are clear cases of figuration and have been the most thoroughly analyzed. First, however, let us back up and place figurative language within an even larger framework.

INDIRECTNESS

The human species distinguishes itself from other animals in many ways. One way is in terms of intelligence, most especially intelligence made manifest through language. Another related way is in terms of indirectness. We humans are highly skilled at reaching goals by symbolic and generally roundabout means. Nonhuman animals have primitive abilities in this realm: camouflage, traps that look enticing to prey but turn out to be foodmakers, and mock displays of aggression. Animals show great intelligence in these endeavors, but the level of complexity does not compare to that exhibited by humans. Moreover, indirectness and subtlety in animals is largely limited to the domains of food-getting, territoriality, and survival in general.

For humans, indirectness is characteristic, a way of life. It occurs in every aspect of human behavior, both linguistic and nonlinguistic. In the nonlinguistic realm there is acting, role-playing, pretending, and other forms of "as if" behavior. In each case, at least two levels of events are occurring: what naively seems to be the case and the more important reality. It can be as simple and innocent as the child who treats a toy block as a truck, or as complicated and pernicious as a money scam.

In the verbal realm, indirectness includes not only figurative language but nonfigurative verbalizations as well. Lies and boasts fit here, as do exaggeration and innocent forms of under-statement. In his study of verbal discourse among the Akan of Ghana, Obeng (1994) found that indirection is a prized skill: "The Akan place a high value on speech suffused with obscurities and semantically dense words. Anyone who skillfully uses such words is said to be eloquent, wise or *akwakora ba* 'A child of an old man'; it is the old who are skillful users of Akan" (p. 38). From his transcriptions of natural Akan discourse, Obeng described and gave examples of various uses of indirection, such as to save face, be polite, or persuade. Proverbs were the most common form of indirection, probably because they are assumed to come from the elders and sages of the society and because their use is immune from any negative consequences. Other forms of indirectness used were metaphor, innuendo, euphemism, hyperbole, and circumlo-cution. Obeng (1994) pointed out that the use of such indirectness is inconsistent with Grice's (1975) maxim of manner, which is an implicit rule that speakers should be perspicuous, clear, and to the point. Of course, users of indirection usually do make their point, but not by directly observing this rule of discourse. It seems that this rule is there to be broken, often and unremittingly.

On a larger nonlinguistic level there are other forms of indirec-tion such as schemes, plots, and subterfuge of all sorts. Such indirection is a major part of human history, but it can be found even at microlevels. For example, there are perceptual forms of indirectness, such as synesthesia, in which experience in one sensory modality is somehow translated into experience in a different sensory modality. One form of synesthesia is chromes-thesia or "colored hearing," in which musical tones are experienced as colors. Chromesthesia is rare, but synesthesia is less so (Marks, 1996). We seem to experience many events in ways that go far beyond the basic perceptual input. Clouds can be seen as cruel, people as cold or warm, bright lights as deafening, and music as dull or brooding. Word meanings can be rapier-like or music to the ears.

Our thoughts, emotions, and behaviors can have multiple layers, and the layers and their connections can be complex. Such layering bespeaks intelligence, a connection taken up in more detail in chapter 6. The layering, embeddedness, circumlocution and distancing inherent in figurative language is not unique to it. When someone says A but means B, it is part of a more general human scheme for communicating. In this sense, there is nothing special about figurative language because its indirectness develops out of a more general proclivity for communicating one thing in terms of another. We often hear people say such things as, "She's a peach" (a metaphor), "George went through the roof" (an idiom), "The Serbian Army are real sweethearts" (irony), "The arm had a bad day on the mound today" (metonymy), "The silence was deafening" (oxymoron). These kinds of utterance are neither rare as linguistic events nor novel as a means of human expression. To the contrary, figurative language is commonplace, and indirect expression is breathtakingly normal.

Some forms of figuration are conscious and intentional; some are not. For example, utterances jotted down by the author over several years from conversations, texts, TV, and so forth seem like clear cases of unconscious uses of metaphor. Much of it is prosaic and corny, but it illustrates a popular approach in contemporary cognitive psychology—*spreading activation* of concepts through automatic *priming*. That is, a concept is used, and its use arouses other related concepts. The latter are said to be activated, and the entire process is one of spreading activation, because a number of concepts might be activated. Activation and its spread need not be conscious and, indeed, there is reason to believe that it often is not (Ashcraft, 1994). The general context of an utterance seems to unconsciously prime the use of metaphor. Here are some examples:

> The town's favorite long distance runner didn't make the Olympic team. She's *taking it in stride* though.

Thursday's pitcher Scott Service didn't *bat an eye* when Reds manager Davey Johnson used him as a pinch hitter.

Food supplies are going to Bosnia. One official said that he looks forward to the supplies *with relish*.

Physicists have concluded that people's concerns that high tension wires cause cancer are *groundless*.

Strippers are going to *get busted* for nudity.

The snow is coming, that's for sure. How much though, is *up in the air*.

Fred is cutting his lawn earlier now. I guess he's *turning over a new leaf*.

This guy stands on the dock and slows all the boats down. He *runs a tight ship*.

This man makes guns for a hobby. It's a *dying art* but he likes it.

Well, I'm *steering* her toward a red color. (Said by a man at a bicycle shop wanting to buy a bicycle for his daughter.)

Well, I tell 'ya, the quickest way to *pass through* customs is to tell them that you have diarrhea.

Farmers stick together. They're *down to earth* people.

The author's impression is that this kind of contextually primed figuration is common but ordinarily goes unnoticed. One need not consult books on the topic or check the latest *Reader's Digest* section, Toward More Picturesque Speech, to find examples. They are all around us. That figuration can occur automatically and unconsciously also conflicts with the popular notion that it is a conscious form of linguistic embroidery. It also contradicts the more fundamental idea that figurativeness is a matter of linguistics, a figure of speech, rather than a matter of the human drive to think in indirect ways and to compare things that come from different categories.

The notion that metaphor is conventional and ordinary has been promulgated since 1980 by George Lakoff and his associates (Lakoff, 1987, 1993; Lakoff & Johnson, 1980; Lakoff & Turner, 1989). In particular, they have argued that metaphor often represents unconscious, noneffortful means of expressing more fundamental cognitive ways of construing experience. For example, Lakoff (1986a) has used the example of the underlying *conceptual metaphor* of "Love is a journey." This conceptual metaphor is presumably responsible for expressions such as "Our relationship is at a turning point"; "We have a ways to go in working things out"; and "I don't think we'll ever get to where we want to go." By this view, all of these expressions and more are related by having been derived from the same conceptual metaphor. Most scholars would say that these expressions are not classical metaphors, although supporters of the conceptual metaphor view might say that their metaphorical status has been overlooked. The more general question of literalness and figurativeness is taken up in the next section.

LITERAL AND FIGURATIVE

A central debate in the area of figurative language is how to distinguish utterances that are literal from those that are not. What is literal? What is figurative? Making this distinction has proved to be a daunting task.

Bear in mind that terms such as literal, figurative, and conventional are theoretical terms and that it is impossible to define them in a sentence or two. Like all important theoretical terms they are located in an extensive web of concepts. Literal and figurative are not precise terms such as "odd number" or "DNA" or "trump card." They are more like "ethical," "alive," and "altruistic." In cognitive psychological terms, literal and figurative are not classical concepts (Smith & Medin, 1981), in that there does not seem to be a set of singly necessary and jointly sufficient criteria by which we could definitely decide that a statement is either literal or figurative. The best we can do is to say that it is more or less likely that some statement is literal or figurative. Of course, this implies that there may be a continuum, with highly literal cases on one end and highly figurative ones on the other, with some murkiness in the middle. No attempt is made here to resolve this issue, but rather to elucidate the reasons for the disagreements and confusion about it.

There are at least three general reasons for this unsettled state of affairs. First, there are different theoretical perspectives on literalness that hinge, roughly speaking, on whether it is conceived as a phenomenon of language, language use, or mind. Second, the term "literal" has multiple meanings, irrespective of one's theoretical perspective. It is used in different ways by different people on different occasions. Third, even if the first two reasons could be discounted, the empirical reality is that many factors will influence our decision about whether a particular utterance is literal or figurative. This set of factors is complex, and they interact in even more complex ways. The three general reasons are now elaborated.

Three Views of Literalness

That there are different views about literalness can be illustrated with the simple statement, "Joan is a peach." Assuming that Joan is an adult human female, the statement qualifies as metaphor. However, different theorists would approach it in different ways, which can be called the semantic, pragmatic, and conceptualist views. The standard position on each view will be presented, with subpositions provided for the latter.

Semantic View. The semantic view might be considered the older, traditional view (see Cohen, 1979; Katz, 1966; Osgood, 1980, for variations on the semantic view). We can get a sense of this view if we call it the stingy view or, more propitiously, the heroic view. By stingy I mean that adherents of this view wish as much as possible to treat figuration as a purely linguistic matter. That is, they wish to be able to account for figuration by considering only the meanings of words and how these meanings are combined by syntax (the compositionality principle), and to do this, as much as possible, without resorting to concepts such as world knowledge, inference, context, and, in general, to extralinguistic factors.

The basic claim of this view seems to be that there is only literal meaning, and that when people say things such as, "Joan is a peach," they mean what they say; it is just that they have said it in an odd way. The task for this view is discovering a way to get a sensible literal meaning out of an odd statement. Usually, this is accomplished by treating meaning in terms of "features," so that, for example, "peach" has features such as tastes sweet, is yellowish, is a fruit, has a pit, has a thin membrane, smells good, bruises easily, and so on. Then some set of rules is put into operation to combine features in a compatible way. In our example, Joan is adult, human, and female, so Joan could not be sensibly combined with has a pit, is yellowish, and has a stem.

Potentially, however, Joan could be combined with smells good, bruises easily, and perhaps with more abstract features such as delightfulness. What is heroic about this approach is that it tries to keep figuration within bounds by not having us guess what is going on in the minds of speakers, which the pragmatic view has us do, or by populating the mind with all sorts of preexisting general metaphors, which some variants of the conceptualist view do. In general, it tries to handle figuration with the same principles that are presumed to apply to literal language.

The semantic view can be found in some psychological approaches to metaphor, those that have analyzed it in terms of semantic features. This position can be found in the neobehavioristic writings of Malgady and Johnson (1980) and of Osgood (1979, 1980), who assumed that there are basic meanings in long-term memory that can be juxtaposed for use in linguistic expressions. In the case of metaphor, they are simply juxtaposed in anomalous ways. What is literal and what is figurative, therefore, are treated in terms of featural similarity, which is greater in the former than in the latter case. Literalness is treated in empirical and mathematical or quasi-mathematical terms. The empirical aspect arises from the fact that researchers who take this approach often use people's associations to words, such as the topic (e.g. "Joan") and vehicle (e.g., "peach") terms from metaphors, to derive statistical norms. These norms are then used to make mathematically based predictions (e.g., of how understandable or apt some particular metaphor might be). For our "Joan is a peach" one could get people who know Joan to give their associations to her and to the word peach, and then compute the similarity and dissimilarity of these associations. Theoretically, there would be some similarity, more than in the case of "Joan is a tree," so the peach metaphor would be judged easier to understand and more apt as well.

This empirical-associationistic approach has the virtue of being objective and of making predictions about actual language performance. Unfortunately, it generally fails to explain how verbal and nonverbal context, intention, immediate shared cognition, and other powerful mental variables can affect metaphor processing by way of reconfiguring, creating, canceling, and otherwise affecting semantic features. It has particular problems in addressing trope functions, such as ironic uses of metaphor and critical uses of proverbs. Neverthess, it is a straight-ahead approach and it has its place.

Alas, there are few adherents of the semantic view. The reasons are legion, but include the fact that there are problems with this view even on its own turf: The concept of feature is not well-defined; exactly how features are to be combined is rarely worked out in any detail, and, in the case of metaphor, it is not clear how just the right features get attributed to the metaphor topic whereas other features are rejected (it should be done mechanically, but there always seems to be a bit of prescience to it). Then there are other cold hard facts: Context can make what seems like an innocent-looking literal statement become a nonliteral one with a wholly different pragmatic force; words can take on new features in new contexts, so that the process of combining features becomes posthoc and ad hoc. In general, what looks like a sleek, pristine, automatically gotten literal meaning in some zero context turns out to be built on all sorts of assumptions, inferences, world knowledge, and what not. Therefore, the stinginess and heroism of this view come at a mighty cost.

The metatheoretics of the semantic view is what bothers its antagonists the most, however. For example, there is the presupposition that there are only literal meanings, and that a metaphorical twist on something is just a new literal meaning. A corollary here is that so-called figurative meanings can be paraphrased in literal terms. Thus the semantic view is reductionistic and, indeed, would have all linguistically engendered meanings be reduced to semantic features or feature combinations, a position that is anathema for many scholars. Then there is the implicit idea that figurative meaning (new literal meaning, actually) is always preceded by and dependent on literal meaning, a position that some scholars believe is inconsistent with empirical findings (Gibbs, 1994).

Some adherents of the semantic view would also claim that tropes do not yield any new meanings, but that they merely package old ones in new ways or suggest things that presumably are already known. This view often connects literal meaning with truth value by making this meaning equivalent to truth value, or even proclaiming that something does not have any meaning if it has an indeterminate truth value. Naysayers such as myself would have truth arise from understanding rather than be equivalent to it. Finally, although this view does not make figuration special, it also does not give it an important place in the everyday language and cognition of ordinary people, a serious shortcoming in the eyes of many scholars.

In conclusion, most scholars concede that the meanings of words, including something like their core, context-free meanings and how meanings get combined, play a role in language comprehension. The problem is that language cannot be comprehended by knowing only these things. Language comprehension, whether literal or nonliteral, is typically dependent on many factors: background assumptions, massive amounts of world knowledge, inference, immediate context, and more. For this reason, we must not fall into the trap of thinking that literal meaning is simple, direct, explicit, or otherwise uncomplicated. Moreover, people are not limited in their communicative efforts to what they say because what they do in the saying can be critical to the communication, particularly when it comes to nonliteral language and all forms of indirect language in general. That is why some theorists have moved the theorizing from the structural linguistic level to the pragmatic linguistic level.

Pragmatic View.   The pragmatic view of figuration is that it is a matter of how language is used rather than of what words or sentences might mean. Words and sentences still mean what they do by the semantic view, but now the critical question is how they are being used. This naturally leads to a distinction, a dissociation, really, between meaning and use. Use ultimately becomes a matter of what the language user is trying to do by saying things, a view that can be traced to Grice (1957, 1975) and Austin (1962). Figuration is not present in the words per se, therefore, but, rather, in the discrepancy between the words and what the speaker intends. As Searle (1979) put it, the question is how intentions (speaker meaning) and actual words (sentence meaning) "come apart" (p. 92).

For Searle, who offers perhaps the most detailed pragmatic theory, the question is how someone can say, "S is P" (e.g., "Joan is a peach") and mean "S is R" (e.g., Joan is a delightfully pleasant person). That is, how can people say one thing and mean another? This way of theorizing places figuration squarely within speech act theory (Austin, 1962; Searle, 1969, 1979). What people actually say becomes literal meaning and, depending on how it differs from what was intended, this meaning can be deemed defective (by some interpreter) and then replaced with a contextually more appropriate meaning (what the conveyed meaning is thought to be by the interpreter). When people say what they mean, that is when "S is P" is taken in some context to be the same as "S is R," then "S is P" is to be taken literally. In other words, when speaker meaning and sentence meaning do not come apart, literal meaning results.

On occasion, however, a speaker will say something that is at odds with the context, or that seems inherently odd, or both, and this will serve notice to the listener that something other than "S is P" is meant. That is, the speaker can conjoin words in odd ways as in a standard "is a" metaphor, or violate some social convention for speaking, such as by seeming to be irrelevant, insincere, mendacious, or otherwise infelicitous. At this point, proponents of the pragmatic view typically add, after Grice (1975), that listeners assume that speakers abide by basic conversational rules, which is to say that, in general, speakers are still trying to communicate something even if what they have said does not make sense in the overall communicative context. By making these assumptions the listener is implicitly guaranteeing that he or she will recognize that there is a problem, namely that what was said is not what was meant, and that he or she will be motivated to find a meaning for the utterance that does makes sense in the context.

In brief, buying into these assumptions makes for problem recognition, but the listener still has the job of solving the problem. Searle (1979) addressed this concern by outlining a variety of strategies that the listener might use to compute "S is R." For "Joan is a peach," for example, this might require abiding by the notion that things that are P are, by definition, R (e.g., pleasurable, emotionally uplifting), or contingently R, or somehow associated with R, and so on.

The pragmatic view does not dispense with the notion of literal meaning. It builds on it. Although theorists such as Searle tend to use terms like "defective" for literal meaning, when this meaning is inappropriate, it might be better to say that in some cases the literal meaning is used for building a different meaning. Of course, such building requires mental powers, so adherents of the pragmatic view gladly endorse concepts such as world knowledge, inference, and so on.

The pragmatic view has a larger following than the semantic view. It is less stingy, if also less heroic than that view. However, it is similar in some respects to it. Literal meaning remains the fundamental meaning. This meaning is comprehended first, before figurative meaning, so as with the semantic view, it too leads to a stage-based view of figurative comprehension.

The pragmatic view also sometimes makes (literal) meaning a matter of truth value and, again, this position makes many theorists uncomfortable. Many tropes evoke meanings that are not so clear-cut or propositional, but, rather, mushy, emotional, and generally imprecise, yet highly communicative. This is the case for even as simple a metaphor as "Joan is a peach." Presumably, such meanings are less capable of truth value analysis.

Nevertheless, the pragmatic view has much to recommend it. It acknowledges the fact that what people say can be complex in the sense that more than this is at stake in communication. Simply put, it acknowledges that it is very difficult to tackle problems of indirectness in tropes and various functions such as overstatement, irony, sarcasm, euphemism, and rhetorical question, without simultaneously considering both what people say and how this can diverge from what they intend. This gives the pragmatic view a depth and scope to which the semantic view cannot lay claim.

This apparent plus, however, comes with a cost—Pandora's box is opened, and all the problems of mindreading come to the fore. How do people ever ascertain what the speaker meant? Is there always some discrepancy between speaker meaning and listener meaning? Are people ever really perfectly in tune with one another? The literal meaning, itself complex and not given just by fixed meanings and syntax, is only one among a set of important variables in a big equation. There may be some ways, heuristics perhaps, that enable the listener to use sentence meaning to get a new meaning, but there are no guarantees. We might just as well say that, contrary to Searle (1979), metaphorical meaning is listener meaning, or at best, what speaker and listener seem to agree the new meaning is, and that this meaning is not what the speaker meant because no one else can ever know exactly what that was. Maybe the speaker does not know either.

An interesting twist on this matter is that it is not the sentence meaning that is somehow odd or defective but, rather, the world or conditions under which it is uttered (Levin, 1979). In this case, the metaphor is taken literally (as Searle would have it), but it is not reconstrued via inference. Instead, *the world* is taken as deviant and in need of reconstrual. By this tack, we take the statement "Joan is a peach" as a direct, meaningful assertion and simply invent a world in which Joan becomes peachy. Such possible worlds accounts of metaphor provide a good example of how the pragmatic view opens Pandora's box.

For some scholars, however, the pragmatic view retains too many faults of the semantic view including, especially, its retention of many of the same metatheoretical assumptions (e.g., literal meaning is primary). It also fails to address certain kinds of systematicity in metaphor usage. That brings us to our third and last view, the conceptualist view.

Conceptualist View. For the conceptualist, metaphors and other tropes are not figures of speech, but figures of thought, motivated, that is, by nonlinguistic knowledge. Whether for cultural or biological reasons, the raison d'être of figuration is not linguistic but conceptual and nonverbal, essentially independent of the linguistic system, though expressible by means of it. Whatever is happening when people use tropes, it is because they have some general mental ability to do so.

Although all subpositions within the conceptualist view comport with the basic conceptualist thesis, there are important differences among them. For example, there is the older Gestalt psychological view that perception is at once technical, physical, and in some sense literal, but also nontechnical, evaluative, and metaphoric, though dependent on technical perception for its existence (Werner, 1955; Werner & Kaplan, 1963). The Gestalists have called the latter *physiognomic perception*, which they consider to be a general, biological tendency to experience the world in dynamic intersensory, wholistic, synesthetic, and feeling-tone/action terms. Physiognomics, in turn, is a differentiated product of the syncretic state of the organism, one in which affective, postural-motor, internal proprioceptive, and imaginal elements are fused. Babies are in a more syncretic state than adults in that these elements are blended and experienced as one.

Mental development brings about their differentiation, and through physiognomic perception, figurative forms such as metaphor, simile, analogy, and even sympathy and empathy come about. Thus, expressions such as, "The clouds are angry," "The music is yellow with black streaks," "Railings are cruel," come about because, perceptually, clouds just do look angry, music somehow evokes an experience of yellow and black, and railings naturally look foreboding and cruel. This subposition is interesting, although the details of the mechanism of physiognomics were never worked out by the Gestalists, nor was much research done on language per se. However, this tradition has been kept alive in some contemporary analyses of synesthesia (Marks, 1996).

Perhaps the most radical conceptualist variant is that of Lakoff and his colleagues (Lakoff, 1987, 1993; Lakoff & Johnson, 1980; Lakoff & Turner, 1989). For convenience, it can be called the conceptual metaphor theory (CMT) because the basic premise of the theory is that metaphoric expressions reflect deep conceptual metaphoric roots. This system of conceptual metaphors "structures our everyday conceptual system, including abstract concepts, and ... lies behind much of everyday language. The discovery of this enormous metaphor system has destroyed the traditional literal-figurative distinction, since the term 'literal,' as used in defining the traditional distinction, carries with it all those false assumptions" (Lakoff, 1993, p. 204).

What is literal for Lakoff is "those concepts that are not comprehended via conceptual metaphor" (p. 205). Examples would presumably be statements such as "The ball bounced on the ground," "She wore a blue dress," and "The CMT is better than the traditional approach."

The arguments that adherents of the CMT use against the traditional view are lengthy and complex. What can be emphasized here is that what many people would think of as literal, the CMT makes metaphoric. Utterances such as "She was struck with his intelligence," "The stock rose 10 points," and "He found success," which may seem literal and conventional, are viewed as manifestations of underlying conceptual metaphors. Only extremely dead sayings such as "foot of the mountain" escape metaphorization.

According to the CMT, much of our reasoning about everyday concepts such as money, love, quantity, death, time, legal matters, disease, foreign policy, and so forth is best treated in conceptual metaphoric terms. Conceptual metaphors are not dead. They are constantly and automatically being used by people every day, so that there is nothing atypical, dead, fancy, or even intentional about most metaphor usage. Metaphor is ubiquitous and conventional for poets and the commonfolk alike.

In the case of "Joan is a peach" the conceptual metaphor is presumably something like, "People are foods." The particular metaphor is merely one manifestation of the deeper conceptual metaphor, in terms of which the surface metaphor is understood. The operation of the deep metaphor would be suggested by the occurrence of a family of surface metaphors such as "She's a real sweet-pea," "Ralph is a MacDonald's Big Mac," or "Georgia's voice is a nectarine with a cold." Scholars using this approach employ examples that seem more systematic and regular, such as anger idioms—"He blew his stack," "She's boiling," or "He flipped his lid"—which are interpreted to be instances of a basic metaphoric way of comprehending anger, expressible in the present case as "Anger is heated fluid in a container," which is conjoined with another conceptual metaphor, namely, "The mind is a container" (Lakoff, 1987). The latter metaphor stems from Reddy (1979).

What is radical about this approach is that it rejects traditional views about literal meaning and literal language and essentially replaces their function with metaphor. By the traditional view, literal meaning is commonplace in communication. It is the basic and perhaps the only means by which truth value can be ascertained; it is used to understand just about all instances of language; and it is the format in which linguistic structures (grammar, lexicon) are writ. By the CMT, metaphor is commonplace, basic, truth-bearing, and used to understand just about everything, including abstract ideas. By the CMT, literal meaning was once king, but no longer. Adherents of the CMT place no faith in the semantic view and reject the pragmatic view as well because of the literalism they believe still pervades these approaches.

The CMT has been extremely influential and has made scholars think twice about the entire area, most especially about what is literal and what is not. It also plays an important role in the great chain metaphor theory of proverb comprehension (see chapter 4).

The conceptual metaphor notion has not gone unchallenged. If there are problems with the concept, then it can be claimed that there may be problems with the way in which the concepts of literal and figurative are treated in the CMT.

First, there are methodological problems. For example, no objective means are offered by which other analysts could come up with the same conceptual metaphors, given the same surface metaphorical expressions. The CMT proponent who creates and names conceptual metaphors is imputing conceptual similarity to literally discrepant pieces of information. These expressions are said to reflect conceptual metaphoric categories, yet we.are not provided with any rules for deciding that they are in these categories, or, more fundamentally, what constitutes these categories or how they should be linguistically described.

Perhaps the fundamental issue is that of semantic primitives (features, concepts, metaphors, or whatever), the stuff of which actual linguistic meanings are composed. This issue has been around for a very long time, and was debated most extensively, in psychology at least, in the 1960s and early 1970s. In some respects, conceptual metaphors have the theoretical status of the semantic feature concept of this bygone era. The problems with this concept, discussed in conjunction with the semantic view, were legion: It was impossible to draw up an exhaustive list of features; context plays a large role in determining what becomes a feature, yet new contexts can always be created, and there are no well worked out ways to combine features. The conceptual metaphor approach is fundamentally a synthetic approach in the sense that preexisting metaphors are pressed into service singly or in combination to create surface level utterances. Yet even at the sentence level, wholistic forces operate, so that one needs to understand a sentence at this level before it is possible to specify the presumed conceptual metaphors that underlie it. This tends to lead to the postulation of an ever-increasing number of conceptual metaphors because there is an infinity of sentences. This leads, in turn, to metaphorization of essentially all forms of utterance just to keep up with the bewildering sets of ideas that people can create. This is a losing battle. Constraints have to be placed on the postulation of any sort of underlying primitive. For example, it would be inappropriate to put primitives *in* words and sentences, although this leads to questions about the interaction between a system of primitives and linguistic expressions (R. Hoffman, personal communication, August 8, 1996).

Is there a conceptual metaphor behind every metaphor, proverb, and idiom? What, after all, is the conceptual metaphor behind our "Joan is a peach" metaphor? The author made one up, but others could be imagined. Should one be made up at all? If so, how broad should its scope be, and in precisely what terms should it be stated? Along these lines, there are likely many other metaphors that do not fit the mold of emanating from a conceptual metaphor, including examples that come from the Gestalt psychologists as well as everyday kinds of metaphors. Part of the problem here is that it is too easy to generate a conceptual structure for any linguistic utterance: Just state it in more abstract terms (frankly, the same can be done with the cognitive ideals hypothesis). "She flipped her lid" could be interpreted as an instance of "Anger is heated fluid in a container," but also as "Anger is highly energetic activity in a physical system." Other anger idioms would fit this conceptual metaphor as well: "George is boiling," "Kathy hit the ceiling," or "Pete blew his stack." It is not clear how it is decided that one characterization of a conceptual metaphor is to be preferred over another.

Furthermore, the CMT appears to treat conceptual metaphors as classical categories, in the sense that all category members are equally good and share the same attributes. The irony here is that Lakoff (1987) has specifically rejected the classical approach to conceptual categories in favor of a more probabilistic approach. Surely, there must be gradedness, and therefore some not-so-good examples of conceptual metaphors. Even if one assumes that well-formed mental structures, or idealized cognitive models as Lakoff (1987) calls them, motivate surface level expressions, then gradation should be found in the expressions. Yet this performance issue seems not to have been treated in the CMT approach.

There is also the crucial issue of whether people actually use conceptual metaphors in real-time processing of figurative language. That is, it is one thing to postulate the existence of deep underlying conceptual metaphors or deep underlying anything, and quite another to demonstrate that these structures serve as the basis for comprehending or producing tropes. Several investigators have expressed contrary views about the role of conceptual metaphors in comprehending metaphors (Glucksberg,

Brown, & McGlone, 1993; Glucksberg & Keysar, 1993; but see Gibbs, 1992) and proverbs (Honeck & Temple, 1994; Honeck & Temple, 1996; but see Gibbs, Colston, & Johnson, 1996). This issue remains unsettled.

Other criticisms of the conceptual metaphor notion have surfaced. Mac Cormac (1985), for example, averred that the CMT overdoes it in making too much of ordinary language metaphoric, thereby robbing metaphor of the unique function of generating novel ideas. The CMT does allow some knowledge to be nonmetaphorical, and unmediated by the filter of conceptual metaphors, but Mac Cormac argued that even this knowledge may be less than direct.

There is also the question of the extent to which generic knowledge is metaphoric. For the CMT it is largely so, but this is an open empirical question to be decided by data gathered on large numbers of people. A related issue is how extensively metaphors enter into the mind's work. In the CMT, metaphor occurs when one thing is understood in terms of another, a cross-domain mapping from a source (e.g., spatial knowledge) to a target (e.g., time). The problem is that zillions of things are understood in terms of other things: people in terms of lower animals, computers as fancy typewriters, atoms as something like solar systems, viruses as miniature robots, and so on. The question therefore arises: What sort of mapping is a cross-domain mapping? The CMT does not answer this question for us in any principled way. Fogelin (1988) argued that Lakoff and Johnson (1980), who provided the first version of the CMT, should have used the term "comparison" but used the term "metaphor" instead. This important observation appropriately makes metaphor, not special, but one of a large number of comparisons people can make among things. Furthermore, if current semantic network models of memory structure are considered (Collins & Loftus, 1975), then essentially all knowledge becomes a matter of comparison in that, to become meaningful, concepts must be related and compared to other concepts. This makes all knowledge, old and novel, more or less metaphoric. It just becomes a matter of where one wishes to draw the line for what constitutes a different domain.

In conclusion, the CMT has provided a refreshing, productive and spirited approach to figurative language. A wide range of scholars have benefited from and used the approach. It is theoretically appealing and appears to have some empirical justification. For example, it is difficult to explain the systematicity that is apparent among different metaphoric expressions without invoking the conceptual metaphor concept or something like it, and abstract reasoning often seems to draw on metaphor. The CMT approach is beginning to be applied to empirical aspects of proverb processing (Gibbs, 1995). Yet nagging questions remain concerning the methodological status of the conceptual metaphor concept itself. The conceptual metaphor construct has its place, but it is not the whole of tropic understanding.

There is plenty of room within the conceptualist view for different positions. In psychology, there is a long history to what is sometimes called the *deep cognition thesis*, which in its broadest sense, holds that thought is primary and language derivative. This tradition predates the CMT view. It can be traced to Piaget (1926), Vygotsky (1962), and Wundt (see Blumenthal, 1970), as well as to the Gestalists mentioned earlier. It finds expression in the more recent writings of Bransford and Franks (1971), Marks (1978, 1996), Miller and Johnson-Laird (1976), Osgood (1960, 1980), Pollio, Barlow, Fine, and Pollio (1977), and other sources.

The deep cognition and CMT theses differ. The major difference concerns whether the thought system is intrinsically metaphorical (the CMT position) or whether it can compute a variety of relationships and comparisons, some metaphorical (the deep cognition position). The best example of this view, as applied to proverbs, comes from the extended conceptual base theory of proverb comprehension (briefly described in chapter 1 and more extensively in chapter 4). Briefly, this theory holds that proverbs get a figurative meaning by a series of processes that draw on a large pool of information in long-term memory and elaborative processes in general. This information exists in a nonlinguistic conceptual memory. Proverb use and understanding is seen, in turn, to result from basic mental capacities for understanding one thing in terms of another, not from an intrinsic *content-based metaphorical* connection in conceptual memory. This version of the deep cognition view distinguishes, therefore, between our immense knowledge base and the processing mechanisms that can access and relate this information, some of which operate to yield products that are deemed figurative when what is related is discrepant enough domain-wise.

In any event, it should be clear by now that the issue of literalness and figurativeness is unsettled, to say the least. Theorists have strong, relatively entrenched opinions about the matter. Perhaps the more reasonable stance is that all three views have something to offer. Each view may be more appropriately applied in some situations, for some tropes, than others. For example, for some kinds of automatic, conventional metaphors (e.g., "Some jobs are jails") the CMT may be more appropriate. For novel metaphors, and depending on their specifics, the pragmatic view may be more viable, or some combination of this view and the deep cognition variant of the conceptualist view. For metaphors that occur in isolation, for which interpreters may be forced into the stategy of breaking words down into features, the semantic view may be relevant. Each view is incomplete, and given that the human mind can function in different modes in different situations, it is unlikely that any one approach will provide all of the answers.

The Imprecision of "Literal"

That there are theoretical differences about literalness is sobering enough. There are also different ways in which the term *literal* is used, and although these usages correlate somewhat with theoretical perspective, it is not always clear exactly what sense of the term is being used. The term is polysemous, a chamelion that resists precise definition, because the definition changes with the context and the user. *Literal* has been variously conceived as: whatever the object or real-world referent for the sentence is, whatever someone believes other people believe something means, the technical meaning of something, the dictionary definition of something, something only experts know, whatever can be capable of being shown to be true or false, how some subgroup of people usually talk about something, and, as Lakoff (1986b, p. 293) points out, whatever is "directly meaningful" by not being understood in terms of something else, the definition he apparently favors.

Such terminological variety is interesting but prohibitive. *Literal* is an important term and, ideally, should be defined theoretically. If the theory stands up, then its construal of the term stands up. Some of the preceding definitions are easily dispensed with, for example that literal is only a matter of dictionary definition, reference, and expertise, although there is some debate about the latter two. Now, the problem comes to life when we consider even simple things that we hear every day, for example someone who says, "I'm dead, and I mean that literally." When we point out, if we dare to, that they can not really mean that because they are obviously not dead, just exhausted perhaps, they might then reply, "Well, but I feel dead." At this point, we might as well go about our business, because hardly anybody knows what it is like to feel dead, unless we believe the stories of people who were clinically dead for a time and were brought back to life. How can we quarrel with the pronouncement that someone feels literally dead? Moreover if we accept the statement as a literal one, in what sense do we understand it as such? The statement is obviously not literal in one sense, but it is also not metaphorical in some other senses. Perhaps part of the problem in trying to identify a statement as literal or metaphorical is that we feel compelled to make it, unequivocally, one or the other. However, just as visual figures can be ambiguous and give rise to contradictory perceptions, so it is with some utterances—viewed in different ways they are variously metaphorical, literal, or anomalous.

What Determines Figurativeness?

The last reason why the issue of literal versus figurative is unsettled is more empirical. Many factors can influence our judgment about relative literalness. The entire envelope of the utterance must be considered. Everything counts—the speaker, his or her intentions, the intended audience, knowledge shared by speaker and audience, the context, and the utterance itself.

Any one of these factors can affect literalness. Make Juliet an 8-year-old who plays the part of the sun in a grade school play. Now the utterance, "Juliet is the sun," becomes less than Shakespearean. Make *A net with a hole in it won't catch any fish* be said by a ship captain who has just lost the day's catch, and it sounds quite ordinary and literal. It becomes nonliteral if the captain uses it to describe a faulty ship compass. If people are led to believe that a computer generated some strange statements, they are less likely to believe that the statements are metaphorical than if they believe that a poet wrote them (Katz & Lee, 1993). Try saying things like "Life is a journey" to 6-year-olds and see what happens. A key factor in understanding metaphor is not only domain-specific knowledge (Winner & Gardner, 1993), but also the ability to synthesize concepts. Entire passages can be read as commonplace (literal?) descriptions of things or as allegory. *Moby Dick* is a good example.

There are degrees of indirectness, so it is hard to tell what counts as a clear case of figurative language. For example, the following sentences seem to move from direct to less direct in their commentary on the moon:

The moon is bright at times.

The moon is a chunk of rock in the sky.

The moon soothes the psyche.

The moon is intelligent in its phases.

The moon is like a child lost at sea.

The moon wraps itself in the warm solar flow.

The moon is a donkey weighed down in gold.

The moon is a $30 bill.

If "the moon" refers to Earth's natural satellite, then the first sentence seems quite literal, conventional, and direct. This sentence merely describes a truth about perception. The second sentence is a literal half-truth. The moon is partially composed of rock but lots of other materials as well. The moon may only seem like a big rock, but this is less odd than saying that the moon can soothe, as if it were a salve that could be rubbed on an ailing body part. However, intelligent the moon is not, because hardly anyone but the most ardent panpsychist would attribute intelligence to such an object. The next four sentences seem increasingly metaphorical with the last two verging on nonsense.

Are they, or is metaphor and indirectness in the mind of the beholder? There would seem to be clear cases of metaphor, cases that many people could agree on, but there are unclear cases. If the speaker of a statement intends the statement to be taken metaphorically, or more generally, as a form of indirectness, but the statement's hearers do not construe it this way, has a metaphor been uttered?

It is hard to understate the importance of context for this issue. If "the moon" in the preceding sentences refers to the name of a particular manned spaceship, then the position of the sentences on the continuum would change. "The moon is a donkey weighed down in gold" becomes less metaphorical and more direct. Manned spaceships carry a heavy load; it is valuable, and the spaceship itself can be hard to maneuver, just like a donkey. "The moon is a $30 bill" becomes more sensible now, taking on a nuance, namely that the spaceship may seem like a waste of money to some people, a phony project.

Thus, by changing the reference somewhat, attributions of literalness may change dramatically. If "the moon" now refers to an expensive new brand of diamond ring, the position of the various statements on the scale changes once again.

These several examples strongly suggest that degree of literalness is not a property of statements. Interactions matter. This is also the case for what, on the surface, look like obvious examples of metaphor such as "The stock prices went down." The example would qualify as a metaphor under the CMT, because prices are understood in terms of a spatial property. The utterance could become quite literal if stock prices were written on a large bulletin board and there was an earthquake. Some financial commentators, such as Louis Rukeyser from TV's "Wall Street Week," would have a field day with this situation. Furthermore, *Make hay while the sun shines* can be good literal advice for a farmer.

The approach to literal meaning suggested by the foregoing discussion is consistent with the "moderate literalism" approach outlined by Dascal (1987, p. 260). Briefly, Dascal argued that there is no set of necessary and sufficient conditions for defining literal meaning. Everything counts, but no one factor is, by itself, able to determine what is or is not literal. Thus, to decide literal status requires that we look at a large number of factors: context, people's knowledge, and the purposes involved in attributing literalness. As Dascal put it, scholars have generally asked too much of literal meaning when a more inclusive treatment of communication is called for.

In conclusion, although the concept of literalness is complex, it is not intractable. Therefore, as applied to proverbs, it becomes feasible to make a distinction between literal and figurative meaning. When a proverb is taken to refer to the commonplace instances of the categories suggested by it, then the proverb statement is being used literally (and should not be called a proverb). But when the proverb is used to comment on a topic that is ordinarily conceived as beyond the scope of the categories suggested by the proverb, then the proverb is being used as a proverb, figuratively that is. Of course, we should have to examine the details of this conception in any instance.

TYPES OF TROPES

With these ideas in mind, we discuss the various major forms of figurative language. How these forms differ and how they compare to proverbs are taken up in the next section.

Fundamentally, figurative language is a form of communication in which some topic is indirectly connected to and commented on by some vehicle. The terms "topic" and "vehicle" were introduced by Richards (1936) in connection with metaphors. The *topic* is what is commented on, whereas the *vehicle* is the concept used to do the commenting. In a simple metaphor such as "Today was electric," "today" is the topic and "electric" is the vehicle. Furthermore, in Richards' terms, what today and electric share is the *ground* of the metaphor. In most metaphors, topic and vehicle are easy to identify but, because the latter are the actual concepts being referred to, they need not be stated explicitly. For example, the entire sentence could be a vehicle, an apt description of the case in which a proverb is used to instantiate some topic. Richards also used the term *tension* to describe the felt conceptual mismatch between the topic and vehicle, a tension that is present in every case of figurative language, from a theoretical though not necessarily from an experiential perspective.

Richards' (1936) scheme for describing metaphor can be extended to all tropes. As it turns out, the way in which the connection between topic and vehicle is accomplished is the primary basis for distinguishing many kinds of tropes.

Metaphor

In the case of metaphor, the topic is classified in an odd way by the vehicle. Here are some examples, the last from Durrell (1959, p. 79):

Man is a wolf.

She's a statue in the wilderness.

The sky broods at dusk.

Joan is a peach.

The time runs downhill on iced feet toward Christmas.

These are part-sentence metaphors in the sense that, in the absence of context, the oddity of the categorization (category crossing) makes for their metaphoricity. There are also whole-sentence metaphors in which a complete sentence (the vehicle) relates in a metaphorical way to some context (the topic; e.g.,"The soldiers are planning their assault," said of a group of people playing poker.)

These are all odd classifications for the topic, because humans and wolves are different animals; a female is an organism that cannot be a statue; only sentient beings can brood; if Joan is human, then she is not a peach; time does not have legs and cannot run downhill; and poker players are not soldiers. The very oddness of the classifications is a clue that something is amiss and that the statements are not to be taken as (literally) true, at least in the contextless way in which which they are all (except for the soldiers) presented. In this sense, the statements are not to be taken literally because they make no sense on a literal, referential level. That is, the apparent intention of their author was not to invite the reader to find a way in which the categorizations could possibly be true. Rather, the invitation was to discover something about the vehicle that could be applied to the topic that would somehow make sense. Of course, the reader/listener must assume that the author/speaker was trying to communicate by saying something relevant about the topics. If this assumption could not be made, then there would be no reason, save for curiosity, for the reader to go beyond the stage of having detected a strange and untrue assertion.

The foregoing analysis flows from an approach to communication that combines speech act theory with the cooperative principle. To reiterate, the basic premises are that people intend to say something (speaker meaning); they actually say something (sentence meaning); and their listener gets a particular meaning (conveyed or utterance meaning). For metaphor, and presumably for all forms of figurative language, there is a mismatch (indirectness) between speaker meaning and sentence meaning. When a listener hears a metaphor, therefore, it sounds as if the speaker is being uncooperative because he or she has said something that is obviously untrue, in violation of the maxim of quality. However, if the listener assumes that the speaker is still cooperating—by being sincere and relevant—then what seems like a real violation of the norms of cooperation can be viewed as merely an apparent violation, so it becomes worthwhile to construct a new meaning for the statement. How this new meaning is constructed is currently the subject of an intense debate. The listener's job is to get the speaker's meaning, but with access only to the sentence meaning and a variety of other situational clues. If the listener does not get the speaker's meaning, then there is miscommunication. Irrespective of this pragmatics approach, communication is the rule, and a tribute to the computational powers of the human mind.

Of course, the position can be taken that people automatically compute metaphorical meanings, sans pragmatic conventions (Gibbs, 1994). For example, Glucksberg and Keysar (1993) claimed that a metaphor is a category-inclusion statement. That is, when, for example, someone says, "Joan is a peach," they mean that Joan is to be viewed, momentarily, as a member of the peach category. It is not the purpose here to take sides on this issue, however, but to provide a general introduction to the topic of metaphor.

Simile

In the case of simile the topic is set within the framework of another category, the vehicle, by explicitly asserting that the topic is similar in some particular ways to that category. Here are some examples:

> Her hair is like a bird's nest.
>
> This newspaper article is like a Hampton Court maze.
>
> Pete's running style is as a locomotive climbs a steep pass.
>
> A diamond is like money in the bank.
>
> She reads metaphors like a baby drinks milk.

Similes use terms, most often "like" or "as," that invite a comparison between two domains that are dissimilar. To say that, "Her hair is like the actress Jessica Lange's" might involve making a literal comparison. Therefore, as was the case for metaphor, it is the very oddness of the categorization that makes simile a form of figuration. Simile goes beyond metaphor in directly stipulating the existence of some sort of similarity of the topic to the vehicle. The listener's job is to mentally conjoin the topic with its new ad hoc category and derive a similarity. In this sense, simile can be viewed as a special kind of metaphor because the set of possible relationships between the topic and vehicle categories has been reduced to one of similarity. Most metaphors are based on similarity but need not be. Metaphors also tend to be seen as stronger statements than similes (Glucksberg & Keysar, 1993). It is not that "Man is *like* a wolf," but that "Man *is* a wolf." Similes hedge, but do so in a way that constrains comprehension.

Metonymy

Metonymy occurs when the topic is referred to by another concept (the vehicle) with which it is somehow associated. Instead of the referent being invoked literally and as a whole, it is alluded to by substituting the vehicle. Examples include the following:

> The legislature said that the Bill won't pass.   (legislature = particular members of the legislature)
>
> Nearly all of the guns passed through this territory.   (guns = soldiers)
>
> We won't have the bat in the game today.   (bat = good hitter in baseball)
>
> The West has failed Yugoslavia.   (West = government leaders in Western countries)   (Yugoslavia = the people of this former nation)
>
> Johnny Carson did a Jack Benny.   (Jack Benny = a gesture that mimics the late comedian Jack Benny)

There are also synesthetic metonymies, such as the connection that exists for most adults between the colors red/orange/yellow and "warm," and between blue/green and "cool." Similarly, smallness connects with high-pitch sounds, largeness with low-pitch sounds. The sounds made by crickets, chalk on blackboards, and electric fans are higher pitched than the sounds made by lions, dropped tables, and foghorns. The correlation is far from perfect but sufficient to drive the connection (Marks & Bornstein, 1987; Osgood, 1960).

Metonymy is figuration, not in the sense of crossing dissimilar domains as with metaphor and simile, but in virtue of using an aspect of something to stand for that thing. Obviously, then, communication could go awry if the vehicle were not chosen carefully. If a receiver of metonymy does not share certain pieces of information (common ground) with the speaker, the utterance may not be interpretable. To use the preceding Johnny Carson example (sic!) with someone younger than 30 years of age is to risk not communicating. Moreover to say "The hat won't be pitching today" to refer to the star pitcher is to risk not communicating unless the listener knows that this pitcher wears his baseball cap in a strange way. The use of metonymy requires, therefore, that there be some principled way in which the listener can make the connection between topic and vehicle. From a purely informational standpoint this connection is perhaps more variable than in the case of metaphors and similes. The latter are commonly based on similarity, whereas metonymy can be based on a much larger set of conceptual relationships. For example, Lakoff (1987) described a number of ways in which metonymic references can come about, including the use of vehicles that are typical examples, paragons, salient examples, ideal cases, social stereotypes, and generators such as the 10 basic digits that generate all other numbers in base-10 notation.

Metonymy is a common form of expression, one that seems to illustrate the law of least effort, because it expresses a larger, more extensive idea in an economical way. It also motivates novel linguistic usages—"The secretary word-processed the article," "He computered his way into a job"—that turn nouns into (denominal) verbs. There seems to be little limit to the ways in which metonymy can come about, so long as the persons on the receiving end have at their disposal some information that will enable the connection. Thus, "steak city" might serve as a private metonymic reference to a favorite restaurant for husband and wife; "desk sitter" can serve as a college student's sarcastic metonymic-based opinion about a particular course; and "the Babe Ruth of experimental psychology," could be a metonymic reference by way of a paragon to an esteemed colleague.

Metonymic allusions cannot be just anything of course. Metonymies often draw on the same domain as the intended topic—arm for the baseball player, legislature for legislator—but not always as in Babe Ruth for psychologist or the mention of green to evoke the experience of coolness. There are some systematic and typical ways in which metonymy comes about. For example, places come to stand for institutions (e.g., "The White House said...,") and objects for their users (e.g., "The computer is at it again"; Gibbs, 1994; Lakoff, 1987). Metonymy captures an essential general characteristic of figuration in that it is a compact way of referring.

Idiom

From metonymy, in which, for privileged communicators, the connection between topic and vehicle is usually obvious, we move to idioms, in which the connection is less than obvious. All languages have idioms, thousands of them. In English they include the following:

He's a *dead ringer* for Bertrand Russell.

She's *turning over a new leaf* with her piano lessons.

The boys *hit the sack* around ten.

That physicist's ideas are *off the wall*.

I'm *bushed*.

The relatively unprincipled distancing of topic and vehicle is the main signal of idiomaticity. Ideas cannot literally be off the wall, and playing the piano has no obvious connection with turning over a new tree leaf. The idiom itself, however, may be more or less decomposable, in the sense that its idiomatic meaning can be computed on the basis of the words and their syntactic arrangement. Many, perhaps most, idioms do not conform to this compositionality principle. However, idioms are variously nondecomposable or nonanalyzable (Gibbs, 1993, 1994).

Because even the most decomposable idioms are not easily decomposed, they make life difficult for the language user who is confronted with one of these beasts for the first time. I remember the first time I heard the phrase, "I'm chillin' out." This was said during final exam period by a college student who was sitting on a hallway floor with her books scattered about. It took me (a college professor) a few seconds to realize that she meant that she was trying to relax, an inference I put together based on the

shared background information, the immediate context, her de-
meanor, and the systematic metaphoric way we have in English
of using coldness to imply nonmovement, hence relaxation. This
was an easy inference, though I was a bit slow on the take.

In contrast, I know an Oriental student with an otherwise good
command of English, but who did not have the slightest idea what
I meant when I said, "Ralph kicked the bucket." I would be
similarly disenfranchised by Chinese idioms, to be sure, even if I
spoke Chinese, which I do not. In some cases, such as "kick the
bucket," no amount of reasoning, save some rather sophisticated
and lucky reasoning, would uncover the meaning of this idiom.
By hindsight, one could reason that in kicking the bucket someone
might fall and injure him- or herself and perhaps die. There is a
historical basis for the idiom, but it is lost on essentially all
English speakers, who must therefore rely on context and some
friendly help to get the meaning.

We would have better luck with some other idioms. For example, "She let the cat out of the bag" may well be construable for
someone who knows English, cats, and bags, but is unfamiliar
with the idiom. A little reasoning can do the trick. The cat is in
the bag in the first place because apparently it is supposed to be
there. Cats can be a nuisance anyway, and if the cat gets out of
the bag it is likely to cause some trouble. Therefore, letting a cat
out of a bag is equivalent to engaging in some act that has the
potential to cause trouble. A similar kind of reasoning might be
used to decipher idioms such as "spilling the beans"—beans are
not supposed to be spilled, so it is a bad thing when it happens.
That the spilling is likely to be accidental contributes to the sense
that the spilling was unintended, although it might not be.

In any event, it is not accidental that "spilling the beans" has
come to mean something like revealing a secret. Partly at issue
here is how this systematicity comes about. Adherents of the
conceptual metaphor theory have argued that systematicity is
based on underlying conceptual metaphors. One piece of evidence
for this hypothesis is that there is more similarity in the images
that people develop for similar meaning idioms, such as for the
anger trio of "blow a gasket," "boiling," and "hit the ceiling," than
for their presumed literal equivalents, such as "blow your tire"
(see Gibbs, 1993, for a review). On the other hand, there is great
commonality of cultural meaning for idioms. Such commonality

is necessary for their idiomatic status, after all, so it may be hard to disentangle conceptual metaphoric effects from relative familiarity and inferential effects. Also, people's introspections about their imagery may import processes and products, especially more reflective ones, that play no role in online processing. Keysar and Bly (1995) have provided some evidence that idioms vary in transparency of meaning, which they view as highly dependent on knowing the idiom's conventional meaning and having selected senses of the idiom's words that are consistent with this meaning.

It would be interesting to test people for whom English is a second language, or youngsters for whom English is a native language, to see to what extent they could reason out the figurative meaning of unfamiliar idioms. Idioms would likely vary a great deal in this respect. The same is probably true for proverbs. The problems that proverb translation causes are notorious. For this reason their use is frowned on in speeches given at the United Nations. Some of the difficulty in translation, humorous at times, is provided in Mieder's (1993a) case study of the Americanization of the originally German proverb, *Don't throw the baby out with the bath water*.

Oxymoron

Our last trope places the indirectness of topic and vehicle in close conjunction. With oxymora, the oddness that permeates all figuration is taken to the extreme of outright contradiction.

Examples include the following:

Thunderous silence
A swinging bunt
A fail-safe hard drive
The kiss of death
A peaceful world
Sweet pain
A deathly existence
Military intelligence
Bitter sweet
Colorless green

Surely, oxymora grow out of the well-developed human ability to conceive of things in anomalous, ambivalent, and generally opposed ways. Many oxymora seem to rest on the yin and yang of human existence: good and bad, life and death, strong and weak, war and peace, dark and light, and so on. They therefore have a universal intuitive appeal. There are some formal ways of describing oxymora, such as whether it is *direct* (e.g., "a hot cold," "a peaceful war") or *indirect* (e.g., "thunderous silence," "the loyal opposition"; Shen, 1987). For direct types, antonyms are used that differ only in terms of a single semantic feature at the same level in some hypothetical semantic hierarchy. For indirect types, a subcategory of the topic's antonym is used as the vehicle. In our examples, silence is connected by the subcategory of loudness to thunder, whereas opposition is connected by means of ally to loyal. This is not to say that such semantic schemes are neatly organized in long-term memory, but that people are quite adept at creating adhoc categories for which some sort of semantic hierarchy becomes manifest.

In general, it can be argued that, like proverbs, oxymora tread in the realms of ideals, prototypicality, and norms. Silence is supposed to be soundless, green is supposed to be colored, and a war somewhere in the world is the norm. For the latter, the topic is implicit in the sense that it is hard to think of a time in the history of humanity when a war was not occurring somewhere. Thus, the juxtaposition of "peaceful" with "world" helps to create and define the topic while simultaneously reducing its magnitude. In any event, if this "normality subtraction" hypothesis is at all valid, then the oxymoron works only by subtracting from the norm. Greens are made less colorful, worlds less warlike, sweets less sweet, intelligence less intelligent. By "normal situation" we mean, of course, that the most prototypical case, usually the extreme on the major semantic dimension, applies. In thinking of silence, one thinks in ideal, absolute terms of the absence of sound. Pain is normatively hurtful, and sweetness diminishes the sense of hurt. One could speak of a "painful pain," a "greeny green" or a "sweet sweet," in which cases the topics would simply seem to be made even more explicitly prototypical and normative. Such redundant expressions should not be considered oxymora.

TROPES AND THE BIG LANGUAGE PICTURE

It is time now to more directly compare the various forms of figurative language. To do this, we first take a look at language from the bird's perspective to see how lexicons are designed. Then we see whether analogous considerations apply to figurative language. To anticipate, there is good reason to believe that figurative genres have been forged under the same general constraints that apply to the construction of lexicons. These constraints provide some clues for distinguishing the various forms of figurative language.

Designing a Language

If we were in the position of being able to design a language how would we do it? Some design features would be obvious: allow for the reuse of words; make it possible to produce novel combinations of words; make a word semantically flexible but not so flexible that the word is not recognizable from one context to the next; make up words that are similar but not identical in meaning. Other features would have to be added.

Theoretically, all languages are a compromise between contradictory ideals. On the one hand, the ideal of economy would be achieved if there were just one word in a language. On the other hand, the ideal of precision would be achieved if there were a different word for every possible meaning. One word such as "polifloom," would make life boring, but it would make language learning a breeze! Of course, this would hardly be a language at all: No syntax is possible, no linguistic creativity, no means of making references precise, except perhaps by intonational changes (in which case we might violate our stipulation of just one word).

In this one-word world, the linguistic processing load would be virtually nothing, but context, and ultimately, personal knowledge and shared knowledge, would assume supreme importance. That is, if "polifloom" were uttered, no one would know what it meant, because it could mean anything, so all those factors that could help to delimit and make meaning precise would have to come from other sources, namely circumstances, context, and shared knowledge. This would place an enormous responsibility on the individual to acquire an immense amount of personal knowledge and have it accessible in all communication situations. Part of the problem is that contexts are innumerable, so our communicators would have to be very good at reading contexts in order to figure out what the other person was thinking, and, of course, this strategy would not always work. Moreover, because there would be only one word, it would not do much good to use it to ask a question.

With the opposite situation, one word for every possible meaning, new sets of advantages and disadvantages would arise. Language learning would be difficult, because there are limitless meanings. Furthermore, each word would have to be independently paired with each meaning, adding to the learning burden. This arrangement, if it could be accomplished, would make semantic precision the norm and easy at that, but the general memory and information processing load would be incalculable. Long-term memory would have to be stupendous, as also would the ability to access a particular word in it, in that if the pure number of words slowed access, communication would be all but impossible. In this big mental dictionary world, context would have little if any importance because the meanings all would be stored a priori in memory. In this case, there would have to be exact shared knowledge, because if someone knew a word but another person did not, then communication about that word meaning would be impossible. This circumstance would present a rather severe teaching problem. Also, if new meanings occurred, someone would have to invent a word for them, and then teach them to someone else, using old words, which might be impossible unless the old words could be organized somehow to convey the new meaning, or if we allowed nonlinguistic meanings to be used along with old words.

Neither of these alternatives is possible or desirable. Economy of expression and semantic precision both come with great costs. Moreover, these alternatives do not by any means exhaust what it is that we would want to build into our made-up language. For example, we would want people to be able to do things with words, to accomplish purposes, including aesthetic ones. We would want the language to articulate with the rest of the mind, most obviously in terms of meaning and goals. Furthermore we would not want language to be either a slave of context, as in the "polifloom" case, or independent of it, as in the mental dictionary case. We would want all sorts of words, not just one kind, and we would want people to be able to work out the meanings they wanted by using a stock of these words, some syntax, knowledge of context, shared knowledge, and a great deal of world knowledge in general. We would, in other words, want things to be pretty much as they are. Although this argument is anthropic in assuming what is, it seems apt.

Theoretically, one way in which language communities have resolved the dilemma of contradictory ideals is by creating words that take up different positions on the underlying continuum of the ideals. At the economy/context-specific end are indexicals and deictic words such as "it," "that," "here," "there," "yesterday," "I," and so on. These words take their meaning from context. Near the indexicals are polysemous words such as "over," which has over 100 different senses (Brugman, 1988), and "about," "among," "on," and many other function words in the language. Next in line are abstract words such as "generally," "precision," "abstract," "meandering," and the like, whose meanings are generally subject to debate although they can be used with some precision. Then there are homonyms such as "to," "too," and "two," and "pear" and "pair." Nearer to the technical end are words for more perceptual categories such as "tree," "fence," "garage," "table," "glasses," and so on. At the noneconomical/context-free end are words such as "voltage," "altimeter," "longitude," and "atom" that have precise or technical meanings.

Comparing the Tropes

When the tropes are placed on the continuum what happens? First, it must be clear that the question is whether a trope can be understood in isolation from a context, not whether it is likely to be used in one. That is, the question is whether a trope resembles "polifloom" or the one-word-one-meaning situation.

Under this interpretation, idioms emerge as the least like "polifloom," so they are the least context dependent. They are like technical words with a conventional, culturally based meaning that remains relatively invariant from one situation to the next.

Oxymora seem to fit this description as well because they create their own context, which can insulate them to some extent from the larger context. Like proverbs, they also seem to operate outside a context as comments on it, implying that they are less contextualizable. Proverbs also arguably have a meaning that is context independent, but because they are decomposable and often require desymbolization, they are more contextualizable than idioms or oxymora. Proverbs emerge as a kind of compromise between the context-means-nothing and the context-means-everything positions.

In any event, idioms, oxymora, and proverbs take up the more technical, context-free, one-meaning–one-expression side of the continuum. Similes and (part-sentence) metaphors juxtapose topic and vehicle in the same expression, so they create their own context. Of course, the expression is ordinarily set in some context that, as we have seen, can have a dramatic effect on metaphoric meaning. Metonymy depends almost completely on specific context or knowledge of the topic, without which it cannot function. Metonymies are like idioms and proverbs in that the topic exists outside the verbal expression, but unlike the latter, they tend to rely more on private rather than culturally shared knowledge of a context. Metonymy is akin, therefore, to indexicals and deictic terms.

Our exercise in language design has turned up some fundamental issues that apply both to individual words and tropes. Let us explore in detail how these issues can help distinguish these forms. The tropes vary along several dimensions: the relationship that each trope effects between topic and vehicle, the extent to which the trope is prelearned rather than computed on the spot, whether the trope can be figured out on the basis of its words and syntax (decomposability), general applicability, and typical functions.

There are at least two aspects to the topic-vehicle relationship criterion: whether the topic and vehicle come from the same or different domains, and how the vehicle relates to the topic.

In the cases of metonymy and oxymoron, topic and vehicle typically come from the same overall contextual domain—"the voice" (for the singer), "screaming silence." "Voice" is a music term and so is singer. "Screaming" activates the loudness dimension, on which silence takes up an extreme point. In the cases of metaphor, simile, proverb, and idiom, the vehicle always comes from a noticeably different domain. Otherwise, it would be difficult to talk of figuration.

How the various tropes have the vehicle connect to the topic is a little more complicated. For oxymoron, the topic's category remains the same, but it changes its position on a dimension of the category from an extreme to a less extreme one. For the other five tropes, the vehicle categorizes the topic in an odd way. The details of the categorization process are, however, somewhat different in each case. For metaphor, category membership is directly asserted: "Joan is a peach," "Pete's lips tripped on the big word." For simile, category membership is only suggested or invited: "Joan is like a peach." Idioms generally recategorize a single domain of events but in a relatively unprincipled way: going to sleep becomes "hit the sack"; dying becomes "kick the bucket"; an odd experience becomes "a trip to the moon." As vehicles, idioms assume an isomorphic relationship to their topics. Proverbs also recategorize events, but in more principled ways, and the events can come from a wide variety of domains. Almost all idioms work only for events that belong to a particular category—going to sleep, dying, and so on. All proverbs work for events that belong to a potentially very large number of categories. Thus, one could say of someone who "spilled the beans" that he or she should have *let sleeping dogs lie*, but this proverb could also be applied to many other events that have nothing to do with telling secrets. Finally, metonymy has the vehicle refer to the topic via an odd classification, but one that is principled in the sense that their connection is socially shared. The connection could seem unprincipled, however, to an outsider.

A second major way in which tropes differ is in terms of their prepackaging, that is whether they have already been learned or are produced anew in some context. Proverbs and idioms are generally learned and used as wholes. That is not to say that they cannot be understood on the first occasion of their use, because they can, especially proverbs (see Forrester, 1995, on novel idioms; see Honeck & Temple, 1994, for a review of research on novel proverbs). The other four tropes are almost always produced on the fly, cases of trope memorabilia notwithstanding. This distinction therefore assumes that people have a stock of idioms and proverbs in mind, but no such stock of metaphors, similes, oxymora, or metonymy, an assumption with notable exceptions no doubt. It also assumes to some extent that cases of dead or conventional metaphor, simile, and so on are not in the picture.

There is some untruth in this assumption, however, because there are probably always not just dead cases, but half-dead cases of each of these tropes.

Then there is Lakoff's (1987) argument that the mind is heavily populated with conventional (i.e., learned) metaphors. Another way to put this is that there is undoubtedly a continuum of familiarity for examples of each of the six kinds of tropes. There is a common stock of metaphors. There are probably even more familiar metonymies that might be produced if we asked people to generate some examples (e.g., "The White House said," "The king (Elvis Presley) was seen today," etc.), although of the set, metonymy would seem to be the most contextually bound, and the least likely, therefore, to become part of a learned corpus. Thus, the claim that idioms and proverbs are more likely to come in prepackaged form is subject to exception.

Third, the tropes can be distinguished in terms of decomposability, the extent to which it is possible to get the figurative meaning of the whole trope based on its word meanings and syntax. According to our earlier discussion, the worst offender on this criterion is the idiom, although we now know that idioms vary in terms of decomposability (e.g., "spill the beans" is easier to figure out than "kick the bucket"; see Gibbs, 1994). Whether the other tropes yield on this criterion depends on how much the would-be interpreter knows about the topic and vehicle, except for proverbs. For metaphor, simile, oxymoron, and metonymy, both the topic and vehicle must be known for the trope to function figuratively. But given this knowledge, these tropes become analyzable in a way that idioms are not, that is without having to get additional pieces of information. Proverbs are unique, however, because they can be understood figuratively without consideration of a topic. Subtract away the topic in the case of metaphor, simile, oxymoron, and metonomy and the trope ceases to exist. Proverbs are topicless tropes, but typically function in conjunction with topics. Having added this important caveat, all of the tropes, idioms excepted, are decomposable. Indeed people can make sense out of nearly any juxtaposition of vehicle and topic, including random ones.

The tropes also differ in terms of scope of application. Does the trope work for just one event in one context in one domain, or can it be used appropriately in conjunction with other events in new contexts in other domains? It is difficult to be precise in answering this because there are innumerable cases of each trope category. However, a continuum of generalizability from very high to very low might look as follows: proverbs, idioms, metaphors, simile, oxymoron, metonymy. Almost no cases of metonymy and few cases of oxymoron are produced in order to be used, as a whole utterance, in a new context. Metaphor and simile seem more movable. Essentially all true proverbs are movable. The same is true of idioms, as discussed earlier, but idioms are more limited in their range of application by the level of abstraction with which they operate. That is, the underlying meaning of idioms seems to operate almost exclusively at the level of basic-level categories: sleep ("hit the sack"), death ("kick the bucket"), anger ("flew through the roof"), talk ("shoot the breeze"), craziness ("lose your marbles"), and so on. Proverbs seem to operate at a more superordinate or ontological level. For example, *A net with a hole in it won't catch any fish* has a meaning that involves the concepts of an instrument, a flaw, and not reaching a goal. The familiar *A stitch in time saves nine* entails the concepts of human activity, time (now, later), quantity (less, more), and equivalence (of a stitch and nine stitches). Idioms are also typically shorter and more syntactically frozen than proverbs, properties that will tend to limit application.

Finally, the tropes also differ in their basic functions. These can be guessed at, but there is empirical evidence on the matter. Roberts and Kreuz (1994) asked college students to provide several examples of a particular kind of trope (to ensure that they understood the trope) and then provide reasons why they might use that kind of trope. The experimenters then classified these reasons in terms of discourse goals. Of the tropes we have examined, only metaphor, simile, and idiom were investigated. The results indicated that the discourse goals overlapped the most for metaphor and simile: "to clarify" was the most common goal (listed by 82% of the participants for metaphor, 94% for simile), whereas "to provoke thought" placed a distant second (35% for metaphor, 39% for simile). For metaphor, "to add interest" was the second most frequently listed goal at 71%. For simile, "to provoke thought" was second. Idioms shared little with metaphors and similes, except for some overlap between idioms and similes on the "to be humorous" goal (44% vs. 33%), which also turned out to be the most frequently listed goal, although "to be conventional" (38%) and "to clarify" (38%) were a close second.

Metonymy and oxymoron were not examined in this study. However, of the discourse goals the authors listed, one might expect that metonymy would rank high on the following: to be humorous, to emphasize, to add interest, and to show positive or negative emotion. Essentially, metonomy functions as a quick reference for people who share particular pieces of knowledge. Thus, it can serve as a sociopsychological laborsaving device that can also bond people, the latter because metonymy often reflects an opinion or attitude about a topic. Oxymoron would likely rank high as attempts to be eloquent, contrast differences, add interest, provoke thought, and show emotion. If, as speculated above, oxymoron is a way of diminishing an ideal, then perhaps the primary function of oxymoron is to criticize, be ironic, sarcastic, or otherwise negative about the topic.

Proverbs also were not examined in the Roberts and Kreuz (1994) study. However, indirect requests (e.g., "Can you reach that salad bowl?") were studied, and the most frequently listed goals were "to guide another's actions" (64%), "to be polite" (64%), and "to protect the self" (57%). Had proverbs been examined, perhaps a similar profile would have emerged, along with the additional goals of emphasis, adding interest, clarification, provoking thought, and showing negative emotion. This all seems to follow from the fact that proverbs are indirect, motivational, pragmatically deviant, instructive, and odd. They therefore share many of the functions of metaphor, simile, and indirect speech acts.

On some occasions, metaphor, simile, and idiom can be nearly indistinguishable from proverbs. Slight changes in wording may be all that is needed to tranform one of them into a proverb, and vice versa. The famous "Man is a wolf" is a metaphor that becomes more proverb-like when transformed to "Man can be a wolf." The metaphor is gone, but the message remains, this time in proverbial form. Alternatively, one could as well say that "Man is a wolf" is a proverb stated in metaphoric form. Its status depends on how it is used. Of course, many proverbs use metaphors to produce their effect. A simile such as "Soldiers are like pawns" has a proverbial message and could be used proverbially in a nonsoldier context, such as that of college athletes in high-profile programs. The simile invites comparisons that become the focus of the immediate statement, whereas the statement qua proverb is suitable for general application outside the realm of soldiers and war.

There are a number of functions that can be performed by each kind of trope: irony, sarcasm, understatement, hyperbole, rhetorical question. These functions are often considered to be figurative forms in their own right. However, it is better to treat them as functions than as forms. The reason is simple: Each of the six tropes that we have examined can serve each of these functions, and conventional language can serve these functions as well. For tropes and nontropes alike, the function turns on context. Examples for each of what amounts to a 30-cell (6 tropes by 5 nonliteral functions) matrix are not provided here, but it can be done. Focusing on just metonymy for example, "the glove" could be used in each of these five ways. For example, the player has just bought an expensive new glove but commits several errors (irony/sarcasm), is just an average fielder on the team (hyperbole), is the best fielder ever seen in a league (understatement), and just makes a fantastic play (rhetorical question—"Is he the glove or what!").

Of course, the tropes tend to serve some functions better than others: Metaphor, simile, and oxymoron naturally tend toward hyperbole and, to a lesser extent, understatement. Idioms are probably not often used for pragmatic point making, although they could be as in "They tripped the light fantastic," said in reference to a couple who sat and talked to one another all night while everyone else at the party was singing, dancing, and cavorting about, which could be meant as hyperbole, sarcasm, irony, or as hyperbole which was intended as sarcasm. Of the five functions mentioned, proverbs are likely to be used for sarcasm, irony, and criticism in general because they are designed to correct someone's thoughts or behaviors, a process that requires pointing out that some ideal was not attained. Generally speaking, people are not happy about having ideals pointed out to them, especially when they were aware of the ideal to begin with: "Dad, I know I should have put the car in the garage but I was busy," said by a teenager who got proverbed with "A stitch" after the car was hit while parked in the street.

Table 2.1 summarizes the various comparisons among the tropes.

TABLE 2.1

Summary of Comparison of the Tropes

| Criterion | Type of Trope | | | | | |
	Idiom	Metaphor	Metonymy	Oxymoron	Proverb	Simile
Context dependence	low	medium	high	low	medium	medium
Decomposable	no?	yes	yes?	yes	yes	yes
Prelearned	yes	no	no	no	yes	no
Range of application	medium	medium	low	low	high	low
Topic and vehicle						
Same category	no	no	yes?	no?	no	no
Vehicle's function	refer to topic	reclassify topic	shorthand reference	reduce value of topic	comment on topic	suggest similarity to topic
Typical functions	humor, be social	clarify, express emotion	add interest, be brief	show contrast	guide, exhort	clarify

Note. The entries are based on the speaker's viewpoint. They would change somewhat if the listener's viewpoint were used.

SUMMARY

Figurative language is a form of indirectness. Something is said in such a way that its topic is classified in an odd way, and thereby referred to indirectly. This happens for metaphor, simile, metonymy, idiom, oxymoron, and proverbs. Different accounts of the oddness have emerged that, roughly speaking, treat it by reducing it to a presumed literal base, by invoking intention and thereby creating a gulf between intended meanings and spoken meanings, and by making thought content either intrinsically metaphorical or capable of yielding figuration through general mechanisms. Furthermore, the term literal is used in different, often unpredictable ways, although factors such as context play a crucial role in determining the judged literalness of an utterance.

The tropes differ in several ways, including how the vehicle classifies the topic, whether topic and vehicle come from the same conceptual domain, how the vehicle relates to the topic, whether the trope is prelearned or computed, whether it is decomposable, its scope of application, and its primary functions. In many respects, the tropes mimic the underlying design of the lexicon.

3

Cognitive Foundations

80 ◆ 03

This chapter focuses on the cognitive view of the proverb. Therefore, the goal is to identify the issues presented by proverb use and to begin to address these issues with cognitive science, the handmaiden of the cognitive view. To some extent, this process began in the first two chapters, but much more remains to be done.

QUESTIONS ABOUT PROVERBS

First we list some important questions about proverbs, then consider the domains of cognitive science that can help answer them. Here are 20 sets of questions:

- What is a proverb? Do proverbs have necessary linguistic characteristics? To be called a proverb, does a saying have to be familiar to both user and recipient? Are there different kinds of proverbs?
- How are proverbs created? How are they learned?
- What sorts of situations foster the use of proverbs?
- When do proverbs occur? Are they part of the discourse or outside of it?
- Why do people use proverbs? Do proverbs have unique functions?
- Do proverbs have a standard meaning? Can a proverb have more than one standard meaning, and does this vary with context? More generally, how much variability is there in interpretations and other illustrations of the proverb?
- How many levels of meaning does a proverb have? Are all of these levels activated during proverb production and comprehension?

- How can proverbs be applied to a variety of situations? Do proverbs vary in their range of applicability?
- How are proverbs represented in memory? If the literal and figurative meanings are different, then what is the relationship between them? Are figurative meanings remembered at all or are they computed anew?
- Are proverbs comprehended in a serial way, with all phases having to be successfully negotiated in order?
- Does a small set of generic meanings motivate the totality of proverbs? Are these meanings the same in different cultures but expressed in culture-specific ways?
- Why does proverb interpretation seem to be so arduous when proverbs are presented without supporting context?
- Why do children apparently not use proverbs? If a child can understand what it means to say, *A net with a hole in it won't catch any fish*, then what prevents the child from using or understanding a proverbial enactment of the statement?
- Where in the brain are proverbs processed? Do different kinds of proverb information get processed in different brain areas? What happens to proverb processing when someone suffers brain damage?
- Are proverbs processed quickly, automatically, and without much consciousness, or are more effortful, reflective, and metacognitive processes involved? Or both?
- How do people put thoughts into proverbs? What are these thoughts? Is proverb use and comprehension related to intelligence?
- How are literal, background, episodic, figurative, and pragmatic meanings integrated when a proverb is used?
- Must proverbs categorize episodes before they can comment on them? If so, what is the nature of a proverb category?
- Are there experts in using and comprehending proverbs? In general, what significance do individual differences in proverb processing have?
- What would it take for a computer to invent a proverb and use it appropriately, or to comprehend it?

To answer these questions, the data and theory that inform at least 10 different domains of cognitive science will have to be brought to bear. These domains are the following:

- Induction and learning
- Intention and conceptual motivation

- Language and thought
- Mental representation
- Categorization, instantiation, and reminding
- Mental effort and automaticity
- Pragmatics and communicative functions in general
- Reasoning, problem solving, and inference
- Online processing and information integration
- Society and mind

These 10 domains overlap. For didactic purposes, however, they are treated separately, and attempts here and throughout the text are made to provide a more integrated understanding of proverb cognition.

The domains will be addressed in an order that accords with the lifeline of a proverb, starting with its original creation and following through to its appropriate use and complete understanding. There is a related reason for this progression: Proverbs represent a classic case in which form follows function. Screwdrivers have the physical properties they do because they are designed to perform certain restricted functions. It is the same with proverbs. Proverbs have the structural, semantic, and even pragmatic properties they do because people want to accomplish certain goals by using them. They are known by the functions they perform, and no statement can be called a proverb until it functions as one, but certain formal properties arise as a result of the need for the statement to perform these functions.

THE LIFE OF THE PROVERB

Like species, proverbs evolve, moving from relatively simple, new memorial structures to well-remembered and figuratively understood forms for understanding, reasoning, educating, making pragmatic points, and, in some societies, making one's mark. Proverbs vary on all manner of dimensions, such as familiarity, ease of learning, pithiness, and imagery. Not all proverbs have the same fate, however. Some will become familiar, be called proverbs by most members of a culture, and serve the culture's need for linguistic forms that moralize and preach. If a statement does not do these things, then it will not be regarded as a proverb. Other proverbs will become less familiar, be less likely to be called proverbs, yet serve typical proverbial functions for select segments of a society or in restricted domains. For example, experts in an area may use unique proverbs that are otherwise unknown. Private proverbs may abound. Therefore, whereas the pool of proverbs that are relatively familiar to large segments of a society—call these *cultural proverbs*—may number in the hundreds or thousands, the number of proverbs that do not attain the status of cultural proverbs is probably very much larger. That is, there are probably *expertise-specific*, and *private* proverbs, and perhaps other kinds of noncultural proverbs as well. The cognitive view is encumbered to address all of these.

Irrespective of a proverb's cultural range, its timeline can vary enormously. For a young child there may be years of exposure to a proverb before the proverb stabilizes in meaning and the child is able to use it appropriately. Because exposure to a proverb is distributed over time and situations, its learning becomes decontextualized. Practically nothing is known regarding the empirical status of such matters, however. For adults who are learning a new proverb the timeline may be highly compressed, with proverb learning, comprehension, and appropriate use taking place within a matter of minutes. This scenario is enacted every week or so for some adults. Indeed, this is precisely what happens in laboratory research on proverbs in which a number of novel proverbs may be presented within a 1-hour experimental session.

PROVERB TASKS

We can now become more systematic in describing proverb cognition. Our discussion up to this point indicates that proverb comprehension and production entail a set of cognitive accomplishments. Call these the *proverb task* (P-task) for short. The accomplishments are somewhat different for speakers and listeners, so there is a *speaker P-task* and a *listener P- task*.

At a minimum the speaker P-task consists of the following:

Understand one's situation.

If there is a relevant topic in the situation, understand this topic and generate an attitude about it.

Access a thought complex that instantiates the topic, and map the two. Colloquially, find an idea in memory that the topic illustrates.

Select an appropriate proverb, using the thought complex and topic as guides.

Produce the proverb, abiding by rules of discourse coherence and whatever rules apply for proverb use in the culture.

Use the proverb so that it makes the desired point.

For the listener P-task, there are the following elements:

Understand one's situation.

If there is a relevant topic in the situation, understand this topic.

Construct a literal meaning for the proverb when it is encountered by computing phonological, syntactic, and basic lexical information, and by generating plausible inferences.

Recognize that the literal meaning does not fit the situation.

Construct a new meaning, using the literal meaning, various computational resources, and whatever background information seems relevant. This will produce a figurative meaning, which should be recognized as a better fit to the situation.

Map the topic meaning and the figurative meaning.

Get the point of the mapping by inferring the speaker's attitude about the situation.

Remember the statement (proverb) and what its nonliteral meaning seemed to be in the situation.

An explanation of these two P-tasks will quickly get us into the details of practically every topic and issue in cognitive science. That being the case, it is time to open the cognitive nutshell.

OPENING THE COGNITIVE NUTSHELL

Induction and Learning

Induction is at the heart of proverb creation and learning because it involves generalization from experience. We push on a door and expect that it will open, praise a friend and expect praise in return, run a melody through our mind hoping to feel better because we felt better in the past when we did. Because there are recurring aspects to our experience, induction is extremely useful. If every experience were unique, then learning would be of no avail, a moot issue. Learning enables us to make sense of our experiences, predict, relate events to one another, make important distinctions, adjust to circumstances, and, ultimately, survive. Nevertheless, induction is a risky business. That melody may not put us in a good mood, and the door that always opens may not do so on some occasion. Not all swans are white. Learning can also be maladaptive. There must be constraints on learning, or its generally beneficial effects would go for naught. These constraints come from a variety of sources, including knowledge, our biology, the feedback we get in using our inductively acquired assumptions, and our ability to critically examine our own thoughts and behaviors. Clearly, induction involves a number of subprocesses such as mental representation (memory format), categorization, inference, analogizing, and problem solving in general. Each of these subprocesses plays a role in proverb cognition.

Inductive learning implies that the learner goes beyond the information given to develop some kind of summary of or hypothesis about particular learning experiences. In Johnson-Laird's (1988) view, inductive generalization creates new information in the sense that it rules out various possibilities, the more the better. With experience, the generalization can be revised to include more possibilities. This happens for proverbs when they become understood at deeper levels and are extended to an increasing range of topics.

There are at least three different kinds of situations in which proverbs can be learned. These can be called discovery learning, guided learning, and self-learning. In *discovery learning*, the most typical case, the learner is in a social situation with another person (the teacher) who wishes to make a point. The teacher makes the point by using a proverb. For example, a young girl notices a tiny hole in her bicycle tire and her father says, *A stitch in time saves nine*. A young executive is hellbent on succeeding at all costs and tramples on the dignity of business associates. In response, a concerned peer says to another, *Frog forgets he had a tail*. The learners may never have heard these proverbs before. In both cases, the learner is on his or her own and must discover what was meant by the utterance.

In cases of *guided learning* the teacher explains to the learner what the proverb means. For example, in the bicycle episode the girl might give evidence that she does not understand how her father's utterance relates to the hole in her tire. In this case her father may explain that unless clothes are stitched when they have a small tear, the tear will get larger, and a much bigger job of stitching will have to be done. Similarly, a small tire hole may become a big hole that requires much more work to fix. In the case of the executive, the teacher may have to remind the learner that frogs start life in the more primitive form of a tadpole. In both cases, the teacher may have to explain something about the meaning of the proverb, taken as a literal statement, concerning the way in which the literal meaning maps onto its intended referent, and about the exhortative nature of the statement. That is, the father is clearly exhorting his daughter to fix her tire now, although she cannot understand this unless she first understands the logic of the proverb as a literal statement. The teacher in the executive scenario is implicitly conveying an attitude of derision or moral turpitude and suggesting that the executive should be more considerate of business associates.

A kind of guided learning also occurs when proverbs are created by groups of people. Something like this happens when there is an attempt to forge a behavioral code or enunciate a set of values. The proverbs that lace the Old and New Testaments of the Bible fit this description. In societies that have a strong oral, rather than written, tradition, proverbs may function as laws and be used to make points and win arguments, legal and otherwise. This seems especially to be the case in certain African countries such as Nigeria (Finnegan, 1970). Even written codes can have a proverbial flavor, including laws, codes for students, codes for members of various organizations, and so on. The Boy and Girl Scout oaths sound very much like proverbs. The danger in calling written codes of whatever kind proverbs is clear, however, because it muddies the status of the proverb.

Arguably the rarest cases of proverb learning involve *self-learning*. Here an individual codes some recurring pattern of significant events in proverbial terms. Having done my share of painting, I have learned too slowly that all paint jobs have common components that, if ignored, can lead to disastrous consequences. My generic proverb for painting is *Plan before you paint*. Actually, painting is the easiest part. Preparing—doing the scraping, getting the right paint, brush, ladder, and day—is really what painting is all about. A few painting disasters, or even a string of minor frustrations, lead even the least reflectively inclined of us to invent guides for more efficient painting. Most people have probably invented something like a proverb that they use with respect to a limited domain of experience. Of course, irrespective of its originating domain, any proverb can take on more general powers.

These three learning paradigms have several common, interrelated elements. First, there is a *primal experience* or perhaps several related experiences. This experience gets encoded in proverbial form. Verbal encoding is passé, but because proverbs code experiences that relate to value-laden ideals, they incorporate an attitude. If my generic painting proverb is used as self-exhortation only in painting contexts, then it is best called a maxim or a weak proverb.

Second, the primal experience has several conceptual components. This requires, in turn, that proverbs be complex enough to map these components. This probably explains why proverbs contain a minimum of two words and why they are ordinarily cast in a propositional format. Even proverbs of the form *Dogs bark* are rare for this reason. As applied to politicians, for example, this proverb might mean that they are verbose, a verbosity that does not amount to much, and it would be better if they said less and said it more directly. It is stretching things, however, to say that *Dogs bark* could plausibly imply all these ideas. An elaborated version, such as *Dogs bark at all hours*, would be better. In any event, proverbs must be fashioned so that even the simplest of them have the potential to convey a set of related components.

Third, the proverb is new, both for its creator and for its more passive learner. Although new, it becomes a mental badge that can be worn for a short time and then put away to be used in new situations. Once familiar, a proverb becomes a mental reminder.

Finally, because induction is a probabilistic process, proverbs have an aura of uncertainty. In this regard, Johnson-Laird (1988) stated that a hypothesis can have one generalization in one context and a different generalization in another. Thus proverbs are approximate fits to situations. This is because their literal meaning was a probabilistic capture of the primal experience, they map in analogically variable ways onto topics, and their use is subject to a variety of felicity conditions. The life cycle of a proverb is punctuated by uncertainty from beginning to end.

Intention and Conceptual Motivation

Proverbs are used to attain some goal. They are a form of serious intellectual work, not idle chit chat. What is this work, and how can proverbs perform it? What are people's intentions in using proverbs?

The answer to these questions depends on one's view of intention, the expressive power of language, and the kinds of constraints that operate on proverbs.

"Aboutness" is the stuff of intentions. In Jacquette's (1994) words, "According to intentionalism, all thoughts are directed toward an intended object or objects. But they may be directed in different ways—by believing, hoping, fearing, desiring, doubting, or dreading something about an intended object" (p. 96). Presumably, intentions can be about anything, including imaginary things. By a strong intentionalist stance, proverb power may be unique to biological minds and incapable of existing in nonbiological ones such as computers.

What intentions are expressible through language? According to the *expressibility thesis,* anything that can be thought can be expressed linguistically. The strong form of this thesis is probably untrue, depending, of course, on one's conception of thought. Many cognitive scientists believe that much mental activity is relatively inaccessible to consciousness. This conclusion comes from a number of sources. For example, people unable to recall or recognize a particular word (e.g., mountain), have been able to supply this information when prompted with fragmentary cues such as letter fragments (e.g., mo__t_in). People can also be primed without being aware that the priming has had an effect on their memory (Schacter, 1987) and show either decrements or improvements in recall without knowing what it was about the materials they were recalling that produced these effects (Wickens, Dalezman, & Eggemeier, 1976). Of course, we cannot equate intention with consciousness. This is interesting, because if intentions do not have to be conscious, then a larger range of intentions can play a role in shaping people's linguistic utterances.

Now, if people have intentions, and intentions can be about anything, and if the expressibility thesis is correct, then to the extent that proverbs can express intentions, proverbs have great conceptual power. In other words, purposes in using proverbs are limited only by people's intentions. It is a truism that proverbs can comment on anything by way of expressing a judgment, attitude, or belief about it. In any event, a complete theory of proverb cognition must take into account people's interests and motivation. The cognitive ideals hypothesis presented in the next chapter is designed to do just this.

Language, Thought, and Symbolism

Several positions are possible regarding the relationship between language, thought, and symbolism. We concentrate first on language and thought, then discuss symbolism.

From a logical standpoint, there are three possible relationships between language and thought: identity, noninteraction, and interaction. The *identity view*, touted by the empiricist philosopher Thomas Hobbes and the behaviorist psychologist John Watson, holds that language and thought are one and the same (Leahy, 1987). Thus, there are no nonlinguistic thoughts and no linguistic utterances without thought. Generally speaking, this position has been held by radical empiricist and positivist thinkers who have found it unnecessary and theoretically inapposite to postulate unobservable causal events for linguistic behavior.

A thorough discussion of this position would take us far afield, but it is generally agreed that it has been discredited because it denies thought to lower animals, preverbal children, profoundly deaf children who have minimal linguistic skills, and in general to people who have some disability (e.g., Broca's aphasia) that prevents them from using language. It is hard to see how proverbs could be placed within the identity view framework. By this view, a proverb that is merely repeated by a 5-year-old child has the same cognitive status as when it is appropriately used by an adult. It is also not clear from the identity view how the same statement could produce different consequences in different situations or how different proverbs could be synonymous (e.g., *Don't count your chickens before they're hatched* and *Runners on base are not runs*).

The *noninteraction view* makes language and thought different and noninteracting activities. Thus, there can be language without thought and thought without language, but no dependency or influence of the one on the other. The language without thought category is fuzzy though interesting. Candidate examples include these: the effect of brain damage that can produce speech that conforms to phonological and syntactic rules but makes no sense (Wernicke's aphasia); ritualistic utterances such as "Hi, how are ya?"; schizophrenic language, which often seems incoherent from a discourse standpoint; and perhaps "TVese," cases of children who mimic language from TV, especially commercials, but who have no idea what it means. Overlearned songs and pledges repeated by children may also qualify, as well as computer talk: Does a computer really know what it is talking about?

Examples of thought without language are clearer and include the following: mental imagery, dreams, problem solving by animals, the cognition of deaf individuals, some forms of language disturbance in which people can understand language but can not produce it (Broca's aphasia), the cognition of preverbal infants, and the cognitive content of feelings.

Although the noninteraction view is more empirically tractable than the identity view, it has some unacceptable consequences. Proverbs are not verbal doubletalk. They could not have the power they do if this were the case. Therefore, they do not fit the language-without-thought category, and, manifestly, they are not thought without language. We must move on to the interaction view.

The *interaction view* holds that language and thought are different but interact on occasion. There are two versions of this view. One, the conceptualist hypothesis, sometimes called the cloak hypothesis, holds that language expresses thought. The Sapir–Whorf hypothesis, also called the linguistic relativity, linguistic determinism, or mold hypothesis, holds that language shapes, molds, and determines thought.

Proverb cognition fits comfortably within the interaction view. A case can be made for both versions. Proverbs can express a large set of meanings. This claim is consistent with the intensionalist stance that thought, and therefore language, is about something, and with the expressibility thesis that any thought can be put into language.

More important, a large number of empirical findings are consistent with the conceptualist version. Work on the conceptual base theory has been conducted within this framework. The essence of the theory is that the figurative meaning of a proverb—a conceptual base—functions as a theory-like core of a category that includes members that are superficially quite different and distinct. That is, concretely stated verbal instances, representational pictures, abstract nonrepresentational pictures, and verbal interpretations of proverbs can all be related to one another in reliable ways (for reviews, see Feldhaus & Honeck, 1989; Honeck & Kibler, 1985; Honeck, Kibler, & Firment, 1987; Honeck, Sugar, & Kibler, 1982). This strongly suggests that some common conceptual core is the explanatory glue that relates these different pieces of information. It is especially notable in the context of the conceptualist version that pictorial information can become part of a proverb category, because this version holds that thoughts and meanings can be expressed in different ways. Of course, there is a long history to pictorial representation of proverbs in cartoons, emblems, tapestries, advertisements, and paintings (Sullivan, 1994). Perhaps the most famous of these is the oil painting *Netherlandish Proverbs* produced in 1559 by the Dutch artist Pieter Bruegel (Sullivan, 1994), paper reproductions of which are now sold in various stores.

Although the figurative meaning of a proverb can be represented in various forms, the fact remains that proverbs can trigger a variety of meanings. There is more to proverb meaning than a figurative meaning. Kirshenblatt-Gimblett (1973) argued that instead of focusing on "base" proverb meanings we should consider the larger picture provided by "proverb performances," which includes participants' evaluation of the situation, the base (figurative) meaning(s), and the proverb user's goals and intentions in using the proverb. Thus, the same proverb can have different base meanings, be used in situations that have somewhat different meanings, and convey different sentiments (sarcasm, praise, disbelief, etc.) on different occasions. Many paremiologists have commented on the different kinds and levels of meanings evoked by proverbs (see Grzybek, 1987, on the historical evolution of this matter). For example, proverbs have functions that are illocutionary (e.g., persuade, explain, scold), societal (i.e., education, norm maintenance and entertainment) and illustrative (i.e., modeling topics in an analogic way). Meanings as such can arise at the literal, logical, figurative, pragmatic and interpersonal levels. Only a detailed conceptualist version of the interaction view would seem capable of handling this level of complexity.

The Sapir–Whorf (Sapir, 1921; Whorf, 1956) version of the interaction view cannot be overlooked, however. By this hypothesis, language can determine what kind of thoughts are possible. At least that is the strong version of the hypothesis. Weaker versions are sometimes offered, for example, that language can strongly influence thought but not affect the ability to fashion certain thoughts (Hunt & Agnoli, 1991, review various versions of the hypothesis). For example, numerical counting can be done more quickly in English than Arabic (Naveh-Benjamin & Ayres, 1986).

The weaker form of the Sapir–Whorf hypothesis may apply to proverbs. Proverbs provide economical and selective codes for events, making information processing more efficient. However, because proverbs provide a perspective, they influence thinking by coloring a situation and by implicitly excluding other perspectives. Like a word in the lexicon, they parse reality and teach people how to represent a similar reality in the future. It is not so much that proverbs dictate people's thinking about the world, but that they provide an efficient means of understanding and organizing similar future experiences. In this respect, proverbs are handy, but they can be overapplied and become ineffective when new situations arise. This is one reason why proverbs may disappear over time.

From the standpoint of cognitive psychology, the use and understanding of a proverb requires a complete mind. Various memory functions are required for successful proverb performances. Because proverbs entail a complex of intentions, meanings, and functions, a fully operational long-term memory and a highly efficient working memory are required. Long-term memory is sometimes organized into kinds, such as episodic, semantic (generic), and procedural memory (see Tulving, 1985). *Episodic memories* are those that are particular, time-dated, and personal, such as remembering an event from childhood or what we had for breakfast yesterday. *Semantic memory* is less particular, less time-dated, and less personal, and includes knowledge of word meanings and various facts, for example that Mars is the fourth planet from the sun and that most socks do not have zippers.

Procedural memory is knowledge of how to do various things, such as opening a door and reading this text.

Proverbs undoubtedly lead to all three kinds of memories. Because proverbs make situations stand out in one's experience, they foster episodic memories. They also draw on generic memory because they require that a connection be made between a particular situation and a prior proverbial meaning. Many elements of situational and proverbial understanding originate in semantic memory. Comprehension of *A net with a hole in it won't catch any fish* draws on people's general knowledge about nets, holes, and fish, as well as abstract notions about instruments, flaws, and desired objects. Moreover, because appropriate use of proverbs may require extensive knowledge of certain preconditions (Briggs, 1985; Gokhan, 1992), they also draw on procedural memory.

Finally, working memory is part of the cognitive system. Currently, this memory is seen as an activated, capacity-limited portion of long-term memory that can contain various kinds of information codes. In Baddeley and Hitch's (1974) model of working memory, there is an executive or strategist which is independent of its slave subsystems, namely an articulatory loop, and a visual-spatial sketch pad. Given the complexity of communication and the informational mix evoked by proverbs, it is clear that they must burden working memory. It is not so much the basic linguistic information (phonological, lexical, syntactic) that is burdensome, but pragmatic meanings and how these relate to the situation. Proverb familiarity will reduce, but not eliminate, the burden. The more serious problem, practically and theoretically, is the constant updating of working memory required by language processing.

There is another aspect to the relationship between language, thought, and proverbs, and that is the compact form of the proverb. Proverbs put a great deal of conceptual power in a small, condensed package. One way to address this property is in terms of mental economy. Proverb compactness is consistent with a mental law of least effort. In the verbal realm, the tendency toward brevity is ubiquitous and includes the foreshortening of names, acronyms, the high frequency of short words (Zipf's Law), and the use of metonymy. The proverb stands in for a number of different but related experiences. Instead of rattling off a long series of examples that are similar to a focal event and then explaining how the examples apply to the event, a proverb is used. When all of the examples have faded from memory, the proverb emerges as a kind of ruin that symbolizes their passing (Siebers, 1992). Obviously, this is not a simple case of metonymy because the proverb must retain in its literal sense some of the logic and force of the original experiences. But the fact that these experiences have been rendered in a condensed symbolic form is consistent with the larger tendency toward mental economy. This tendency is due in no small measure to limitations on short-term memory and attention.

Mental Representation

A basic axiom of cognitive science is that knowledge comes in organized packages and that these packages, or mental representations, can differ. Various candidate formats have been proffered including images, propositions, schemas, frames, scripts, mental models, and others. Parenthetically, there are those who eschew the entire idea of mental representation, such as proponents of the ecological view (Honeck & Kibler, 1985, discuss representation and figurative language).

At various points in proverb processing, from initial exposure to complete understanding and use, different aspects of proverbs are mentally represented. In some cases, different representations may be present simultaneously or interact in rapid, recursive ways.

Proverbs are already sufficiently complex at the literal level that all sorts of information may be present, including images, fleeting associations, schemas, and so forth. Perhaps the notion of a mental model best captures what is meant by literal level because, theoretically, mental models can retain various kinds of information and because there is an internal logic to them (Johnson-Laird, 1983). It is the logic, not the particular kind of information, that is crucial at the literal level, because the same figurative meaning can be expressed by proverbs that sample different conceptual domains.

At first blush, a literal mental model would seem straightforward, as if literal were synonymous with simple. For example, many proverbs, perhaps the most interesting ones, use concrete nouns and verbs that can evoke a great deal of imagery, and imagery, naively viewed, does not seem especially mysterious. That is, there are clear real-world, basic-level (Rosch, 1978) mappings and referents for nouns and verbs. This seems to describe many common proverbs such as *The grass is always greener on the other side of the fence*; *A bird in the hand is worth two in the bush*; *Birds of a feather flock together*; and *A rolling stone gathers no moss*. Some of these mappings are pragmatically deviant or hypothetical, such as having a bird in the hand be worth two in a bush, but the point is that the literal mappings are generally easy to construct. Essentially all proverbs capitalize on the proverb user's familiarity with the referents of the proverb.

However, lexical familiarity and concreteness do not a literal representation make. There is always more to it. Regarding imagery, it is clear that nonimagistic interpretive processes are almost always required to get an adequate mental model. For example, for *The grass is always greener on the other side of the fence*, the implicit logic is that the grass on this side is less green and so less valuable. For *A bird in the hand...*, one can easily imagine holding a bird in one's hand and seeing two birds in a bush. The key word is "worth," however, which has no representation in the imagery, nor the value of bird, nor the idea that having something in hand symbolizes personal possession. Therefore, although proverb concreteness may arouse an imagery-laden mental model, it does not guarantee a satisfactory model, even on the literal level. Furthermore, many proverbs are not stated in concrete terms, including familiar ones, such as *Opportunity knocks but once*; *Haste makes waste*; and *An ounce of prevention is worth a pound of cure*. Furthermore, some highly concrete proverbs are figuratively opaque (e.g., *Eat peas with the king and cherries with the beggar*). In conclusion, a complete literal mental model is likely to contain an integrated multiplex of varied information.

What can be said of figurative meaning? This meaning cannot be the information contained in the literal mental model. It is simply not the right kind of information, which must be abstract, general, precise, and yet retain the schematic logic of the literal model. When these properties are absent, the proverb lacks general applicability. A candidate mental structure that seems to have these properties is the proposition. The problem, however, is that propositions are composed of concepts, so that our search is pushed another step away. Unfortunately, there is no theory of concepts that specifies the content of the concepts or how concepts are to be combined. We are therefore left in the somewhat unsavory position of knowing the effects of a figurative representation but little about its content. Furthermore, in all this there is a paradox that an originally concrete statement can, by being pragmatically deviant, push the mind to create a representation that is abstract and conceptually powerful.

This representation cannot be just anything, however, for several reasons. Like all inductive learning, proverb learning is constrained by prior knowledge and context. Only a handful of the possible inferences on a proverb will ever be drawn. Moreover, if the cognitive ideals hypothesis (see chapter 4) is on the right track (i.e., that a generic ideal, norm, or standard underlies proverbs), then this ideal will tightly constrain how the proverb will be interpreted and represented.

Proverbs ordinarily occur in a context. This means that whatever representations develop for a proverb, they may be embedded in a more global discourse representation. This applies most obviously to figurative meaning representations, including whatever pragmatic points may attach to this meaning.

Categorization

Proverbs, as everyone knows, apply to things. The key to application is categorization, however, because proverbs could not serve other functions if they did not first categorize. A father who says *A stitch in time saves nine* to his young daughter on seeing the nearly flat tire on her bicycle has exhorted her to do something about it. Whether she will get the point depends on her having understood how the proverb categorizes the flat tire situation. Can cognitive science shed any light on this matter?

Most views of categorization rely on the concept of similarity. The more similar some event is to the way in which a category is represented in memory, the more likely it is that the event will be instantiated and become a member of that category. Similarity functions as a causal variable in this scenario. For instance, in the flat tire example, something about the situation is similar to something about the proverb, so the latter instantiates the former.

Different similarity-based views have arisen over the past 50 years. Smith and Medin (1981) called these the exemplar, probabilistic, and classical views. Briefly, the *exemplar view* has categories represented in terms of examples or sets of disjunctively arranged examples, without summary information as such. This would imply, for example, that the category of furniture is represented in terms of particular pieces of furniture without any overarching principle of what constitutes a piece of furniture. We categorize something as, say, a piece of furniture because it reminds us of the couch in our living room, not because it reminds us of the average couch.

The *probabilistic view* does stipulate that categories are represented by summary information, but category membership is seen as graded, with some examples being better or more typical than others. The furniture category might be represented by the average couch because it shares the most features with other members of the furniture category. A television would not represent the category very well because it would share few features with other members. Clearly, the idea that categories might be represented by a prototype or best bet of some kind is consistent with the probabilistic view.

The *classical view* also has categories represented by summaries, but category membership is all-or-none. A member must share all of its features with the category, making it a full-fledged member, or lack even one critical feature and be rejected for membership. By this view, a television would be rejected as a member of the furniture category by many people. Honeck et al. (1987) described in some detail how these views and others apply to proverbs and figurative language in general.

The problem with these or any similarity-based views vis-à-vis proverbs is that similarity is derivative rather than causal. If a proverb is applied to a topic whose significance is already understood, then the proverb interpreter has to construct a correspondence between the topic and the figurative meaning. That is, the interpreter has to *make* the topic and the figurative meaning similar, in which case similarity becomes a goal rather than a causal variable. If the significance of a topic is poorly understood and a proverb sheds some light on it, then the derivative nature of similarity becomes all the more transparent.

The three traditional views of categorization do not apply to proverbs for other reasons as well. Instantiation of a proverb is a matter of satisfying mutual conceptual constraints, yet each of the three traditional views is based on a kind of reference-based, one-way logic. By this logic, proverb topics are compared to an already existing stable category structure; similarity overlap between topic and proverb meaning is computed; and category membership is determined. For proverbs, this scheme sounds much too pat because of the uncertainty in proverb application. The core process in this categorization scheme appears to be analogy, yet, as Lieber (1984) has persuasively argued, analogic correspondences between proverbs and topics are inherently ambiguous. Categorization by proverb often seems instead to have an ad hoc or goal-derived character (see Barsalou, 1983, on these kinds of categories). Proverb categories may not be as stable as they seem, a tacit assumption that seems to flow from the cultural view. They may be continually reconstructed as the proverb gets applied in different contexts.

If the three traditional views of categorization do not apply to proverbs, the possibility remains that similarity may yet have a role to play. This is a complex issue that depends on one's conception of the processes at work when categorization occurs. Even if one assumes that proverbs categorize topics in top-down ways, this categorization may have strong elements of pattern matching in which components of figurative meaning interact with components of the topic. In this case, similarity of components may produce a settling-in to a stable overall pattern that synthesizes and harmonizes the interacting components. Under different circumstances, having largely to do with how well learned proverb meanings, topics, and situations are, similarity may play either a predominant or a subordinate role (Sloman, 1996, discusses cases of similarity versus theory-based categorization). Well-learned patterns may lead to more automatic, associative-similarity forms of mental activity. In either case, however, the conceptal nature of the interacting patterns must be emphasized. There is good justification for calling proverbs miniature theories. These theories are more complex and tentative than clear-cut propositional structures. Like all theories, however, proverb categories serve to summarize, integrate, and economically code a large number of superficially distinct events.

Proverbs vary in their range of application, which has important theoretical implications. It is well documented that as the range or variability of category examples increases, the category itself becomes more abstract and flexible (Homa & Vosburgh, 1976; Nitsch, 1977; Posner & Keele, 1968), a process that occurs with proverb categories as well (Honeck & Firment, 1989). The category becomes decontextualized, and the ability to instantiate new examples increases. Proverbs applied to narrow or highly defined domains would accordingly be less likely to be used in new situations. This circumstance describes aphorisms, maxims, and weak proverbs. However, the ability to generalize, and therefore the size of a proverb category, is not overdetermined by the nature of the topics to which proverbs are applied. If people develop more abstract, complete, and decontextualized interpretations, irrespective of the situations in which they develop, then generalization is facilitated on more remote instances (Honeck & Firment, 1989). Finally, a mental set to search for applications in different domains also contributes to the scope of generalization, even in young children (Brown, 1989). In effect, people's a priori beliefs about the variability of a category will have an impact on the kind of mental representation they develop for it.

There is a vexing complication, however. Transfer of ideas across dissimilar domains is not automatic by any means. People often do not apply ideas learned in one context to analogous ideas in another context. This applies to children but also to adults (for reviews, see Brown, 1989; Gentner, 1989; Holyoak, 1985). However, the universality of proverbs provides a prima facie case against the thesis that analogical transfer is rare. When one examines the sort of factors that promote transfer in laboratory studies, the reasons for the discrepancy become clear. Brown (1989) described some of these factors, namely the need to teach learners about analogies, to develop a mind set in the learner that expects and searches for deep similarities in situations, and to train for the flexible use of information in different contexts. When these conditions are met, even young children show analogical transfer. These conditions are rarely addressed in laboratory studies with adults, however, hence the pessimism regarding the ability to show deep analogical thinking.

These factors are undoubtedly present when proverbs are learned in everyday circumstances. When children are the audience, adult users of proverbs are generally not content to utter a proverb, hoping somehow that their listeners have understood. Explanations often accompany proverb utterances.

Moreover, the universal, gnomic aspect of proverbs carries with it an implicit promise that similar circumstances will recur. That proverbs get used in varying situations no doubt helps the learner to look beyond surface similarities to underlying structures and to retain this as a permanent problem-solving strategy. The concept of coverage applies here (Osherson, Smith, Wilkie, Lopez, & Shafir, 1990). For example, if one says that a mouse has a heart and a human has a heart, the coverage is greater than saying that a mouse has a heart and a rat has a heart. Because the coverage is greater in the former case, then for phylogenetic reasons, people are more willing to generalize the premise and say that mammals have a heart. With proverbs, the analogy would seem to be that if proverb X applies in situation A, but also in an apparently very different situation Z, then X has great generality of application. Coverage seems to increase the psychological weight of the evidence for a hypothesis, proverbial or otherwise.

Mental Effort

How quickly and effortlessly can a proverb be understood? The answer depends on one's view of proverbs. All views except the cognitive view would seem to say, "fairly quickly and effortlessly." The noncognitive views make proverbial status synonymous with both literal and figurative familiarity and, of course, familiarity implies automatic processing. According to the cognitive view, proverb familiarity should speed up but not automatize comprehension.

A more complex answer emerges when we consider the life cycle of a proverb and the various subprocesses involved. The original creation of a proverb is hardly automatic, being more a hard-won conclusion based on conscious reflection about a string of experiences. The person hearing it for the first time may also be faced with a task that requires effortful, conscious processing, sometimes called controlled processing (after Schneider & Shiffrin, 1977). As the proverb is used over and over, what was originally a jolt to the ordinarily rapid pace of discourse becomes less of a jolt, with subprocesses running off in a more smooth, integrated way. A solid finding in research on skills, both mental and physical, is that practice reduces time and errors, also allowing people to perform efficiently on a secondary task while maintaining good performance on the primary task (Anderson, 1982). But sometimes practice is to no avail because the task is too resource demanding.

Because proverb cognition involves a number of subtasks, they may each be undergoing practice effects at different rates with different results. As we have seen, each P-task entails a number of subtasks. These subtasks are affected by somewhat different variables, so the P-task will be more or less effortful depending on the subtasks involved. For example, figurative and pragmatic meanings are probably more influenced by experience with non-literal communication, working memory capacity, and metacognitive skills than is the case for syntax and lexical retrieval.

There is another reason why proverb processing may retain nonautomatic elements, namely strategies. Proverb users want to get people to think or do things. These goals are likely to be conscious and calculated. Moreover, the same proverb can be used for different purposes on different occasions, a factor that is likely to keep strategies at a conscious level. Proverb task consciousness, therefore, has much more to do with its functions than with its linguistic structures. Proverbs have been known to "stop people in their tracks," not because the words were unfamiliar, but because of the difficulty in relating the proverb to the discourse context.

If proverbs often involve effortful processing, then it is clear that they should not be regarded as frozen, prepackaged entities whose meanings just sit in long-term memory waiting to be used on a moment's notice. There is much more to it than that because proverbs are multilayered and multifunctional. This leads to the next topic.

Communication

What is communication? The simple answer is that it is a process by which an information sender and an information receiver engage in processes that result in a temporary sharing of information. To the extent that this information is not shared, there is miscommunication. The process can be mechanical as for most animal forms of communication, or nonmechanical as in most human communication. Moreover, for human communication, it seems necessary to add that there is an intention that information be shared, and that the information be mental content. These additions complicate matters enormously. The following discussion of this complication follows the general guidelines but not the detailed theorizing provided in Sperber and Wilson's (1986) enlightening presentation of communication.

The complications can be addressed in terms of two concepts: *manifest factors* and *substantive factors* of communication. If the communication situation involves two people in a face-to-face conversation, then several factors are manifest. These are the physical surroundings, the presence of the two people, what the people do, and what they say. These factors have perceptible qualities: The people perceive their environment, which includes the other person, nonverbal actions, and verbalizations. Theoretically, these factors have some communication value, and they have it without benefit of significant mental involvement. Much of animal communication may operate at this level. The problem is that the manifest level does not provide the information needed to solve the riddle of what intentions and other mental contents might be. Intentions and mental contents are not manifest.

The riddle can only be addressed by moving to the substantive factors level. In our two-person exchange, these factors are Person A's mind, Person B's mind, situational meaning, the speaker's intended mental contents, the semantic content of what the speaker says and does, the semantic content derived by the receiver, and the momentary mental content that the receiver constructs in relation to the speaker's total communicative act. These factors are not manifest. They are hidden and hypothetical, yet fundamental to the communication process.

The hidden aspect of substantive factors would not be so vexing if it were not for one fact: the factors are related in nonlinear ways. That is, there is rarely if ever a one-to-one relationship between the factors. Speakers' intentions or thoughts in general can map in many-to-one or one-to-many relationships to literal semantic contents. People can think one thing (e.g., they do not like radishes), and verbally express this idea in a variety of ways (e.g., "Radishes are at the bottom of my vegetable list"; "Grass comes before radishes for me"). But then, different thoughts can sometimes be alluded to with the same verbal expression. For example, the question "Are Hollywood movies worth seeing?" might be used to turn down an offer to see a movie, to render a general opinion about modern movies, or to suggest a different mutual activity. Moreover, as Sperber and Wilson (1986) state, "The same sentence, used to express the same thought, may sometimes be used to present this thought as true, sometimes to suggest that it is not, sometimes to wonder whether it is true, sometimes to ask the hearer to make it true, and so on" (p. 10). In general, any two of the hidden factors on any given occasion will not match up completely. That is why communication is a roll of the dice. Successful communication, however, seems to be the rule rather than the exception, which is a tribute to the computational powers of the human mind.

The problems presented by the substantive level of communication have given rise to a variety of theoretical solutions. One general approach is pragmatics theory, which assumes that people are trying to do things with words, and that they do so by observing basic conversational rules. This approach, which has been discussed previously, typically makes a distinction between the things people intend, what they say, and the effect of the saying, or intended meanings, sentence meanings, and utterance (listener) meanings, respectively. These meanings may not match up. In effect, speech act theory puts the receiver in the position of mind reader and allows the sender to be direct and clear or variously roundabout. People often intentionally say important things in an indirect way. Criticism, sarcasm, parody, digs and maledicta of all sorts often take an indirect form. Sarcasm and parody demand it (e.g., "These modern teenagers, they sure do have a strong interest in being grammatical"). One can damn with faint praise by using just the right combinations of words (e.g., "She sang that old song beautifully, every note was nigh unto closing onto target"). By the pragmatics model, therefore, language is a tool that can be used in an enormous variety of ways to attain a goal. Our biology constrains the way we can put words together, but at the same time it allows us to use all of our mind to get language to do what we want it to do.

The problems posed by substantive communicative factors are painfully evident when proverbs are considered. These factors include the semantic content of the proverb (i.e., literal meaning), the meaning of the proverb topic, the proverb's figurative meaning, and propositional attitudes (i.e., opinions, views, beliefs) conveyed by the proverb. There is another hidden factor: If we follow the cognitive ideals hypothesis, proverb usage represents an attempt to communicate an ideal, norm, or standard. That is, the intention in uttering a proverb is to get a receiver to discover an ideal. Add to this the constants of substantive communication, namely, minds and situations, and a high order of nonlinearity becomes evident in any proverb performance.

What is most clear in proverb communication is that proverbs are used with some purpose. For example, they are ideally suited for conflict resolution. Finnegan (1970) makes this a key element in her insightful discussion of proverb usage in African societies. She writes: "First, there is the sense of detachment and generalization inherent in proverbs. The speaker stands back, as it were, from the heat of the actual situation and draws attention, for himself or others, to its wider implications. And secondly, there is the oblique and allusive nature of expression through proverbs which makes it possible to use them in a variety of effective ways" (p. 27).

Proverbs are a tactful use of speech. On occasion, however, proverbs may be used in Yanja (African) as a kind of malicious double talk in which the proverb user deliberately says something that seems clear but in reality is clear only to the user and people in the know. A secret language is employed. Proverbs also can be used in formal initiations, as embellishments, and as a general way of adding color to one's speech. There are even contests in which users exchange proverbs, sometimes buying one to get a new one (Finnegan, 1970).

The substantive level of communication is hard on the receiver, who must integrate a significant subset of substantive factors. The receiver need not know the whole of another's mind but must come to appreciate and integrate all the other factors. To do this the receiver must have acquired a great deal of information about the world and other people. This nonlinguistic knowledge sets the stage for the use of indirect speech acts because any one of the innumerable things that people may have in mind can guide and motivate a single speech act. Figurative language is marked by indirectness between these things and what people actually say, and proverbs represent a classic case.

The foregoing presentation describes the basic theoretical problem inherent in communication, but does not resolve the problem. The latter requires a foray into our next topic.

Reasoning

If there is nonlinearity in substantive elements of communication, how might they be made linear, matched up, or otherwise integrated? The traditional answer is that inferential processes play this role. Inductive inference has been discussed already. In formal logic, the other major form of inference is deductive inference.

To take a simple example of deduction, if someone says, "Tom went to the movies," then we might infer several things: Tom is a male human; he changed from some location to where the movie was shown; he bought a ticket, sat in a theater, watched a movie for two hours or so, then left the theater. In fact, innumerable, though perhaps less plausible, inferences could be drawn. Even so, our initial inferences could be wrong because even though they seem logical, they are not really logical in the pure, formal logical sense. If the context for uttering "Tom went to the movies" was that a cat watched a videocassette recording of its own backyard play, then essentially none of our initial inferences were valid.

In a nutshell, this is the dilemma posed by using inference as the solution to the substantive communication problem: Inference is needed to integrate and make pieces of information coherent, yet (nonformal) inference can be wrong or imprecise. The major issue here is whether the laws of logic are equivalent to the laws of thinking, the so-called *doctrine of mental logic* (Johnson-Laird, 1988). Most modern scholars would answer this question in the negative, but those who are computationally minded would probably add that the mind nevertheless operates by complex logicomathematical formulae. Any cases of reasoning would therefore be a fortiori logical, though perhaps not logical in the deductive logic sense.

In formal deductive logic one begins with premises, then uses explicit rules for generating further pieces of information, such as a conclusion. If the premises are true and the rules are followed precisely, then the newly generated information is guaranteed to be true. Deductive reasoning does not yield any new information because the conclusion simply makes explicit what is already present implicitly in the premises (Johnson-Laird, 1988). But deductive reasoning is powerful nonetheless. For example, we could argue this way: On Sundays it rains; today is Sunday; therefore, it is going to rain. We could also say it this way: On Sundays it rains; it is not raining today; therefore, it is not Sunday. In propositional (if–then) logic the first argument is called modus ponens (if P then Q; P, therefore, Q) and the second, modus tollens (if P then Q; not Q, therefore, not P). Deductive logic works well only when the information being reasoned about is part of a closed system whose characteristics are known, such as mathematics. Certain pockets of science and even limited domains of everyday life also qualify. Thus, we can be assured that if our car is out of gas, it will not run. In logic terms one could say, "If a car is out of gas it will not run; my car is out of gas; therefore, it will not run," an example of modus ponens. Of course, we would have to be driving a gas-powered car, not some other kind of car. For the "On Sundays it rains" argument, it might not rain on Sunday even if it is Sunday, and if it is not Sunday it might rain anyway. Weather is not a closed system. Thus, valid arguments, the kind that conform to the rules of deductive logic, may not be true in reality. Indeed, logicians are fond of pointing out that perfectly valid arguments can be totally false, whereas invalid arguments can be true. Humans seem to be more interested in truth and falsity than in soundness of argument, however. This makes good sense from an evolutionary standpoint. If people (e.g., the progeny of Star Trek's Mr. Spock) were very logical but only came up with conclusions that were true about the world half of the time, they would die out in a short period of time. People who were good guessers—that is all of us—would fare much better.

Even under optimal circumstances, people are poor logicians. We reason best when the argument conforms to the two valid forms, modus ponens and modus tollens, but much more poorly when it does not. Suppose we reason that "If she loves me, she will kiss me; she doesn't love me, so she will not kiss me." This is an invalid argument by logic standards, but it is easy to imagine a circumstance in which, even if she did not love us, she would kiss us. Maybe she likes to kiss people or we just met. If we reason that "She didn't kiss me, so she doesn't love me," we are equally illogical and could be wrong. Much of everyday life seems to defy (deductive) logic. Again, the issue is whether we are dealing with a closed or open system. Kissing is an open system. We might be able to predict when we will be kissed, but you may as well kiss perfect prediction goodbye. Factors outside the system always seem to impinge.

A variety of factors make people notoriously poor deductive logicians. The basic problem is that deductive logic is concerned only with the formal structure of an argument, that is with its syntax, not with its content. Humans are heavily influenced by content, however. Thus, irrespective of its validity, we are more likely to accept a conclusion with which we agree and to reject a conclusion with which we disagree. Our reasoning worsens as the content of the argument becomes more abstract, suggesting that our reasoning depends more on a semantically based than on a syntactically based logic. We spontaneously invert arguments (e.g., turning "If she loves me she'll kiss me," into, "She kissed me, so she must love me"), implying, once again, that empirical probabilities drive our reasoning rather than strict logical necessities. We are biased toward the confirmation of premises rather than their disconfirmation, a result perhaps of our reliance on palpable experience rather than logical possibility. Moreover, we are poor at combining premises (see Matlin, 1994, for a basic introduction to these matters, and Johnson-Laird & Byrne, 1991, for a more advanced treatment).

Aside from conditional (if–then, propositional) logic there is the syllogism, another form of deductive logic. There are a variety of syllogistic argument forms. A common form looks like this:

All planets are smaller than all stars. (major premise)

Pluto is a planet. (minor premise)

Therefore, Pluto is smaller than all stars. (conclusion)

The conclusion is valid, but probably false, inasmuch as astronomers have claimed evidence for the existence of very small stars such as the neutron star.

Sometimes deductive reasoning works. It is hard to imagine anyone not reasoning at times by using modus ponens, or more precisely, whatever the psychological equivalent is for modus ponens. How could we communicate with someone who did not go along with the logic that "If today is Monday, tomorrow is Tuesday; today is Monday; therefore, tomorrow is Tuesday"? If the person claimed that tomorrow is Friday, we would surely believe that we were dealing with Martian logic. In Western culture, at least, the days of the week are a closed system.

As a model for human reasoning, deductive logic is inadequate. In the absence of a closed system, humans reason in messy ways, using trial and error, hunches, guesses, heuristics, blind leaps of faith, and generally old ways of reasoning that seemed to work, especially what works. Often what works is a guess based on perceived similarity to a prior problem, analogies in other words. People are model builders for just about everything, and reasoning flows from the constraints of the model. Because almost all models are not and cannot be worked out in every detail, and also because the logic of the model may not be evident even after prolonged reflection, people are typically in the position of having to draw conclusions based on incomplete data. That makes us, not logic machines, but pragmatists who try what seems plausible, appropriate, and consistent with our experience.

The fact is that even if we could somehow became familiar with the intimacies of deductive logic, it would not suffice because it has too many inherent difficulties. It does not tell us what to infer, what not to infer, how to deal with hedges and might-be's, or what to do with the practically infinite set of valid inferences that would flow from the deduction machine. Pure deduction would quickly overload us and make the simplest problems unmanageable. (Hunt, 1982, provided a highly readable discussion of these matters, and Kahneman, Slovic, & Tversky, 1982, gave a technical presentation.)

What relationship exists between proverbs and reasoning? A number of scholars have noted the connection. Some have likened proverbs to riddles such as "What has eyes and cannot see? A potato." Dundes (1975) argued, for example, that although the topic of a proverb is shared by speaker and receiver, in the case of the riddle it has to be figured out. Of course, the topic of a proverb might not always be shared because the user may on some occasions have to clarify the topic, its significance, and even how the proverb relates to it (Briggs, 1985). Chapter 1 showed that proverbs also share certain features with Zen koans, which are notorious for bending the mind to produce a hoped for insight. The famous "What is the sound of one hand clapping?" can easily be made proverbial by turning it into an assertion—"It is the sound of one hand clapping"—although even the original question form could be used in a proverbial way.

As for all language understanding, proverbs rely on the listener to fill in the gaps. As such, proverbs have enthymemic qualties (Green & Pepicello, 1986). Technically, enthymemes are incomplete syllogisms in that there is a missing premise, conclusion, or both. For example, to say "Scott is a football player" is to imply that Scott is bigger than the normal person. The missing premise is that football players are bigger than the norm. Sometimes this kind of pragmatic implication is called a plausible inference because it is probable, though not inevitable, that Scott is bigger than average. Less often, the inference is necessary and logical as in these statements: Joe is taller than Carol, Carol is taller than Pete, so Joe must be taller than Pete. Proverbs call on the listener to make both kinds of inferences. These inferences may be variably automatic. They are less automatic, for example, for proverbs that are opaque or paradoxical such as these: *At the foot of the candle it is dark; A candle lights others and consumes itself; At night all cats are black; Who is last shall be first.*

On initial reflection, therefore, P-tasks require varied forms of reasoning. Proverb creation depends on something like induction. The literal meaning for a proverb contains a schema-based logic. The mapping of proverb and topic seems to be built on analogical reasoning. Proverb use is a kind of metonymic reasoning in which the proverb stands in for a cognitive ideal. And on the larger level, proverb cognition looks like enthymemic reasoning, implying that, if we knew what they were, we could take all the relevant substantive elements in a particular proverb communication and lay them out in a neat logical arrangement.

For example, suppose Bea is a young lawyer trying to decide whether she wants to join a new business firm that specializes in international trade. A friend of hers is trying to persuade her that global economics is producing a call for this kind of expert and so she says *Make hay while the sun shines.* If Bea understands this to mean that the time is ripe to take this kind of job and she takes it, then presumably she has understood her friend's point. Apparently, Bea has made a number of inferences: Hay is grass; grass is best turned into hay when the weather is warm and dry, so grass should be put out in the sun; making hay is a matter of timing; the job situation is one in which timing is important; there is a general idea that goals are best accomplished at some time rather than others; the topic (her job situation), the figurative meaning of the proverb, and the cognitive ideal (there is an optimal time for goals to be accomplished) have been blended by analogical inference.

These seem like the major forms of reasoning performed by Bea, although other pieces of information would have to be inferred as well. It looks like a nifty piece of syllogistic reasoning. Cognitive ideals become universal statements that act like a major premise: In all cases, there is an optimal time for goals to be accomplished. The topic becomes a minor premise stated in the particular mood: Some job is a goal. The conclusion is that there is an optimal time to do the job. The proverb seemingly has initiated a basic deductive chain. The pragmatic force of the cognitive ideal, set in the context of the overall communicative situation, is that Bea should take the job offer. Although none of Bea's deductions are guaranteed (i.e., she has engaged in pragmatic reasoning), it appears as if she has fundamentally engaged in deductive reasoning. Pragmatic reasoning has led to a purely formal logical pattern, or has it?

There is another perspective on Bea's successful negotiation of her P-task. Specifically, she has engaged in a complex pattern-matching task, the major elements of which are the cognitive ideal, the proverb's figurative meaning, and the proverb's topic (Bea's job situation). That is, there must be some matching and integration of the conceptual properties of these three elements. These properties are essentially that there are goals and that there is an optimal time to accomplish them. There is undoubtedly some mental fitting that occurs in this process in which the topic and the proverb constrain one another's meaning and invite a common generic ideal in the process. This process would not in itself seem to operate by a deductive mechanism. Rather, several conceptual constraints have operated to produce a single, overall conceptual fit. In general, this might be called the *proverb triangle equation* in a comprehension P-task. In this scenario, the topic serves as the referent, the proverb as the symbol, and the cognitive ideal as the thought that relates the other two. It does not look like pure logic, except that the three elements are mutually consistent, a logic-like property.

Perhaps the safest conclusion is that a successfully negotiated comprehension P-task involves a combination of pragmatic reasoning and pattern matching. In turn, these result in something like a deductively arranged pattern of thoughts.

The less than pristine deductive mental processes are necessary for the deductive pattern to emerge, however. This pattern is epiphenomenal. Whether there is a more fundamental mental logic that guides and constrains the communicative process is anybody's guess.

This two-pronged view of reasoning is echoed in recent work in the area. For example, Sloman (1996) distinguished between rule-based and associatively-based forms of reasoning. The former involves sequential operations on symbols, is likely to involve hierarchically related pieces of knowledge, and could be productive, strategic, and involve explanation, among other things. Associatively based reasoning is more likely to involve association, similarity-based pattern matching, automatic processing, and intuition. Thus, a proverb may function as a short-cut representation for a cognitive ideal, but one that must be figured out by a complex-pattern matching process on the part of the would-be comprehender. Connectionistic processes may apply at this level of reasoning (chapter 7 describes connectionism in more detail).

The need for pragmatic reasoning, and perhaps more rule-based processes in proverb comprehension becomes clearer when we look at some of their everyday uses. In Igbo society in southeastern Nigeria proverbs play an important role in the education of children (Penfield & Duru, 1988). Ancestors are venerated, as are their proverbs, which act therefore as quotes. Because proverbs operate at a distance from their larger discourse, what Penfield (1983) called *foregrounding*, they mentally arouse the listener. One of Penfield's respondents said, "The proverb makes somebody think twice. It has an effect on the other person that literal words may not have. It puts someone in a line of relaxation to think" (p. 120) Igbo children, all children actually, not only must solve the problem of what a proverb means in a given situation, but must also come to appreciate that the same proverb can have a different meaning and a different illocutionary force in different situations and yet have a constant philosophical meaning. Proverb users, who are held in high esteem in Igbo society, are prized for their intelligent use of proverbs, and intelligence in this society partakes heavily of indirectness, a premier quality of proverbs. From about 5 years of age on, Igbo children are exposed to the proverbs of caregivers who therefore contribute to the "development of such reasoning processes as analogy, analysis, generalization, deduction, and inference" (Penfield & Duru, 1988,

p. 126). It is mainly by using these basic cognitive processes that the Igbo child comes to understand the norms, values, and customs of society. In general, in nonliterate societies proverbs and other forms of nonliteral and unconventional language may play a role in the mental development of children that reading and formal instruction play in literate societies. Proverbs become a "sacred metaphorical way of speaking (that) teaches children abstract thought and social rules in a natural, culturally relevant interactional context" (Penfield & Duru, 1988, p. 127).

Along these lines, it has been suggested that proverbs constitute cultural lessons in how and how not to reason. For example, proverbs can help people limit their generalizations (*The hood makes not the monk*), make people reflective about cause and effect (*He who lies down with dogs, will rise with fleas*), teach analogy (*Fish see the bait but not the hook; men see the profit but not the peril*), teach about generalization (*Once bitten, twice shy*), teach about arguments based on classification (*Call one a thief and he will steal*), and teach about various follies of reasoning (*If folly were grief, every house would weep*) (Goodwin & Wenzel, 1979). Goodwin and Wenzel concluded that:

> It is generally true that proverbs (a) reflect an implicit typology of patterns of reasoning or argument, (b) illustrate and comment upon legitimate patterns of inference, and (c) caution against general and specific fallacies. Taken as a body of conventional wisdom, proverbs serve the common run of humanity in the same way that a textbook on logic or argumentation serves the formally educated. Proverbs offer a general set of rational strategies for deliberating about life's problems. (1979, pp. 301–302)

In conclusion, proverbs call on a range of reasoning and reasoning-like processes for their comprehension and production. They also provide, by virtue of these activities, implicit instruction in these processes, and in their figurative content, explicit instruction in how to reason in general.

Online Processing

Spoken language is an ephemeral and fleeting thing. It always occurs in some context, typically as part of some discourse. The rapid, ongoing, context-sensitive, constantly in need of updating quality of language has far-reaching implications for our understanding of proverbs. As has been noted, a number of conceptual elements must be integrated in realtime for effective proverb use and comprehension to occur.

Because P-tasks have subtasks and people have short-term capacity limitations, proverbs present a challenge. New proverb information must be added to an old but continually developing discourse model. In this respect, proverbs function like stories, with casts of characters, themes, plots, motives, beginnings, and endings. As discussed previously, most of this information will have to be inferred. No writer or speaker can provide all of the information necessary to understand even the simplest of their statements or would they want to. All language users are at the mercy of the cognitive machinery of their audience.

The analogy with story comprehension may provide some insight into online proverb processing. Research on story comprehension reveals that processing load is greatest at the beginning and end of a story episode (Haberlandt, Berian, & Sandson, 1980). Beginnings present problems because ambiguity is high and the reader has yet to construct a coherent model of the story, yet ambiguity is high at first. Endings call for integration and summing up. As it turns out, proverbs are beneficial for both. When proverbs are presented as headings for abstract passages, people remember more facts, details, and relational information about the passages than when a typical textbook heading is provided (Moreno & Divesta, 1994). For example, a passage about critical periods in development is remembered better if accompanied by A stitch in time saves nine than by "some theories of timing of experiences in development." Presumably, the proverb acts to summarize, invite plausible and valuable inferences, and promote salient connections between the proverb and various propositions in the passage. The proverb may also function as an easily remembered cue for generating information in the passage (Moreno & Divesta, 1994). In general, the use of a proverb as an advance organizer (Ausubel, 1968) serves as an act of categorization such that propositions and relationships among propositions are made coherent in terms of the conceptual basis of the category. In general, there is abundant evidence for the beneficial role of categorization and organization in general on understanding and memory (Matlin, 1994). In any event, this analysis suggests that proverbs are focal points in any discourse, conceptual pegs that help to organize old information and integrate new, incoming information.

If proverbs are valuable setups for ensuing episodes, they are also very useful endpieces, their typical role. It is as if the proverb user were saying, "Keeping all of this prior situation in mind, here is how I would like you to look at it." In this way, the proverb provides a frame for organizing, remembering, and thinking about the information. Proverbs are symbolic ruins (Siebers, 1992). It is interesting in this connection that summaries can be as valuable and sometimes more valuable than the material they summarize by reducing information load, making important pieces of information salient, allowing easier connections among these pieces, and often providing the macrolevel information needed to get the connections (Kintsch, 1988). So it is with proverbs.

Consider the comment of a sales manager to a salesperson who has just presented a plan for selling "Munchos," a new brand of potato chips: *A net with a hole in it won't catch any fish.* The sales manager has rendered a judgment, indirectly, without impugning the salesperson's intelligence or skill in making up sales plans. The salesperson knows that the manager is commenting on the plan and not just making idle, irrelevant chatter about fishing, and that the sales plan must be revised. The salesperson's conclusion is forged on the basis of a great deal of information integration: he or she wants the plan to be accepted; the logic of the proverbial statement is that something that has a crucial flaw can not perform its intended function; a correspondence must be forged between the salesman's goal vis-à-vis the plan and the statement, and the force of the statement is that the flawed instrument must be fixed. The salesperson's next step should be to ask some questions, such as, "Where did I go wrong?".

In conclusion, effective proverbial cognition requires great skill in information integration. Proverbs therefore place correspondingly great stress on working memory where the integration occurs. Breakdowns in this process or in any of the proverb subtasks can doom successful integration. However, because proverbs are salient pragmatic tools, they serve as focal points for organizing and integrating information in an online P-task.

Society and Mind

Proverbs are primarily a social phenomenon. They are learned through social interaction for social purposes. Proverbs do more than familiarize their listener with the proverb, however. Lessons are learned about three interrelated realms: social norms and values, language, and other people's minds.

Perhaps the quintessential function of proverbs is to foster the learning of societal values, expectations, roles, and norms. At this message level, proverbs can be considered lessons in life, that they are ideally suited to convey. That proverbs are used by persons in authority ensures that the following potent social factors will make for their survival and value: the reward function of authority figures, their imitation, and the fact that we use a social-referencing process of looking for guidance in ambiguous situations to certain persons (Small, 1990). As discussed earlier, in nonliteral societies proverbs can become a source of bonding, secret codes, and social cohesion in general, a way of promoting the legacy of a community.

Proverbs also teach their hearers, children especially, a great deal about the language game. In the section on reasoning the claim was made that proverbs provide implicit instruction in levels of meaning and cognitive flexibility. Language is ideally suited for these purposes. It can turn reality on its head in a way that perception cannot. Perceptual illusions occur, but perceptual veridicality is the rule not the exception. When we perceive what seems like a tree, it ususally does not turn out to be a dog. In contrast, language allows people to say one thing and mean another. Proverbs optimize this bifurcation. Yet, proverb comprehension also requires that what was said be taken into account, using context and conversational rules of various kinds. Because proverbs are used in indirect ways and can diffuse responsibility for the pragmatic and social message, the listener is taught that language is a tool. Thus, proverbs may facilitate the development of crucial conversational skills. They may also teach metacomprehension skills that will allow the listener to detect and resolve discrepancies between their current understanding and a more appropriate understanding.

Because proverbs teach about social norms and about language, they also teach about other people's minds, arguably the most difficult lesson. If adults always acted and verbalized in perfectly consistent ways, then there would be no social ambiguity for the child. The drawback of consistency, however, is that it is not conducive to developing a theory of mind. Appreciation of literal aspects of people's verbal and nonverbal behavior would be redundant and sufficient guides to understanding. It is when behavior is inconsistent and people mean something other than what they say that things become interesting and challenge the listener to resolve the discrepancy. In the case of proverbs, because intended meanings and actual meanings come apart, and because there is some rationality in how this happens, the listener can begin to close the gap between appearance and reality. This scenario gets repeated, so that the child can begin to impute a proverb's message, not just to immediate contexts, but to those more permanent things called minds.

SUMMARY

From its original conception and use to its comprehension by others and, occasionally, its cultural enshrinement, the proverb engages an enormous set of mental structures and processes. In fact, most of cognitive science must be pressed into service to account for proverb cognition. Still, proverb cognition cannot at present be fully explicated, a testimony both to the complexity of the proverb and to the need for improvements in cognitive science.

4

Theories of Proverb Cognition

೮ ◆ ೮

A theory, that's the thing! A debate that occurs in the halls of science from time to time concerns the role of theory in the development of a science. Can a science progress by accumulating facts or is theory necessary? For most scientists, data gathering is indispensable to science, but as an end in itself it is unaethestic and inefficient. Whether in science or everyday life we create theories because they are more satisfying than simple lists of facts and ideas because they explain, summarize, predict, and make things coherent. We want the facts to be explained on a higher, more abstract level, using concepts that are independent of the ways in which the facts are stated. One way or another, all theories do this by making distinctions between observation level statements and nonobservational statements whose interrelationships constitute a theory.

Most scientists are therefore both inductive and deductive in their approach to science. The 17th-century philosopher Descartes said as much: Rational processes are needed to order the evidence of the senses. One cannot be done without the other. Some scientists even maintain that inductive, data-gathering activities are a product of, if not well-developed theory, then at least an unspoken point of view. Furthermore, scientists cannot and do not work in a vacuum. There is a history and context to all scientific work.

COGNITIVE THEORY AND PROVERBS

The cognitive view assumes that the same set of principles apply to all cases of proverb cognition. It does not matter whether one is interested in initial proverb use by a teenager or how biblical proverbs might be interpreted. The optimal circumstance is that they are addressed by the same theory. Until recently, however, no comprehensive theories of proverb cognition have been offered. This chapter looks at the available theories, but first we examine earlier approaches.

Early Theoretical Approaches

As early as 1944, Benjamin (1944) wrote a treatise on proverb understanding by individuals diagnosed as schizophrenic. Benjamin asked these individuals to interpret proverbs such as *When the cat's away the mice will play*. He found that their interpretations were quite literal and sometimes nonsensical or idiosyncratic. Benjamin theorized that proverbs are built out of symbols that reflect everyday objects and events and that these symbols combine with predicates. An interpretation required that the person get a literal meaning, desymbolize the symbols, get a general meaning, and then, as the occasion demands, apply the general meaning. However, no details of how this happens were provided by Benjamin.

In the late 1960s Seitel (1969) emphasized the role of analogy in proverb understanding. A proverb is connected with a referent in terms of the standard a:b::c:d analogical relationship. Grzybek (1987) wrote that, in a less well-known paper, Crépeau (1975) stipulated an analogical relationship between denotative and connotative elements within the proverb itself. These elements are then integrated, and the basis of the analogy is constructed to form a "proverb idea," or abstract idea that connects with referent situations. In Grzybek's terms, there is a double analogy. This notion is interesting, but it is unlikely that proverb interpreters first form analogies for the proverb itself.

Numerous authors have acknowledged the multiple levels of proverb meaning. Dundes (1975) described three levels: the image, message, and architectural (formulaic), which roughly correspond to the literal, figurative, and linguistic structural levels. Other authors, notably Krikmann (1974) and Kirshenblatt-Gimblett (1973), have made the ambiguity of proverbs the centerpiece of their discussions. Krikmann held that proverbs have only a semantic potential, with multiple functions, meanings, and situations of use. Kirshenblatt-Gimblett (1973) asserted that we should consider, not proverb meaning(s), but proverb performances. She alluded to anecdotal showing data that the proverb, *A rolling stone gathers no moss*, can mean different things in Scotland, England, and Texas. The Scots make the moss a negative because it could make a stone roller ineffective, so a common interpretation is that people need to stay active and current. In England, moss is viewed positively, as one might envision in a bucolic scene in which moss grows on stones in a stream. The English interpretation therefore affirms the positive aspects of stability. In Texas, college students often interpreted the proverb to mean that it is desirable to keep moving and not be encumbered by family and possessions. The encumbrance here is the moss, and it is a negative of course. These students, however, also provided something akin to the Scottish and English interpretations.

In a further analysis of *Money talks*, Kirshenblatt-Gimblett (1973) described a number of episodes for which the base meaning of the proverb remained the same—giving money favorably disposes someone toward granting your wishes—but at least three other factors varied. These factors were whether the money actually had a positive effect, whether one conversant thought that the money had a positive effect, and whether saying that the money had an effect was concordant with what the conversants wanted to accomplish. The author concluded that "convergences of social situation, partipant evaluation, and interactional strategy" all contribute to proverb meaning and use (p. 118). Nevertheless, base meaning can vary, as the "rolling stone" example illustrates, and Kirshenblatt-Gimblett (1973) stated that this meaning is influenced by how the concrete image in the proverb is understood, what the general principle of the image is understood to be, how this principle is evaluated connotatively, syntactic ambiguity, lexical ambiguity, and key (sarcasm, humor, etc.). She concluded that proverb meaning should not be the focus but, rather, proverb performances, which she defined in terms of participants' evaluations of the situation, their understanding of the proverb base meaning, and the proverb user's strategy.

Finally, in Grzybek's (1987) semiotic approach, the proverb has three functions: its intended pragmatic effect, its social and educational effects, and its modeling or representational effects (i.e., how the proverb categorizes its instances). This approach, however, does not address the mental activities that subserve these functions.

Although the earlier approaches highlighted various issues in proverb cognition—levels of meaning, analogy, pragmatic functions, and so on—they did not provide details about how to resolve the issues. Furthermore, no general theory of proverb cognition developed out of these efforts. What follows is an initial look at the information-processing framework, which does attempt to model mental activities in detail. Of course, much of the material described in chapter 2 derives from this framework, so it should look familiar.

The Information Processing Framework

The early approaches provide a direction for theorizing, but none focus on microcognition: the interplay among memory structures and mental processes that enable proverb processing.

The predominant framework within which microcognition has been addressed is information processing. There are other views, such as connectionism, sometimes called parallel distributed processing, but essentially all of the issues and most of the research has the stamp of information processing. Connectionism will be taken up in the last chapter as one of the new ideas that may bear fruit.

The information-processing view likens the mind to a computer that takes in inputs and converts them into outputs according to certain rules. Various structures, such as a long-term memory and a working memory (limited capacity, data manipulation system) are postulated, with inputs being operated on and transformed by various processes that operate in series or in parallel. Thus, the major theme is that inputs are recoded by being cycled through a series of processes. The human is seen as limited in real-time capacity, although practice can free up capacity by making a process automatic. Nevertheless, capacity limitations have major consequences for how much and what kind of information can be processed online. Depending on the particular phenomenon being modeled, the details of the information-processing framework change, but its basic conceptual elements remain.

Here is an example. Take a statement such as "The old man the boat." The light patterns aroused by this statement are transduced by the visual system into nervous impulses that travel to the back of the brain, the primary receiving areas for visual inputs. The input has already been sliced and diced into a number of dimensions, including size, shape, and intensity, that are handled by different parts of the brain. Because the reader is an expert at reading, the visual inputs are perceived as wholistic units including letters and words. As the sentence is read, a syntax is computed, perhaps driven for this example by the fact that the words are familiar and immediately group into a larger pattern, "The old man." The problem, of course, is that if this grouping is constructed, the sentence becomes ungrammatical and nonsensical, so we have been led down the "garden path." "The old man" and "the boat" look like two different, nonsynthesizable ideas. A revision of syntax and meaning is therefore required. Given the constraints of the words and allowable syntax, the only sensible revision involves making "man" a verb instead of a noun, leading to the new interpretation that the old (people) handle the boat. This meaning has easy literal interpretations. However, because the sentence is stated in the generic, gnomic sense, it is also a potential proverb. For example, it could occur in a debate about the proper age for a president and congress. Someone could say, *The old man the boat*, and imply that they are in favor of the ship of state being run by its elders.

This brief example illustrates the major assumption of the information-processing view: Inputs undergo a series of recodings. Outputs can therefore be very different from inputs. In the example, what started out as a light pattern was ultimately used as an opinion about government. Moreover, several things were left out, including the perceptual processes involved in reading (e.g., saccadic eye movements) and how these interact with syntax and meaning. It would take a small book to discuss all the details of how the "old man" sentence gets processed.

The information-processing view has been criticized on many grounds. One criticism goes briefly as follows. This view presumes a computational metatheory. However, almost all modern computers are symbol-manipulating systems using syntactical rules that operate on data that is coded in an on or off (1 or 0, digital) form. Because the syntactical rules are content free, some thinkers have claimed that a computer could not possibly "understand" what it is doing. There needs to be a semantics, some kind of conceptual underpinning to the rules.

For some scholars, support for this claim comes from the famous "Chinese room" argument by the philosopher John Searle (1980). Searle had us imagine a person in a room, someone who speaks and reads English but not Chinese. This person gets three sets of materials written in Chinese symbols, a set of rules written in English for correlating the symbols in the first with those in the second set, plus a second set of instructions in English for correlating the third set with the first two. Searle told us to think of the three sets as a script, a story, and questions. We are then to presume that the person becomes an expert at "answering the questions," so good, in fact, that the answers are indistinguishable from those that would be provided by native Chinese speakers. Of course, for the material written in English, this person can also provide answers that are indistinguishable from those of other English speakers.

The question now arises, what is it exactly that this person has understood regarding the Chinese inputs? Nothing, said Searle. The output (i.e., the answers) passes the Turing Test (named after Alan Turing, a signal figure in the early artificial intelligence movement) because it cannot be discriminated from the output of native Chinese speakers. But the person really does not understand anything other than how to use rules to relate symbols. There is syntax but no semantics. Searle (1980) claimed that computers do not have the causal powers that brains do. That is, there is something unique about biological systems and, in this sense, computers provide a poor model for explaining human mental activity. This argument raised a storm of protest from the artificial intelligence community when it first appeared, and some in this community reject it altogether.

The computational assumption behind the information-processing view has been attacked for other reasons as well. Many thinkers claim that computers are too inflexible, rule-bound, serial, and exacting, in that if one aspect of a process goes haywire, no sensible output is possible.

Whatever its drawbacks, the information-processing view provides a useful approach to understanding proverb microcognition. It plays a key role in one of the theories we now consider.

CURRENT THEORIES

Currently, there are three theories of proverb cognition that fit within the cognitive view in the sense that they have attempted to explicate proverb processing by means of a set of interrelated microlevel processes. The theories are (a) the *extended conceptual base theory* (ECBT), an update of the conceptual base theory and its new version, the extended conceptual base theory-2; (b) the *great chain metaphor theory* (GMCT); (c) the *dual coding theory* (DCT). These theories emphasize comprehension rather than production, although ECBT-2 attempts to explain a wide range of proverb phenomena.

The Extended Conceptual Base Theory

The ECBT (Honeck & Temple, 1994), which is an extension of the conceptual base theory (Honeck et al., 1980) placed proverb understanding squarely within a problem-solving framework. A problem exists whenever there is a discrepancy between a current state and a goal state. Proverb understanding involves a number of small goals, largely ill-defined, that must be reached for complete understanding to take place.

In any communication situation, language user and language interpreter share certain background conditions. By background conditions I mean packets of information such as culture, language, interpersonal knowledge, and knowledge about the current topic of communication. Sperber and Wilson (1986) called this shared information a "cognitive environment." To the extent that this environment is not shared, communication will be made difficult.

First, consider how the ECBT handles proverb comprehension in irrelevant context situations. In these situations a proverb is received "out of the blue" without any supporting context and without a topic. The theory assumes, per Sperber and Wilson's (1986) analysis, that all communication comes with an implicit guarantee that the communicator is intending something and that it is relevant to the situation. Bear in mind that proverbs are communicationally bizarre in the sense that they mention things that are not part of the cognitive environment, even when the proverb has a clear referent. If a stranger walks up to us on the street and says, *Not every oyster contains a pearl,* how do we respond? First, we build a *literal meaning model*, in this case what is probably a simple, easily accessed model. Having gotten this model, do we ignore it? Is the stranger just a little weird, or perhaps trying to tell us that he or she just picked up our purse or wallet and found nothing worth taking? It is not as if they said something like, "Nice day, eh?" or "Cities, how frustrating!" Such comments seem relevant. The oyster utterance does not. But we probably will not have any difficulty understanding the utterance as a literal assertion.

Thus, the *development of a literal meaning model is the first phase of the overall proverb understanding process*. It is hard to imagine how this phase could be bypassed. However, because the utterance has no immediate referent and because it is stated in a gnomic, nonpast tense way, *a problem recognition phase* results. We might therefore be tempted to think about it, but we probably will need some motivation. This is supplied by a *communication appraisal factor* that involves setting a criterion for deciding whether an utterance is worthy of further thought. Two variables play a role here. First, a cognitive efficiency variable entails judging whether the utterance said anything valuable enough to override a tendency toward least mental effort. Second, a social payoff variable holds that when people say something to us we should respond, because it would be impolite, condescending, unintelligent, or even dangerous not to.

Together, the linguistic form of the proverb and the appraisal factor push the receiver off the literal level toward an ill-defined something else. This is the *literal transformation phase*. The linguistic form and basic communication modes seem to make the receiver say, "Something needs to be done with this utterance, but what? I do not know this person and why is he or she talking about oysters and pearls? There are no oysters and pearls around here, not on this street by any means, so maybe they mean something else." This is the beginning of deeper understanding, of course, because now the receiver can use whatever clues are at hand to get the newer, and now more preferred meaning.

But the receiver's major clue is the utterance itself, more precisely whatever literal meaning model the receiver has developed for it. That is, the receiver has a hunch that the utterance is about itself, not the model for it per se, but what it might mean on another level. The ECBT now postulates that people follow an *ostension maximization principle*, which holds that a meaning should be developed that is general enough to instantiate anything that the literal meaning model could possibly be about, including itself. That proverbs are self-instantiating makes them recursive, showing "strange loops" (see chapter 5). Although the newer, preferred meaning should instantiate the literal model, it is also constrained by it. But it is not determined by it because new information must be gotten, information that is outside the literal model. Getting this information will require inferences, associations, and elaboration in general. Most people already know about oysters and pearls, that oysters make pearls, and that pearls are valuable. That is part of the power of proverbs: They use familiar concepts to engender a more abstract meaning. Without supporting information to provide elaborative processes, one would think that getting a new, consensual meaning would be all but impossible. But language draws on built-in, schema-based logic. Some oysters contain pearls, some do not. What needs to be made salient is the positive value of pearls and the generic quality of oysters as a thing that makes something of value. This information can be synthesized in a new meaning: Not everything that makes valuable things does it all of the time. This is the figurative meaning (more precisely, an expression of this meaning), so the *figurative meaning phase* has been entered.

Now that our receiver has constructed a figurative meaning, what is to be done with it? People are born pragmatists. American pragmatists of the early 20th century wanted to know the "cash value of an idea." The cognitive marking property of proverbs facilitates the push toward using their figurative meaning. That is, because of their linguistic, poetic, and odd communicational quality, proverbs make people think that their meaning should be remembered and used in new situations. This helps explain why there are numerous proverb dictionaries, written as well as in memory.

The point is that once in possession of a figurative meaning the receiver can use it in new situations with new episodes. In this case, the receiver has entered the *instantiation phase*. Further inferences could yield meanings such as "Not every investment I make will grow"; "Even masterful quarterbacks sometimes fail"; or "Planet earth is our mothership, but it can get nasty at times." Almost any domain of reality in which normally productive processes fail to deliver becomes a candidate for application of the oyster proverb. Moreover, each application of the proverb will undoubtedly change its figurative meaning to some extent, so the instantiation phase could also be called the *revised meaning phase*.

What happens if the scenario for application of the ECBT is changed from an irrelevant context situation to a relevant context situation? In the latter, the proverb (as vehicle) has a clear referent or topic. All of the mechanisms that operated in the topicless situation operate here as well. However, the major subproblem is not whether the utterance should be processed further, or what might motivate the receiver to move from the literal level, but how to connect the utterance with the topic. Call this the *connection problem*. It is a categorization problem in that the topic, in whatever state of understanding, is instantiated by the utterance. When the topic is mutually understood, the proverb utterance serves to categorize it. Use of the proverb glosses as, "This is such and such a kind of situation," and typically provides speech act information about it as well. When the topic is not well understood, the proverb serves both to clarify its meaning as well as to categorize and comment on it. Proverbs are most enlightening when used in this fashion, although it makes the receiver's task much more complicated. In all cases of proverb application, however, the ECBT assumes that an analogical process is at work and amounts to saying that the figurative meaning can be used as a kind of grid that can be matched up with the topic. Proverb usage is a good example of pattern matching on a conceptual level.

Theoretically, a number of constraints operate to effect a match. Information about the situation, the topic, the literal meaning model, the figurative meaning as currently developed, and occasional hints from the proverb user all must be processed to connect proverb and topic. Whenever a connection is made, it must be abstract because although the proverb and topic match ideationally, they do not match perceptually. That is part of the intrigue of proverbs because they force people to synthesize information at a high level in a totally abstract medium. This medium has been termed a *conceptual base*, and hence the name of the theory. It must be emphasized that the notion of a conceptual base is only a claim that the representational format for the figurative meaning of a proverb is nonimagistic and nonlinguistic. The ECBT makes no claim about the specific nature of the information encoded in a conceptual base. Because that information is writ in mentalese, and the stuff of mentalese has yet to be explicated to anyone's satisfaction, any claim about the contentive details of a conceptual base would be premature. To be sure, a conceptual base has to have some precision, so it is proposition-like. Moreover, because this base can be widely instantiated, expressed in synonymous ways, and, in some cases, represented in abstract nonlinguistic media, the base must be abstract and general.

In summary, the ECBT holds that someone who receives a (potential) proverb may judge, in irrelevant context situations, and according to basic communication rules, that the proverb is about itself but at a more general level. In relevant context situations, the receiver's problem is to reconfigure the literal meaning model and the proverb topic so that they are conceptual matches. Then, in accordance with the standard pragmatic model, the conventional meaning of the utterance is rejected as the intended meaning, but used, along with reasoning and problem-solving processes, to build a newer, preferred meaning that solves the problem of what the user intended. Because proverb mention yields a cognitive marker, the receiver may attempt to use the preferred (figurative) meaning by way of applying it to various domains. Once the proverb is applied, a normal inductive process will occur by which the figurative meaning is revised.

The ECBT is diagrammed in Fig 4.1. The flow of processes therein will be different depending on whether a relevant or irrelevant context is involved.

The ECBT has been buttressed by a great deal of empirical data, which have come primarily from experimental laboratory work done at the University of Cincinnati. Most of the participants in these studies have been college students, although two studies were conducted with young children. One could argue that the studies were artificial in the sense that they did not observe proverb cognition as it typically occurs in everyday life. However, as in all experiments, the goal is to isolate some phenomenon so that factors influencing the phenomenon can be identified and irrelevant factors ruled out. Observation of phenomena in vivo, especially those that occur quickly and capriciously, are difficult

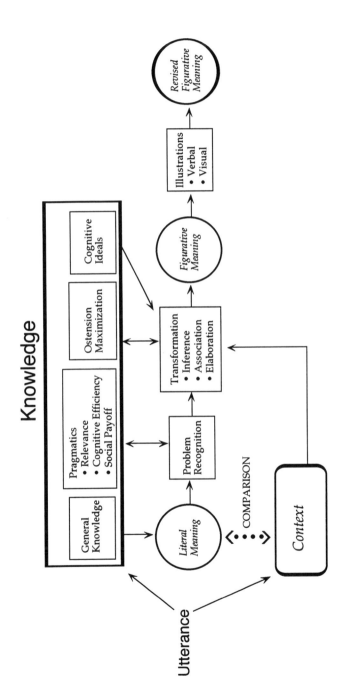

FIG. 4.1. Diagram of the extended conceptual base theory.

if not impossible to study in any depth in nonlaboratory situations.

Our research has demonstrated that people can reliably perform a number of mental tasks in which proverbs are used. Many tasks have involved explicit tests of memory, whereas others have involved judgments of some kind or quick reactions to proverbs or proverb-related materials.

Perhaps one way to understand the large number of studies is to think, not in terms of isolated proverbs, but in terms of proverb families. A *proverb family* potentially consists of all the following elements: a proverb; verbal interpretations of the proverb's figurative meaning, verbal instances of the figurative meaning, realistic pictorial instances of the figurative meaning, and abstract pictorial representations of the figurative meaning.

An illustrative proverb family follows:

Proverb: *Great weights hang on small wires.*

Verbal interpretation: Important outcomes can depend on seemingly minor details.

Verbal instances: The surgeon's hand slipped and the patient died; A shot rang out and a war started.

The literal and abstract pictures for this proverb are left to the reader's imagination (some examples of abstract pictures are provided in the figures in chapter 5).

Research has demonstrated that people are able to reliably connect any two pairs of proverb family members (for reviews of this research, see Feldhaus & Honeck, 1989; Honeck et al., 1987; Honeck & Temple, 1994; Honeck et al., 1980). People's ability to make these connections is theoretically interesting because there are obvious differences in the inputs. That is, the literal meanings of the various inputs do not comport (except for proverbs and literal pictures), so people must be matching them on a nonliteral basis. In addition, cross-modal matching of verbal and visual stimuli strongly suggests that the matching is being done in an abstract modality-free medium, the language of the mind. This is what is meant by a conceptual base: a modality-free, nonimagistic, nonverbal structure. For proverbs, it is the figurative meaning. The conceptual base for a proverb, therefore, is its figurative meaning, but conceptual bases develop for nonproverbial inputs as well. Indeed, there is a great deal of evidence that long-term memory does much of its work in terms of a modality-free medium (Marks, 1996; Snodgrass, 1984).

The research story does not end here. Demonstrations of people's ability to match inputs on a nonliteral basis only tells us that something unitary and fundamental is happening: The action is beneath the surface of the inputs. Other pieces of the puzzle have provided more specific information. For example, as people provide a better interpretation for a proverb, they are better able to use an abstract prompt (verbal instance or story) to recall the proverb (Honeck, Riechmann, & Hoffman, 1975). Furthermore, proverb categories are graded in that the instances can be reliably ordered from excellent to poor. Significantly, it does not matter whether a proverb or a verbal interpretation of the proverb or even an abstract pictorial interpretation of the proverb is used as a standard for ranking the instances. The rankings are very similar. That is, if an input is judged to be an excellent instance of the proverb, it is also judged to be an excellent instance of the interpretation or picture. Proverb, interpretation, and picture are apparently tapping into a common conceptual representation that is relatively precise even while being abstract. Indeed, if the representation is literal and non-abstract, then people cannot distinguish novel positive instances from novel negative ones. For example, if experimental participants focus on the literal imagery evoked by a proverb, they are unable to recognize novel instances of the proverb's figurative meaning (Honeck & Kibler, 1984). Similarly, people judge the interpretation to best represent the basic meaning of a family consisting of a proverb, an interpretation, and some verbal instances. The interpretation is the closest and best representation of the figurative meaning that binds the family members. This result is repeated when a memory test is used and people are asked whether an input was related in meaning to a previously learned family (Dorfmueller & Honeck, 1980). Finally, figurative meanings are more flexible when instances are used that sample a wider rather than a narrower set of domains (Honeck et al., 1987).

These several results indicate that although figurative meanings are wholistic, they have parts whose presence or absence in other inputs will affect how these inputs are judged and remembered. For example, the extent to which a story is rated as having certain figurative components correlates highly with rankings of how well the story illustrates the proverb behind the story (Kibler, 1985). Finally, there is now good evidence that the familiarity of the proverb affects how quickly its figurative meaning can be accessed and constructed (Case, 1991; Temple, 1993). Only highly familiar proverbs seem to have anything resembling prepackaged meanings, and even these seem to undergo some quick editing and reconstruction. The proverb is remembered as a wholistic verbatim form, but its figurative meaning is not. There always seems to be a constructive element to figurative meaning, a momentary, dynamic, on-the-spot building that takes time and effort and that can be difficult to put into words for even the most familiar proverbs.

The major theme of the ECBT is resolution of uncertainty and, therefore, problem solving. For proverbs without a topic, a criterion has to be met just to begin working on the proverb. The literal meaning model is exactly that, a working hypothesis about the things mentioned in the proverb. It can change with time and circumstances. Inferences on the literal model are probabilistic and yield indefinite outcomes. Sometimes poor or inadequate inferences are made because people are not perfect inference machines. There is always some trial and error as well as guessing in the dark. An emerging figurative meaning is therefore tentative, ephemeral, and subject to revision.

Figurative meanings, therefore, are not the stuff that should be put into dictionaries and made out to be the official meaning of a proverb, especially when such meanings, or rather, verbal translations of them, are not empirically derived. Proverbs can have somewhat different meanings, even on the literal level, on different occasions. The connection problem (i.e., relating a proverb to a topic) can be especially daunting. Even when the proverb topic is clearly understood, the problem of setting the proper elements into correspondence can be ticklish. If we have to generate our own examples of what a proverb means, it becomes clear how sketchy the process can become. Finally, putting proverb meanings into words can be especially difficult. People often show evidence that they understand a proverb, but are unable to articulate that meaning satisfactorily. This translation process is just the last in a series of processes that bespeaks uncertainty and requires problem solving.

ECBT-2: The Cognitive Ideals Hypothesis

Two major additions have been made to the ECBT: the cognitive ideals hypothesis and the DARTS model. The former has implications for a number of topics: proverb creation, the occurrence of oppositional concepts in the proverb, a typology of proverbs, the literal content of the proverb, comprehension, the conceptual motivating power of the proverb, production, and pragmatics. Proverb creation, production, and literal specifics are taken up in the next chapter. The DARTS model, presented in chapter 6, has been developed to help pinpoint the right cerebral hemisphere's contribution to proverb comprehension. The reader should note that the ECBT-2 is new and has not as yet been put to empirical test, although it has some rational justification.

First, we discuss the basics of the cognitive ideals hypothesis and then we pursue its implications.

The concept of marking was discussed previously. What is it that people mark with a proverb? One possibility is that they are attempting to capture an ideal, norm, or standard. Societies and individuals judge that there are ideal, normative, and standard ways by which events should and do occur. Call these *generic ideals*. Proverbs tell us what these ideals are, how to attain them, and what constitutes a deviation. In other words, proverbs tread in perfection. Perfection, or givens, exist in many realms, including the physical, biological, psychological, and sociocultural. For example, the physical world places severe constraints on what is possible. Pencils cannot be pushed through iron walls; water does not run uphill. Biologically, organisms must meet basic needs to survive. Psychologically, people know that there is an optimal time for a specific thing to be accomplished. Success in reaching a goal requires flexibility. A part of a whole needs to fit a whole, and so on. On a cultural level, every society values some thoughts and behaviors rather than others. In general, thoughts of perfection derive from multiple constraints that operate on every level of existence. Thus, each generic ideal can potentially be instantiated in different ways in different realms.

However, a proverb must be expressed with particular words and syntax. Call this the *specific ideal*, because it represents a particularization of the generic ideal that underlies and motivates the proverb. The generic ideal is general and universal. It comes about because of human commonalities on the biological, psychological, and cultural levels. The specific ideal is fashioned in more culturally or personally unique terms. Thus, it is rendered in a specific language, using concepts that are familiar. People therefore use the perfection encoded in generic ideals to create specific ideals, the proverbs themselves.

The cognitive ideals hypothesis can be applied to show how it operates. For the proverb, *Not every oyster contains a pearl*, there is the recognition of a deviation from a specific ideal, namely that oysters contain pearls. This ideal can be derived from the generic or superordinate ideal that "some things produce valuable products." For the example, the instantiating generic ideal is that "biological organisms can produce valuable products."

We can also analyze *A stitch in time saves nine* and *The grass is always greener on the other side of the fence*. The "stitch" proverb explicitly acknowledges the specific ideal of the fewer stitches the better. The proverb would make no sense without the underlying belief in a more perfect state of affairs, namely that the least number of stitches is the best. However, this surface level ideal seems to derive from a more basic psychological ideal, namely the law of least effort. This is the generic ideal, and it is instantiated on the physical level.

In the "grass" proverb, the logic is that the grass somewhere else is at some time going to be greener than the grass in one's purview; it is a truth that must be accepted. The proverb therefore asks that people accept the norm because it is inevitable, and by implication, being jealous of the greenness of grass that is elsewhere is fruitless and should be shunned. The generic ideal is the realization that value is relative and, in particular, that instances of the same natural kind (i.e., grass) differ in value. This ideal is undoubtedly acknowledged by all humans, as well as the idea that there is an optimal time to do something, which would seem to be the generic ideal for proverbs such as, *Make hay while the sun shines* and *Strike while the iron is hot*. Thus, the same generic ideal may underlie more than one proverb.

Oppositions in Proverbs.   The cognitive ideals hypothesis makes it clear why proverbs often use binary contrasts, opposition, and comparisons in general. Perfection abides no half-way points. Ideals are either attained or not. Furthermore, the easiest way to point to an ideal is by expressing a contrast between what the ideal is and a state of affairs that deviates from it. The yin and yang of existence comes into play in proverbs, therefore, because ideals partake of a state of perfection that has only one alternative state, namely that of nonperfection, its opposite. For this reason, proverbs contain the many dualities—good–bad, one–many, whole–part, beautiful–ugly, and so on—that scholars have noted through the years.

A Proverb Typology.   The cognitive ideals hypothesis also has clear implications for a typology of proverbs. Specifically, proverbs can be seen to fall into two basic categories. First, there are *ideal-confirming proverbs*, those that explicitly express what the ideal is and how to attain it. Second, there are *ideal-disconfirming proverbs*, those that implicitly express what the ideal is by explicitly describing some deviation from it.

To try out this hypothesis, the author examined a set of 160 proverbs that have been used in the laboratory at the University of Cincinnati. Most are unfamiliar. Many were in fact composed anew, and some were taken from proverb dictionaries. This preliminary examination suggested that a case could be made for the typology.

Here is a sample list of proverbs, potential proverbs at least, that tell us what the ideal is and how to reach it. Thus, these are ideal-confirming proverbs:

A patch on the tire saves a trip to the garage.

A stitch in time saves nine.

A peacock should frequently look at its legs.

Make hay while the sun shines.

If your clothes don't fit make them into a quilt.

Better to fall from the window than the roof.

A rolling stone gathers no moss.

Better be the head of a dog than the tail of a lion.

A bird in the hand is worth two in the bush.

Cows run with the wind, horses against it.

The first two proverbs tell us what to do in a direct way, and they are synonymous in this regard. We are exhorted to engage in some activity now before things get worse, because if they do, more work will be involved. The specific ideal is explicit in the sense that we are told how to reach it, although the value of less work is implicit of course. In "A rolling stone..." we are told explicitly how a stone avoids gathering moss. The ideal state of affairs is to keep moving or stay active and to not have moss affect the stone. The ideal state of affairs in "A bird in the hand..." is to have something in one's possession rather than nothing, generically to preserve maximum value to the self, even if what one has is less than what exists.

Notice that the means by which the ideal is made explicit is almost always accomplished by means of binary contrasts: one–nine, moving–static, beautiful–ugly, window–roof, head–tail, and so on. Moreover, the rhetorical force differs. Some proverbs call for certain actions; some simply ask us to note a state of affairs; others implicitly ask us to consider the implications of a possible state of affairs. However, and this provides the beginnings of a theory of the pragmatic force of proverbs, recognition of the ideal provides the motivation for their particular practical message.

Here are some proverbs that point to the ideal by expressing a deviation from it. Thus these are ideal-disconfirming proverbs:

Too many cooks spoil the broth.
The army with one strategy is easily beat.
Crows mourn the dead sheep and then eat them.
You can't sell the cow and drink the milk.
A knife can't whittle its own handle.
Blind blames the ditch.
You cannot shoe a running horse.
A soft tongue can strike hard.
Even a hair casts its shadow on the ground.
Great weights hang on small wires.

For the "army" proverb, the specific ideal is that an army should have more than one strategy. The generic ideal is that achievement of goals requires flexibility. The (ethical) ideal in "Crows mourn..." is that crows should mourn and engage in behavior that is consistent with mourning, which the eating of the sheep clearly is not. The generic ideal of behavioral consistency, instantiated as ethical consistency, is violated. Similarly, the ideal time to shoe a horse is when it is still; generically, the physical world is such that a physical activity is carried out better at some times than others (the generic ideal behind the "Make hay..." and "Strike while...hot" proverbs). Great weights would normally be thought to hang on large, not small, wires; generically, physical principles of support apply. For all of the proverbs in this category, the ideal, norm, or standard is made prominent by describing a situation that deviates from it.

Like those in the ideal-confirming category, these proverbs use a variety of oppositions, expressed or implied: many–few, great–small, hard–easy, physical possibility–impossibility, and so on. What is significant about these ideal-disconfirming proverbs is that they tell us what *not* to think or do or expect. We are not supposed to sell the cow; the blind are not to blame the ditch; one must not have too many cooks, and so on.

Comprehension. A major thesis in this volume is that proverb comprehension requires a large number of memory structures, memory interactions, and mental operations. Theoretically, cognitive ideals must be accessed as part of this process. It is not claimed, however, that generic ideals are somehow built into proverbs. Rather, proverbs provide information that arouses thoughts about generic ideals, and these ideals provide a basis for assembling an understanding of the proverb.

Moreover, no claim is made that generic ideals are represented in semantic memory. This memory system is characterized as declarative and propositional. For example, we know that Wednesday follows Tuesday, Earth has one moon, and pi is 3.14159. Generic ideals are better viewed as being part of an intuitive or tacit memory, that is, things people know that are so obvious that they are hardly ever singled out, thought about, or verbalized. This intuitive memory contains what, from a scientific standpoint, contains facts but probably also beliefs, such as why physical events happen the way they do, beliefs that are often incorrect. It would seem inappropriate to consider this knowledge declarative, at least in the sense that cognitive psychologists use the term. People know a great deal that is not declarative or propositional: Some things are more valuable than others; physical events have a certainty to them; some tasks are harder to do than others; events that stand out tend to evoke the most attention, and so on. Proverbs tap into this tacit knowledge system, and in this sense there is no news in proverbs (see chapter 7 for an elaboration of this claim).

Proverbs therefore say things that people are expected to know already. When someone, such as a child, has not had sufficient experience to build up a tacit knowledge system, then proverb understanding may become difficult. If the word concepts used in the proverb are also unknown, as for someone who is from another culture, then an appropriate generic ideal cannot be aroused. For example, the author drew a blank upon first reading the proverb, *Any weather, chicken's pants are rolled up*. According to Lakoff and Turner (1989) it has its origins in the behavior of Asian peasants who, when working in fields, roll up their pants and test for puddles by sticking out a foot, looking like a chicken in the process. Because this behavior looks awkward and stilted, the proverb connotes someone consistently behaving in this manner. Thus, the specific ideal encoded in this proverb is culturally quite specific, and ignorance about its reference blocks a culturally appropriate figurative understanding. The proverb, however, draws on a generic ideal: The intrinsic character of something is a constant. This same ideal occurs in less culturally idiosyncratic proverbs such as *A rotting porch can't be fixed with a coat of paint*.

Pragmatics. The cognitive ideals hypothesis leads in a straightforward way to proverb pragmatics. The proverb typology it generates tells us that there are ideals-confirming and ideals-disconfirming proverbs. Ideals are goals that are positively valued and sought, whereas deviation from the goal is negatively valued and to be avoided. Thus, ideals-confirming proverbs exhort us to act in a way that is consistent with the generic ideal expressed by the proverb. Ideals-disconfirming proverbs exhort us not to act in a way described by the proverb. For example, *Too many cooks spoil the broth* is built on the generic ideal that any given task has an optimal number of participants for attaining the task's goal. In this case, the ideal is instantiated in the realm of human endeavor. Because the proverb as a specific ideal tells us that there is a discrepancy from the generic ideal, by way of a specific illustration of it, and because discrepancies are to be avoided, the proverb can be used to exhort people not to have too many people engaged in the same activity. More generally, this proverb can comment critically on any situation that does not conform to the ideal. This will usually be some human activity but does not have to be. For example, we could apply "Too many cooks..." to a beaver dam that is poorly built because several families of beavers worked on it.

What are the pragmatics of an ideal-confirming proverb, *Make hay while the sun shines*? This familiar example is built on the generic ideal that there is an optimal time for desired effects to occur, and it is instantiated in the realm of biophysical material. The proverb explicitly states the optimal time to attain the goal, so it tells us in a direct way what to do to attain it. Thus, the proverb would exhort us in a particular instance to act at the right time to reach a goal. Again, this proverb, though typically applied to human activity, can be appropriately applied, say, to animals that engage in sexual intercourse during the female estrus cycle.

This general approach to pragmatics will be taken up again after consideration of the great chain metaphor theory. This theory's approach to exhortation will compared that of the ECBT-2.

Of course, we know that proverbs do more than exhort. To capture this, a theory of proverb pragmatics will need to consider all the elements of a communication situation: the people involved, their relationship, their shared cognitive environment, the topic of the proverb, and the proverb itself. The eighth-grader who has a paper due but is having trouble getting started might be told by a parent that *An ounce of prevention is worth a pound of cure*, which could be the parent's way of saying that the consequences of not getting the paper in on time could be rather severe compared to the work it takes to meet the deadline. The pragmatic force of the proverb comes from all of the communication elements: the child, the parent, their relationship, the topic (the paper is not getting done and there is a deadline), what they both know might happen if the deadline is not met, and the standard set by the proverb's generic ideal.

This seemingly simple case indicates that proverb pragmatics will almost inevitably require consideration of, not just the proverb, but the entire communication situation. The trick, from the cognitive view, will be to provide a viable theory of how all of this information gets coded and integrated for effective communication.

Conceptual Motivation. The approach to pragmatics and exhortation just described is lacking at least one important element: If proverbs can exhort in various ways, whence comes this power? It would be hard to say that someone fully comprehended a proverb without appreciating the motivational punch behind it. Theoretically, for "A stitch..." someone could understand that work is saved by stitching something now, rather than waiting and having to do more stitches later, but without the underlying value that conservation of labor is a worthwhile goal, the logic remains in behavioral limbo. Similarly, *Spilling wine is worse than spilling water* assumes the ideal of conservation of value, also worthwhile because without it there can be no rational exhortative force. In that case a proverb would become thought without energy or direction, qualities, of course, that represent the essence of pragmatics. The cognitive ideals hypothesis therefore holds that proverbs have strong potential for activating the motivation for effective rhetoric and message making.

Note, in the "wine" proverb, how generic ideals do double duty by providing the rationale for exhortation and the specific form of exhortation as well. The "wine" proverb is an ideal disconfirming proverb, so it tells us not to spill wine. But it could not have this particular force without its appeal to a prioritization of values. In simple terms the proverb says, "Favor the better things, so don't lose them," thereby reflecting a motivation that legitimizes a particular exhortation.

To summarize, the claims of the cognitive ideals hypothesis are that (a) generic ideals describe a mentally created state of perfection; (b) generic ideals are universal and common to most cultures; (c) generic ideals can be instantiated in different ways at the generic level; (d) generic ideals motivate and constrain specific ideals without overdetermining their content; (e) specific ideals are more culture and individual specific; (f) a generic ideal can result in two kinds of proverbs, those that affirm the ideal and those that express a deviation from it; (g) because ideals are either attained or not, in discrete fashion, proverbs often use contrasts to allude to them; (h) a proverb's exhortative and pragmatic effects in general are partially determined by the generic ideal that underlies it; (i) generic ideals provide the rational motivation for a proverb's pragmatic force; and (j) proverbs are created and produced to satisfy a generic ideal. (These two topics are covered in the next chapter.)

Two issues remain vis-à-vis the cognitive ideals hypothesis. First, what is the source of ideals? According to the cultural view, they would be learned through socialization. This occurs, of course, but it leaves out biology and individual experience of the physical world. These factors can also serve as the source of a large number of ideals, and because they are more likely to be universal than culturally based ideals, they increase the overall likelihood that the grand, worldwide population of proverbs tap into universals.

The second issue concerns the way ideals are related to a conceptual base in the ECBT. Because ideals are not viewed as part of a figurative meaning (conceptual base), but are recruited and assembled, the ECBT does not necessarily make these mental contents identical. It would be better to say that a variety of factors outlined in the ECBT converge on a figurative meaning, but that cognitive ideals play a large role in this process. Therefore, in some circumstances the two may converge, whereas in others they may not.

From the ECBT, which assumes the cognitive view of proverbs, we move on to a different theory, one that assumes the cultural view. Although many concerns of the two theories are similar, it will become evident that the theories approach these concerns with different perspectives, and to some extent, different constructs.

The Great Chain Metaphor Theory

A different perspective on proverb understanding is provided by the GCMT. This theory grows out of a cognitive linguistics approach developed since 1980 by George Lakoff and his associates (Lakoff, 1987; Lakoff, 1993; Lakoff & Johnson, 1980; Lakoff & Turner, 1989). A basic premise, discussed briefly in chapters 2 and 3, is that much of the mind is structured in terms of conceptual metaphors that allow one domain of knowledge (the target) to be understood in terms of another domain (the source). Examples include general metaphors such as "purposes are destinations" and "events are actions," as well as more specific metaphors such as "time is a pursuer"; "death is sleep"; and "argument is war." Conceptual metaphors are just that—conceptual, part of the mind—and not mere figures of speech, which are a purely linguistic phenomenon. These metaphors are presumed to operate in a relatively automatic and effortless way. They are unconscious, so we do not notice them, but they play an enormous role in the way we think and reason about things.

For example, Lakoff (1986a) wrote that there is a "love is a journey" conceptual metaphor that underlies expressions such as "look how far we've come"; "we're spinning our wheels"; and "we've hit a dead end street." The root metaphor ties these and other expressions together, provides a basis for reasoning about love relationships, and allows an understanding for new expressions that tap into the metaphor. Lakoff (1986a) explains the correspondences between love and journey this way:

> The lovers correspond to travelers.
> The love relationship corresponds to the vehicle.
> The state of being in the relationship corresponds to the physical closeness of being in the vehicle.
> The lovers' common goals correspond to their common destinations on the journey.
> Difficulties correspond to impediments to travel. (p. 217)

Such metaphors are shared by members of a culture and become conventional ways of construing events within their purview. One special kind of metaphor is the image-schema metaphor (Lakoff, 1987), which embodies general pieces of knowledge about centers and peripheries, paths, boundedness, tops and bottoms, and other topological concepts. Image-schemas are said to underlie some spatial reasoning and the spatial senses of prepositions such as "over," "from," "out" and "beside."

Although conceptual metaphors are central to the GCMT, several other general considerations should be taken into account in our exposition of the theory. These considerations stem from G. Lakoff (personal communication, July 26, 1996) who is quoted in this discussion.

First, the GCMT flows from a general description of thought and language. Therefore, "the entire apparatus of cognitive linguistics is available to be brought to bear on proverb analysis". In this case, the term GCMT is somewhat inappropriate inasmuch as it is part of this larger theoretical apparatus. Nevertheless, for reference purposes, the GCMT label is used here.

Second, Lakoff rejected the information processing view as biologically untenable, preferring instead a structured connectionistic view in which there is massive parallel processing. Accordingly, literal meaning is not given a priority either in general or in terms of temporal aspects of processing. In fact, the term literal is not used in the theory. Third, proverb understanding should be considered to occur always in some context that ordinarily predates and embeds the proverb. Fourth, the GCMT is not specifically concerned with a processing model but with the immense conceptual prerequisites for proverb understanding. Finally, it is assumed that a "frame semantic account" in people's minds allows for an understanding of proverb particulars.

The frame semantic account includes the following ideas. Proverbs are syntactically and semantically generic but they can be used in nonwhole ways in utterances. For example, in some contexts one can appropriately ask, "Did she stitch in time it?" Furthermore, as part of a culture's memory stock, conventional proverbs are typically understood by using moral precepts, folk theories, some notion of the kind of contexts in which the proverb could be used, the frame semantics that apply to these contexts, certain conventional conceptual metaphors, mechanisms such as the generic-is-specific metaphor and the great-chain-of-being (these latter two are described next), and constraints on the linguistic form of the proverb.

Although the GCMT is embedded in a larger theoretical apparatus, it relies on four basic concepts: the *generic-is-specific metaphor*, the *great-chain-of-being*, *the-nature-of-things*, and the conversational *maxim of quantity*. These concepts work together to produce proverb comprehension, although in some cases not all of these constructs need to be invoked.

We briefly discuss these four constructs. Note first, however, that because the GCMT sees proverbs as a form of metaphor, proverbs become sources for which there must be targets. The GCMT is basically designed to effect a source-to-target mapping by using some combination of the four constructs. Also, the GCMT postulates that people assume proverbs to be about humans and human affairs in general.

The great-chain-of-being is essentially the idea that things are arranged hierarchically, from humans, their thoughts, and societies on the top, down through animals, plants, complex physical objects (e.g., TVs), and natural physical things at the bottom. Each of these levels can be further subdivided into more levels. However, the highest properties of a level are what characterizes that level. Humans, for example, are cognitive organisms with refined sensibilities, whereas animals are instinctive. These characterizations are folk theories, of course, not scientifically based pieces of knowledge. Theoretically, the "great chain" is implicitly known by most members of Western cultures.

The nature-of-things concept postulates that different forms of being "have essences and that these essences lead to the way they behave or function" (Lakoff & Turner, 1989, p. 169). For example, candles have basic characteristics that make them behave in certain ways rather than others, but quite consistently compared with animals, which can be much more variable in their reactions. Beliefs and knowledge, especially knowledge of the causal structure of items, is encoded in the nature-of-things. Thus, the great chain and the-nature-of-things link up knowledge about items that are lower on the great chain with knowledge about items that are higher on the great-chain, such as humans. The knowledge that forms these two structures is seen as unconscious, automatic, and culturally shared.

The generic-is-specific-metaphor is a mechanism that "maps a single specific-level schema onto an indefinitely large number of parallel specific-level schemas that all have the same generic-level structure as the source-domain schema" (Lakoff & Turner, 1989, p. 162). The generic-is-specific metaphor is analogous to all "isa" metaphors in that (generic) topics are placed in the category of (specific) vehicles. A specific-level schema is essentially the information aroused by the words used in the proverb, so it includes images, schemas, and other mental structures or parts thereof. It is similar to literal meaning in the ECBT, but this term is not used in the GCMT. Generic-level schemas are contained in specific-level schemas. They are more abstract and general than specific-level schemas and can therefore instantiate other specific-level schemas such as proverb topics (targets). The generic-is-specific-metaphor, in the case of proverbs, "maps specific-level schemas onto the generic-level schemas they contain" (Lakoff & Turner, 1989, p. 163). In commonsense terms, the generic-is-specific-metaphor is a mechanism by which the basic meaning of the proverb is set into correspondence with an already contained, higher level, abstract meaning. For example, the elements of the basic meaning for *A net with a hole in it won't catch any fish*—a net catches fish; fish are valuable as food; nets with holes may not catch any fish, and so on—are mapped to the abstract schema. This schema would presumably include elements such as: Instruments are designed to have a purpose; the instrument must be in working order to achieve this purpose; flawed instruments cannot achieve this purpose; and so forth. These abstract elements could then be set into correspondence with, and instantiate, various proverb topics. In the GCMT, these basic meanings for topics are also referred to as specific-level schemas. In conclusion, the generic-is-specific-metaphor allows the specific-level schema of a proverb to connect up with its own generic-level schema and ultimately with the generic- and specific-level schemas of proverb targets.

The maxim of quantity is a conversational maxim (Grice, 1975), which says that listeners assume that speakers will provide only the information that is needed for understanding, no more, no less. It is a tacit form of cooperation between the speaker and the listener. The major role of this maxim is to constrain "what can be understood in terms of what" (Lakoff & Turner, 1989, p. 173). This maxim applies to the great chain and picks out information that is characteristic of a level on the chain because listeners assume by default that this is the information to which reference is being made. If lower ranking information at a great chain level was of interest (e.g., humans have legs), then it would appear that in referring to characteristic information (e.g., humans can think) that a speaker had implicated too much information, and would therefore have violated the maxim. However, listeners generally assume that speakers are not violating the maxim, so the higher level, characteristic information is deemed of interest. The maxim of quantity pulls double duty because it gets the listener to accept the high level information, and it selects and activates this information for the source and target domains. In general, the maxim of quantity acts as a brake on the great chain and the generic-is-specific processes, thereby restricting the meanings that a proverb could have.

We can now see how the GCMT operates. As for the ECBT, its operation can be explicated in irrelevant-context and relevant-context situations. Because there is seemingly some difficulty in deciding which elements of the GCMT and its larger theoretical framework come into play in explicating a particular proverb, an example from Lakoff and Turner (1989) is used.

The illustrative proverb is *Big thunder, little rain*. If someone hears this utterance and there is no topic for it, what happens? Aside from the comparison of thunder and rain in the proverb itself, there is a causal relationship between the two, information that is focused on by the nature-of-things. This information concerns part–whole relationships. The maxim of quantity therefore picks out information on the great chain that relates to this kind of information. Thus, irrelevant information (e.g., that rain is water, water is wet, wetness is slippery, etc.) is excluded. Together, the maxim of quantity, the great chain, and the-nature-of-things provide information that pertains to the causal relationship between thunder and rain. This information comprises a specific-level schema to the effect that there is thunder and rain; the thunder precedes the rain; thunder produces expectations of rain; and ordinarily the magnitude of the thunder is matched by the magnitude of the rain. Of course, the proverb itself is inconsistent with this schema because big thunder has led to little rain.

Thus far, we have a specific-level schema that has resulted from the relatively automatic operation of three mechanisms. The schema is then recognized somehow as a proverb from an individual's culturally given memory stock. But because there is no topic for the proverb, the generic-level schema of the specific-level schema becomes an acceptable target. That is, the generic-level schema is built into the specific-level schema, and it is automatically aroused when there is nothing for the proverb to be about. Because proverbs are about human affairs, this knowledge is activated as well.

The constructs that have operated thus far are the nonmetaphoric aspects of the theory. The metaphoric aspects now spring into action. The generic-is-specific mechanism extracts the generic meaning from the specific-level meaning, maps it to a human target (on the great chain), and picks out human attributes that preserve the proverb generic meaning (Lakoff & Turner, 1989). The generic-level information for *Big thunder, little rain* is essentially that: There are two natural events; one comes before the other; an occurrence of one signals the occurrence of the other; the second can affect us; the magnitude of the first correlates with that of the second; and for the case at hand, the magnitude of the second is less than would be expected. Generic knowledge about thunder and rain is now connected to generic knowledge about humans. Thus, the "thunder" proverb should theoretically be interpreted to mean something like "ineffectual bragging," "speaking softly with a little stick," "talking a lot and not saying much," and the like.

We now examine the GCMT in a relevant-context situation. Here, essentially all of the same GCMT concepts come into play except that because there is a proverb topic, the step of having to realize that the proverb is about itself is bypassed. The proverb is about the topic (e.g., an animal that seems dangerous because of threatening moves but is otherwise quite tame). In this case, the GCMT has moved to a lower level on the great chain, but the generic meaning of the proverb remains the same.

For the foregoing "big thunder" example, all four major components of the GCMT played a role. On some occasions this is not the case. This can be illustrated for *Not every oyster contains a pearl*, which was used in connection with our description of the ECBT. Lakoff's (personal communication, July 26, 1996) comments help in the description of this case. For this proverb, the great chain, the nature-of-things, and the maxim of quantity are not used. Instead, essentials of standard folk theory about oysters (i.e., they make pearls; opening oysters is work, most oysters do not have a pearl, etc.), and two conventional metaphors, are "sufficient to characterize much of the standard understanding of the proverb." The two metaphors are "well-being is wealth," in which the pearl symbolizes well-being, and "achieving a purpose is getting a desired object." Moreover, Lakoff indicated that the oyster proverb is understood relative to a moral system in which only hard work brings rewards and pragmatic realism is a virtue. Theoretically, the proverb would acquire a meaning via the operation of the generic-is-specific mechanism, which would extract the generic schema from the specific schema and apply it, in topicless situations to humans or, in a relevant-context situation, to a target.

The GCMT is diagrammed in Fig. 4.2. Bear in mind that this theory places more emphasis on parallel processing than the ECBT and that the arrows in the diagram do not necessarily indicate a serial process.

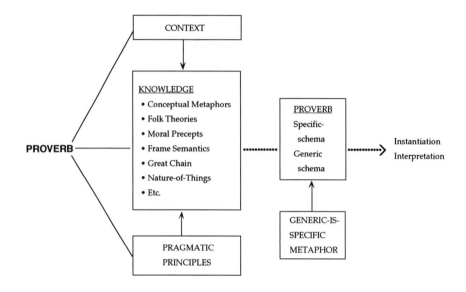

FIG. 4.2.   Diagram of the great chain metaphor theory.

Comparing the ECBT and the GCMT

The ECBT and the GCMT are similar yet different. They both implicitly acknowledge the power and significance of proverbs for individuals and in cultures. They are both cognitive theories that use concepts about cognitive structures and processes. Neither is an ethnographic, neurological, or purely linguistic theory. Presumably, both are capable of being informed by data and theory in cognitive science. They also share the assumption that language expresses thought and that proverbs therefore can only be understood in terms of basic nonlinguistic mental structures. This is the basic premise of the deep cognition view, as discussed in chapter 3. Furthermore, the ECBT uses terms such as *generic ideal* and *specific ideal* that seem related to the GCMT's generic schema and specific-level schemas, respectively. Finally, both theories obviously acknowledge the significance of certain issues in accounting for proverb cognition.

There are serious and fundamental differences between the two theories, however. The most important is that the GCMT derives from the cultural view and the ECBT from the cognitive view. The cultural view basically holds that proverbs are familiar cultural products. This assumption has several important implications (see chapter 1). First, by default, proverbs comment on human concerns. People use proverbs to talk about things that are important to them and those that have a cultural significance. The ECBT does not make commentary on human concerns a default position, being concerned with application in any domain. Second, there are only familiar proverbs and no unfamiliar ones because proverbs are a shared cultural product and no proverb as such could be known by a single individual. The ECBT identifies proverbs in terms of their form and function, not their familiarity. Third, proverbs are viewed as having built-in, socially shared and generated generic meanings that are prestored in memory. In this sense, there is a cultural lexicon of proverb meanings that transcends individual minds and meanings. The ECBT takes a more computational, online view of meaning construction. Fourth, the knowledge that proverbs entrain on the great chain and nature-of-things is culturally shared. In effect, folk theories are assumed to be essentially the same across individuals in a culture. The ECBT does not make special use of the great chain and the nature-of-things in accounting for proverb cognition. Finally, because all this knowledge underlying proverbs is shared, their understanding assumes an automatic quality, with little or no room for misunderstandings. That is, people either know what a proverb means or they do not, and when they do they get the meaning very quickly and effortlessly. This seems to happen even though the GCMT acknowledges that the same proverb can take on different meanings in different contexts that frame the typical proverb meaning. In contrast, the ECBT makes proverb processing variably automatic, with meanings being anywhere from good and whole to poor and fractious.

The ECBT begins with a different fundamental premise, one that originates within the cognitive view. Proverbs are mental entities that get understood by virtue of their form and function, not because of their status as a special cultural genre. Generic ideals are assumed to be supercultural, although the specific proverb ideal may not be. As discussed earlier, the ECBT places proverb understanding squarely within a general problem-solving framework, and this has implications for proverb understanding quite different from those for the GCMT.

First, there is problem recognition, not proverb recognition. When people hear a (potential) proverb, its utterance presents a problem, not unique to proverbs, that has to be recognized for what it is. If the problem goes unrecognized, the proverb cannot be understood because recognition motivates a search for new meanings.

Second, a proverb is recognized and processed as such by virtue of its form and function, not because it is already known. Form is not enough, because a proverb could be uttered in some context as an appropriate literal statement.

Third, having proverbs recognized by form and function further implies that proverb familiarity is treated differently. There can now be proverbs at any point on the continuum of familiarity, and unfamiliar proverbs have a chance of being understood because they are mentally decomposable by a vast range of mental structures and nonproverb-specific, inferential mechanisms.

Fourth, the figurative meaning of a proverb is constructed partially on the basis of literal meaning. However, this meaning is not built into the figurative meaning. Literal meanings are themselves constructed online on any given occasion, so figurative meanings cannot be built into them and somehow remain constant from one context to the next. Similarly, the same proverb can give rise to different interpretations. The GCMT acknowledges this, but it is not clear how this theory can account for variation in interpretation across individuals who share a culture.

Fifth, proverb understanding becomes uncertain, with a lot of guesswork and a settling in to a preferred meaning. There can be vast differences in understanding, with fragmentary meanings, irrelevant meanings, and no figurative meanings engendered at all. Interpretive variability across individuals and proverbs is totally consistent with this premise.

Finally, proverb understanding is not viewed as wholly automatic. Some aspects may be, such as lexical access and, for familiar proverbs, literal meaning models. But other aspects of proverb performances require more effortful processes. It may be effortful to assemble a figurative meaning for even a familiar proverb. Novel application of a proverb may be effortful for both the speaker, who may be using strategies, and the listeners, who will have to get pragmatic meanings to fully understand the speaker.

Aside from these basic differences regarding the status of proverbs per se, the concepts of generic ideal and specific ideal in the ECBT, and the generic- and specific-level schemas, in the GCMT, are significantly different. The content of a specific ideal and specific schema may well be similar on many occasions, but it seems to result from different mechanisms for different reasons. The ECBT has literal meanings develop out of a vast range of domain-specific mental structures by means of inferences that yield a basic logical structure. For example, for *Big thunder, little rain*, people merely call on their domain-specific knowledge about thunder, rain, and storms. There is no accessing of information on a great chain or nature-of-things and no maxim of quantity to use in picking out the correct information. The proverb stated as a sentence provides a context that strongly constrains possible inferences. That this proverb might be interpreted as "talking a lot but not saying much" could be accounted for by the parsimonious assumption that "thunder" is connected via sound to speech. "Thunder" becomes a metonymic, synesthetic, albeit hyperbolic, way of referring to talking.

In general, in the ECBT, literal meanings are more ambiguous, in a word, messier, than in the GCMT. People seem to infer all sorts of things, including irrelevant and unusable things. In this sense, the GCMT seems too inflexible in the sense that it appears always to generate only the right, useful, and relevant information.

Second, in the ECBT, people get literal meanings because they are a necessary first step in any communication scenario, and they echo past successes in solving problems in communication. In the GCMT, people seem to get specific schemas because the words and grammar of a proverb automatically select mental structures and mechanisms based on contextual constraints. These elements are there waiting to be activated by just the right proverb input information.

The situation regarding the generic ideal and generic-level schema concepts is more divergent in the two theories. Unlike a generic schema, a generic ideal is not viewed as being contained in the specific ideal or as being stored in a wholistic, already assembled, pristine way. Proverbs are stated in ways that arouse literal meanings that probabilistically evoke the assembly of generic ideals. More fundamentally, a generic ideal is viewed as a state of perfection, something that motivates thoughts that flow from it and not just a particular package of information, as might be contained in the great chain, for example. If we took generic schemas, placed them outside the proverb, made them less pre-packaged and more capable of assembly, more variable in auto-maticity of access, harder to set into correspondence with target events than the GCMT suggests, computed more online and less directly accessible, then generic schemas would look very much like cognitive ideals. Therefore, these concepts in the two theories are related but differ in important ways.

A generic ideal is more similar to Lakoff's (1987) concept of an "idealized cognitive model," which he views as a kind of standard used to judge the fit between the model and some variant of it. This is the premise behind the cognitive ideals hypothesis as well, except that the ECBT-2 places more empha-sis on the ideal as a state of perfection. The ECBT-2 also does not consider an ideal to have other properties that Lakoff attributes to idealized cognitive models, such as using proposi-tional, image-schematic, metaphoric-mapping, or metonymic structural principles. Generic ideals are things that people know but not in any organized propositional fashion. In addi-tion, Lakoff and Turner (1989) did not use the idealized cogni-tive model concept in their discussion of proverbs, nor did Gibbs (1995) in his discussion of the possible role of conceptual meta-phors in proverb processing. Gibbs, for example, asserted that the proverb, *One rotten apple spoils the whole barrel,* is com-prehended partly on the basis of the underlying metaphor of "People are inanimate objects" (p. 136). The premise is that this proverb is about people, which is understood via the presumed underlying conceptual metaphor. Thus, rotten apples and a whole barrel can, metaphorically, become people.

The cognitive ideals approach to "rotten apple" postulates a cognitive ideal that physical objects have intrinsic properties that from the human perspective should be retained. Physical deterio-ration is a process that denies this ideal and allows the deterio-rating object to taint the intrinsic property of other objects. The proverb is an ideals-disconfirming one, which implies that the bad apple should be prevented from having an impact on other apples. In American culture at least, "bad apple" is idiomatic for someone who has behaved in nonsanctioned ways. Therefore, to understand this proverb we need not invoke a systemic metaphor that depicts people as inanimate objects.

Finally, the ECBT does not make proverbs understood by metaphoric mechanisms or underlying conceptual metaphors. (That is not to say that some proverbs may not rely on a conceptual metaphor, but there is no good reason to search for conceptual metaphors beneath every proverb.) Proverbs often use metaphors, as they do many poetic devices, but these are somehow nonessential aspects of proverbs. That proverbs apply to things outside their commonplace references also does not make them metaphors. It is important here to maintain a distinction between a mechanism (e.g., analogy) that creates a nonliteral mapping and nonliteral mental contents (e.g., conceptual metaphors). The ECBT relies heavily on the former, but hardly at all on the latter.

The two theories differ substantially in empirical foundation. The GCMT treats proverbs as poems, and in this sense it has forged an interesting connection to literary analyses. It has not as yet addressed the large volume of experimental and field study data on the proverb. In contrast, the ECBT grew out of early experimental research on semantic memory in which proverbs were used, and it has been refined and extended to be commensurate with existing data. This data has been presented throughout the text. The cognitive ideals hypothesis has been developed in part to address the field study data.

Most of the empirical implications of the ECBT have been borne out (though the cognitive ideals hypothesis is new and undocumented experimentally). With increasing unfamiliarity, proverbs become more difficult to process, as indicated by the increased time it takes to understand them (Case, 1991; Temple, 1993). Yet, unfamiliar proverbs can be understood, both by adults and by children as young as 7 years of age (Honeck, Sowry, & Voegtle, 1978). That unfamiliar proverbs can be understood, albeit more slowly than familiar ones, destroys any claim that proverbs must be familiar, prestored, and culturally embedded. The reaction-time data are also consistent with the premise that literal meanings are computed before any nonliteral meanings, however they are construed. It is not clear how it could be any other way. People must process something about the meanings of words in conjunction with their syntax before moving on to something else. This is transparently true as a statement decreases in familiarity.

Furthermore, there also is no good evidence indicating that the figurative meaning of a proverb is encoded in complete form in the proverb's literal meaning. Studies have shown that when people judge how well a picture represents the objects mentioned in a proverb or develop mental images for the literal meaning of the proverb, they are less able to recognize novel instances of the proverb's figurative meaning (Honeck & Kibler, 1984). If the figurative (or generic) meaning is built into the literal meaning, this should not happen.

Figurative meaning must indeed be figured out. Proverbial meaning is not a simple matter of extracting preexisting meanings. If this were true, these meanings would just pop out whole and good. But often enough they do not. Proverb interpretations, and by implication proverb meanings, can be fragmentary, vague, and overly literal. This is certainly true for children, but adults often have difficulty with proverbs as well. One of the author's favorite examples showing the difficulty of proverb interpretation is *Eat peas with the king and cherries with the beggar*. What does it mean?

Finally, proverbs can be about anything, although they are ordinarily about human concerns. Humans, not chimpanzees, create proverbs, so what else could proverbs be about? Yet, when proverbs are presented in an illustrative context, the context often has the effect of promoting a more general, abstract meaning. This is somewhat inconsistent with the notion, according to the GCMT, that a stable generic-level schema is built into a specific-level schema. Paradoxically, context can serve to decontextualize the meaning of a proverb, thereby increasing its conceptual potential (Honeck & Temple, 1994).

Pragmatics is another area in which the two theories yield somewhat different perspectives. Bear in mind, however, that what the two theories have to offer on this is quite speculative.

As part of the GCMT, Lakoff and Turner (1989) hypothesized that "proverbs exhort us to exert voluntary control with respect to the behavior described metaphorically by the proverb" (p. 182). For example, *Burned lips on broth now blows on cold water* exhorts us not to engage in the behavior described, whereas *Cows run with the wind, horses against it* would have us act like horses. This is accomplished by an implicit rule that states that when the "metaphorical description" is consistent with voluntary control, "then the proverb exhorts us to behave as described; if it is not consistent with voluntary control, then the proverb exhorts us not to behave as the proverb describes" (Lakoff & Turner, 1989, p. 182). In the case of "Burned lips...," the behavior of blowing on cold water after an experience of burnt lips, is presumably relatively automatic, so we are exhorted not to act this way. For "Cows...," the behavior of the horses is less automatic, so we are exhorted to act more like horses than cows. A basic premise here is that we can only be exhorted when what is being exhorted is under voluntary control.

It is not clear how extensively this voluntary control hypothesis could be applied. A minority of proverbs involve a distinction on the literal level between voluntary and less voluntary elements, and there are many occasions for which the best advice or exhortation would be that someone make some thought or behavior automatic because it would be beneficial. There may in any case be a more general principle involved. The cognitive ideals hypothesis describes two kinds of proverbs: those that confirm ideals and those that disconfirm them. Because ideals are things that are accepted and observed, they tell us what it is we should be doing in thought or deed. If what the proverb describes deviates from the ideal, it tells us what should not be done.

By this construal, the "Burned lips..." proverb is based on the ideal of limiting our generalization from single experiences. People know, intuitively, that if they stubbed their toe on a door mat, this does not allow the inference that they will stub their toe on all door mats or that they will stub their toe on the living room rug. There are intrinsic limits to the generalizability of experience. Blowing on cold water after a bad experience with broth constitutes a deviation from this ideal. This makes "Burned lips..." an ideals-disconfirming proverb. It therefore tells us what not to do by pointing out a deviation from the ideal.

Let's return to the "cow" proverb. Using the ECBT, it becomes an ideal-disconfirming proverb. The generic ideal is the "law of least effort" to which the cows conform (by running with the wind) but the horses do not. The proverb also draws, subtly, on our beliefs about cows (slow, herd-like, dumb) and horses (faster, more prone to maverick behavior, smarter). The truth of this is illustrated by reversing the original proverb to get *Horses run with the wind, cows against it.* The exhortation now seems to shift toward emulation of horses. Whether this shift is consistent with knowledge that we could assume to find on the great-chain-of-being (i.e., horses are smarter than cows) is debatable. In any case, the new proverb confirms the ideal. For both proverbs there is an underlying physiognomic connection between the wind and "going with the flow," which is idiomatic in American culture for "conformity." Exhortations to conform or not conform depend on beliefs about the two entities being compared in the proverb.

Lakoff and Turner (1989) also claimed that some proverbs do not exhort (e.g., *Knife can't whittle its own handle*). Their reasoning is that the descriptive reading concerns an inability to change one's own makeup or character, but, "An exhortation reading of this would be exhorting one to change what is unchangeable, and therefore the reading is impossible" (p. 183). In contrast, by the cognitive ideals hypothesis, the "knife" proverb involves a proscription due to physical design, an intrinsic property of the natural world. It is an ideals-disconfirming proverb, so it can have an exhortative force, namely not to try something that is all but impossible. Thus, if someone overweight for hereditary reasons were trying to slim down by exercise and diet watching, someone aware of the hereditary situation could utter the "knife" proverb with the intention of saying, "Stop the charade, you're wasting your time." Similarly, it could be uttered with exhortative force in reference to someone trying to do self psychotherapy. This proverb can be used to exhort because ideals, prototypes, and norms generally are reference points for thinking and acting, and thus implicitly approve, sanction, or prescribe what is consistent with the reference point while disapproving, not sanctioning, or proscribing what is inconsistent with it (see Rosch, 1975, on reference-point reasoning). Indeed, it is hard to think of a proverb that could not, in some situation, be used to exhort.

In some cases, the voluntary control and cognitive ideals hypotheses converge, or nearly so. For example, Lakoff and Turner (1989) considered the example of *Charcoal writes everybody's name black*. Here charcoal is viewed as something with a fixed black property that will transfer to anything it touches. The word "black" is used metaphorically to mean "bad"; the word "name" is used metonymically to refer to reputation; and the word "writes" symbolizes communication in general. Thus, this proverb, after being processed on the great-chain-of-being, comes to mean that someone is slandering someone's reputation and that they really cannot help it. The proverb could be used to exhort someone not to slander, that is to act in a more reflective, voluntary way, rather than a fixed, indiscriminate way.

Analysis of the "charcoal" proverb via the cognitive ideals hypothesis would proceed as follows. The generic ideal is that physical objects have an intrinsic, constant physicochemical character. This ideal is instantiated to mean "physical objects that have characteristics that can be naturally and easily transferred to other objects" and is expressed as the particular proverb. The charcoal violates the integrity of other physical objects, however, which have their own intrinsic characteristics. It is, therefore, an ideal-disconfirming proverb, so it exhorts against the natural effect of charcoal.

These considerations apply before any application of the metaphoric, metonymic, or otherwise symbolic decoding that would be involved in constructing a particular figurative meaning, most especially one that involves human beings and how they behave or, in this case, misbehave. Thus, the proverb undoubtedly would be applied most often to humans, but it need not be because it has a fundamental meaning that supercedes and motivates its entrance into any kind of figurative meaning. For example, it could be applied in a chemistry setting in which some material has a charcoal-like property that befouls what would otherwise be a desired chemical product. Thus, it would be perfectly acceptable for the chemist to say about this material that *Charcoal writes everybody's name black*. The quest would thus be enjoined to mute or eliminate this particular material, an exhortation in other words. Despite this significant difference in treatment of exhortation, there are some important similarities in the way the two hypotheses operate.

In conclusion, the picture of proverbs painted by the ECBT is much more consistent with the current data. This is not to say that the concepts that the GCMT uses are irrelevant to proverb understanding. However, these concepts are by themselves inadequate, and different assumptions about the nature of the proverb, its levels of meaning, and its pragmatic effects seem to be called for.

In general, the ECBT would have the proverb listener and user draw on all of the faculties of the mind. Thus proverb comprehension requires a complete, whole mind. The lesson of chapter 3 was that a wide array of cognitive structures and processes are involved in proverb cognition. Enabling abilities, perceptual and memorial skills, and good working memory skills must be in place. A vast range and depth of knowledge must also be in place because proverbs are a form of creativity. People can make up and comprehend novel proverbs as well as understand their application in virtually an unlimited number of contexts. There must therefore be extensive knowledge about a large number of domains to undergird these abilities.

The issues that separate the ECBT and GCMT have been extensively debated by Gibbs, Colston, and Johnson (1996), who defend the GCMT, and by Honeck and Temple (1994, 1996), who challenge it. Despite the differences between the two theories, it is clear that the GCMT has already made a significant contribution to our thinking about proverb cognition, and the constructs and mechanisms it proposes cannot be ignored.

We now move on to a third theory, one that stems from the cognitive view of proverbs but uses a combination of neobehavioristic constructs and pragmatics theory. This theory has only recently appeared on the scene, so it is the least well- developed of the three.

The Dual Coding Theory

The DCT stems from a dissertation completed by Walsh (1988), which used Paivio's (1986) dual-coding approach to mental representation. This approach is a highly empiricistic one emphasizing that knowledge is based on perception, is modality specific, and is associationistic in nature. So-called concrete words such as "table" and "seabird" are coded in long-term memory in terms of *imagens*, whereas abstract words such as "promise" and "ineluctable" are coded in terms of *logogens,* which are the articulatory-phonetic representations of a word. Of course, concrete words are also coded in terms of logogens, which gives these words an advantage over abstract words. Concrete words have two codes, whereas abstract words have only one, unless the latter also get hooked up somehow with imagens. Associations between abstract words and imagens are generally weaker than those between concrete words and their more direct representation in imagens.

Thus, in the DCT meaning ultimately resides in the nonverbal system, a set of imagens, and to some extent in the associations between logogens. Even function words—prepositions, articles, and conjunctions—rely for their meaning on their relationship to other words, but also on images and concrete referential connections in general. Logogens get ordered in sequential ways in ordinary language use, whereas imagens contain visuospatial information that is presumably organized nonsequentially. Simply said, words come one after the other in discourse, but knowledge of concrete objects is all of one piece in memory. The two systems, verbal and nonverbal, are independent but have associative connections. Abstract words can have connections with imagens, but the connections are weaker than those for concrete words. As for any truly empiricistic theory, abstract interpretive processes are anathema. Meaning must be directly traceable to an original perception, to a learned perception (an imagen), or to associations among perceptions.

A number of findings have been interpreted as evidence for the dual-coding view (Paivio, 1986; Paivio & Walsh, 1993). For example, inputs that are concrete, including both pictorial and verbal inputs, tend to be recalled better than more abstract inputs, presumably because concrete stimuli arouse two codes, and for memory purposes, two codes are better than one. People who have good imagery abilities can decide more quickly than those with poorer imagery abilities which of two clock angles is larger (Paivio, 1978). For example, which angle is larger, 5:45 or 6:30? Verbal abilities do not seem to predict performance on this task. Concrete terms are learned faster than abstract words, by both children and adults, and more concrete concepts generally are easier to learn than less concrete concepts (Katz & Paivio, 1975). Concrete sentences, compared with abstract sentences, are remembered better, are evaluated more quickly for truth value, and generate imagery more quickly. Even the sometimes beneficial effects of mental practice, (e.g., mentally practicing a golf swing) have been interpreted as being consistent with the dual coding approach, and has the (oversimplified) fact that the left cerebral hemisphere is specialized for linguistic functions, whereas the right cerebral hemisphere is specialized for nonlinguistic functions. These various effects are complex, of course, and different experimental conditions may produce data that are differentially consistent with the dual coding idea (Paivio, personal communication, Oct 8, 1996). In general, however, proponents of the dual coding view claim that there is substantial evidence in favor of this view (Paivio, 1986).

What of proverbs and the DCT? We begin with the premise that proverbs differ. For practically any psycholinguistic dimension proverbs will vary. There are standard dimensions such as familiarity, comprehensibility, and concreteness. For example, *You can't tell a book by its cover* is stated in relatively concrete terms; it is familiar to most adult speakers of English; and it is highly comprehensible. *An ounce of prevention is worth a pound of cure* is also highly familiar and comprehensible but not as concrete as the book-cover proverb. Proverbs that are familiar but not comprehensible are hard to find, but there are highly concrete, unfamiliar proverbs that are hard to understand, such as *Even a hair casts its shadow on the ground.* These three dimensions do tend to be correlated, but only modestly so. Other dimensions on which proverbs vary include humorousness, truth value, paradoxicalness, metaphoricity, emotionality, grammaticality, and quaintness.

A particularly important dimension is the extent to which the proverb is used in different domains—its range of applicability. Proverbs that are applied to only one domain do not seem so proverbial. For example, *A penny saved is a penny earned* is used to comment on money matters and rarely, if ever, on other things. That does not mean that this proverb could not be applied to nonmoney matters. It just usually is not. Many abstractly stated proverbs, including some studied by Walsh (1988) seem to be similarly restricted, and furthermore, seem not to require a figurative interpretation. This would include proverbs such as *Haste makes waste*; *Practice makes perfect*; and *Money talks.* Indeed, many paremiologists do not consider such proverbs to be proverbs at all, precisely because they are applied to episodes that are literally connected to the concepts mentioned in the proverb. Their presumed proverbialness seems to derive from their pithy, poetic style plus the fact that they can apply to a large number of different episodes within their literal domain. Some, such as the author, would prefer to call these proverbs something else such as maxims, aphorisms, or apothegms. Concretely stated proverbs such as *While the cat's away the mice will play*; *All that glitters is not gold*; and *A soft tongue can strike hard* are twice removed from their domain of application, once by interpretive necessity, then once again because their concepts are applied to referents that are unconventional and unrelated to gold, soft tongues, and mice. Additionally, they seem capable of being applied to a more diverse set of domains than abstract proverbs are.

We are now in a better position to understand how the DCT applies to proverbs. To the author's knowledge the only study on proverbs within the dual coding framework is that by Walsh (1988). Using college students as participants, Walsh presented evidence indicating that, compared to concretely stated proverbs, abstract proverbs (a) tend to be judged as more literal (their intended and expressed meanings match up better); (b) contain a subject topic that is more likely to be used in an interpretation of the proverb; (c) produce more consistency in interpretations; and (d) yield a higher correlation between judged ease of interpretation and actual interpretive ease. In other words, Walsh's data confirm what many scholars have only conjectured: Many abstract proverbs do not seem to be very proverbial at all. Walsh concluded that a figurative interpretation requires a highly concrete, imagery-packed verbal input. Searle's (1969) speech act theory is appended to the basic dual coding idea to yield the DCT. That is, abstract proverbs have literal meanings that are closer to their intended meanings. In this sense, abstract proverbs are not proverbial because for something to have a figurative meaning, intended and literal meaning must diverge. Concrete proverbs are more likely to meet this criterion. Theoretically then, concrete proverbs arouse imagery that becomes the source of a figurative interpretation.

The real purpose of Walsh's dissertation, however, was to challenge a central tenet of the conceptual base theory, namely that figurative meaning is nonverbal and nonimagistic. Working within the framework of this theory, Riechmann and his associates found in several experiments that if you ask one group of people to form images for unfamiliar proverbs (without telling them they are proverbs) and another group to try to comprehend the proverbs, then later on in a memory test, the comprehension group does a much better job of distinguishing verbal interpretations of these proverbs from other proverb interpretations (for a review, see Riechmann & Coste, 1980). This result is inconsistent with the DCT because it downplays the role of imagery in getting a figurative meaning for a proverb. Moreover, Riechmann and Coste claimed that imagery may actually interfere with getting a figurative interpretation by leading to a "representational rivalry." They suggested that two codes may be better than one only if the two codes are consonant, and that when concrete proverbs arouse only literal information, this information clearly is not what a proverb means.

Walsh (1988) carried out a study that challenged this anti-DCT position. She presented both concrete and abstract proverbs to different groups, which were instructed either to image or try to comprehend the proverbs. Notice, however, that both groups were asked to interpret the proverbs. It was just that the imagery group had to use imagery in doing this. All subjects wrote an interpretation for each proverb, after which they got a questionnaire that probed for their use of imagery, then another questionnaire that assessed whatever general strategy they may have used. Then interpretations constructed by the experimenter were presented, which the groups used in trying to recall the original proverbs. Finally, the groups were given back their own interpretations to use in recalling the proverbs once again.

The results were unlike those reported by Riechmann and Coste (1980) in that the imagery group recalled the proverbs as well as the comprehension group. The interpretations of the particpants were more effective recall prompts than those of the experimenters, but only for abstract proverbs. Walsh concluded that, contrary to the conceptual base theory, imagery may be part of figurative meaning. A subsequent study used the same procedure except that instead of receiving an experimenter's interpretation as a recall prompt, the participants got another participant's interpretation before getting their own. Once again, the imagery and comprehension groups produced comparable recall, and self-generated interpretations produced better recall of abstract than concrete proverbs.

Note that these two studies of memory for proverbs were set up differently than the studies reported by Riechmann and Coste (1980) and by Honeck and Kibler (1984). In these latter studies, the task was designed to elicit imagery for proverbs, but without the goal of constructing a nonliteral meaning.

In Walsh's (1988) studies, the task intentionally provided multiple cues that a nonliteral interpretation was desired. The subjects were told that the sentences were proverbs; they were asked to write interpretations of their meanings; and they were pushed generally toward getting a nonliteral meaning. The issue here, though, is not whether imagery can be useful in getting figurative meanings, because that is obviously true. It is whether imagery is part of the figurative meaning, something the conceptual base theory denies.

Walsh's (1988) data do not appear to directly bear on this question, for two reasons. First, the memory studies are hard to interpret. Both groups got two questionnaires before they entered the recall phase. This procedure undoubtedly aroused some of the proverbs, and in conjunction with them, imagery and more general comprehension strategies, thereby obscuring the effect of the instructions. The instruction factor was the major manipulation in the study, of course. Another complicating factor is that the participants interpretations' contained content words, such as nouns and verbs, that overlapped with the proverbs. Such overlap provided easy memory access to the original proverbs. Indeed, Walsh found that 41% of the subjects' interpretations shared some wording with the concrete proverbs, whereas only 25% of the experimenter's interpretations showed such overlap. Arguably, even the 25% figure is too high. It should have been as close to 0% as possible because the experimenter is essentially asking whether someone can make a symbolic connection between an abstract interpretation and a to-be-recalled proverb, not whether they can use simple lexical overlap to recall the proverbs.

Second, the results are ambiguous because the imagery and comprehension groups did not differ in performance. This result is uninformative about the content of the meanings that participants formed while interpreting the proverbs. Indeed, if imagery is as powerful as the DCT makes it, then perhaps the imagery instruction group should have outperformed the comprehension group.

The Walsh study tells us that under the conditions in which they were studied, concrete proverbs act differently than abstract proverbs. The empirical confirmation of the difference is valuable. But the study sheds no light on the issue of the contentive status of figurative meaning.

It is not clear that any single empirical study can do this. Although imagery is indeed informationally rich, there is no good evidence that, in the absence of nonimagistic interpretive elements, it can be a figurative meaning. This was the lesson of the Riechmann and Coste (1980) and Honeck and Kibler (1984) studies. Participants in the latter study, replicated by Oliver (1991), were not misled as Walsh (1988) claimed, by virtue of developing images for proverbs (in ratings tasks or by means of direct instruction). They simply were not in the crucial figurative mind mode that would have yielded a figurative meaning. A possible counterargument is that if pictures can arouse figurative meanings, then why can we not attribute these meanings to images as well? (Paivio, personal communication, Oct. 8, 1996). One reply to this question is that pictures are not images and vice versa, and it is difficult to rule out the role of abstract, interpretive processes in picture processing.

Interpretations have to take place either when an image is first learned or when it is aroused and processed. Proverbs typically require us to compare and contrast elements (e.g., in *The sweeter the cherry the bigger the pit*). They also often call for desymbolizing operations that ask what significance the objects and events mentioned in the proverb have. We may get a rich image for the "cherry" proverb, but we understand that cherries are good and pits are not and compute the relative sizes of the cherry and pit. The imagery helps us to do this because we can hold the image before the mind's eye like a picture and mentally play with it. But the information about the relative goodness of cherries and pits and of the cherry and pit proportionality is not, strictly speaking, in the image. Of course, it is just this information that seems necessary to develop a plausible meaning for the proverb such as, "The goodness of things is often matched by some inherent badness." Moreover, this sort of interpretation invokes generalities, whereas the image is particular. The proverb also carries an implicit warning—"watch out, what looks to be good carries a hidden badness"—a warning that is arguably not contained in an uninterpreted image. From the standpoint of the ECBT-2, the "cherry" proverb seems to derive from the cognitive ideal that positive aspects of something tend to be correlated with other positive aspects of that thing, an ideal that underlies other, synonymous proverbs such as *No rose without a thorn,* and *Bees have honey in their mouths and stingers in their tails.*

Without an accompanying detailed theory of imagery itself, imagery hypotheses regarding mental representation can be seductive and almost impossible to disconfirm. This is particularly true when more concrete verbal materials are under consideration. If such materials could arouse imagery, then, the argument goes, it is likely that it is being aroused and playing a significant role in producing some effect. Incidentally, the debate between proponents of imagery hypotheses and more abstract interpretive processes has been going on since the classical Grecian era. Aristotle, the archetypal empiricist, believed that knowledge was primarily imagistic, whereas Plato, his teacher, believed that it was primarily nonimagistic. As a rationalist, Plato populated the soul with innately given "forms" (concepts), eternally existing, abstract, perfect, and true.

This controversy survives to the present day with some, mainly empiricists, holding fast to the fundamental role of imagery, and others, less enamored of bold empiricism, wanting to invoke abstract mental structures such as propositions, schemas, frames, idealized cognitive models, and the like. In the history of psychology the issue erupted in the late 19th and early 20th centuries in the form of the so-called imageless thought controversy. The results of experiments done by the University of Wurzburg psychologists suggested that people have knowledge that is nonsensorial (i.e., for which there was no palpable imagery). This conflicted with the views of Wilhelm Wundt, founder of experimental psychology and leader of the Content school of psychology, which was psychology's first. In his experimental work, Wundt took the position that, according to the current Zeitgeist on the matter, perceptual knowledge existed in an imagistic and associationist format. Thus, the claims of the Wurzburgers were at odds with Wundt's assumptions. A brief battle occurred and when the dust settled, no major victories were won. (Leahy 1987, discusses these matters.)

Presently, many experimentally inclined psychologists take the position that some knowledge takes an imagistic form and some does not. Moreover, the fact that people can imagine things by putting them into a working memory system is not automatically taken to mean that the imagery is actually what is stored in long-term memory. The imagery could well be constructed on the basis of nonimagistic knowledge. Unlike Plato, however, very few thinkers believe that the whole of, or even most, knowledge is inborn. Regarding our ability to distinguish imagery from nonimagery, the current attitude might be characterized as somewhat pessimistic. Fundamentally, the problem is that cognitive science has not been able to specify the properties of imagery or nonimagery well enough to allow a definitive experimental test of their distinction. Scholars therefore tend to pick one side or the other, using heavy theoretical arguments.

The position of the author is that the weight of the evidence, both theoretical and empirical, does not favor an imagistic position. Briefly, the story is as follows. People ordinarily get meanings before they get imagery (Pylyshyn, 1973). Therefore, imagery is derived. Images seem to be stored, in the first place, as interpreted descriptions (Reed, 1974) and thus are retrieved and used as interpreted pieces of knowledge. Images are particular rather than general, yet people are often required to deal in generalities, which includes proverbs. Proverbs that evoke quite different imagery can be synonymous on the figurative level, so how can figurative meaning be represented in particular images for particular proverbs? Images are too ephemeral and dependent on attentional-constructive processes to serve as the basis for the long-term memory basis of figurative meaning. For example, some proverbs (e.g., "An ounce...") are abstract yet have figurative meanings, and some proverbs are concrete but nearly incomprehensible (e.g., *Better the head of a dog than the tail of a lion*). Proverbs often contain negativity, yet images present only positive, palpable information to the mind's eye. Whether images can directly present information about negative states of affairs, however, is debatable.

Some of the empirical data that argues against the imagistic basis of figurative meaning has already been presented, but there is more. For the recall of a proverb, abstract interpretations are better cues than concretely stated verbal instances of the proverb's meaning (Dorfmueller & Honeck, 1980). If people are presented with a family of verbal materials, including a proverb, an interpretation, and some instances, and asked to select the item that best represents the meaning of the family, they overwhelmingly select the interpretation, which is stated in general, abstract terms (Dorfmueller & Honeck, 1980). Furthermore, exposure to a wide or diverse set of instances produces a more productive figurative meaning than does a narrow set of instances (Honeck & Firment, 1989). It is highly unlikely that a wide set would produce an encompassing, summary image.

Thus there is little empirical comfort for the notion that imagery is in or a part of figurative meaning. Proverbs often arouse imagery, which in conjunction with inferences of various kinds, may produce a figurative meaning, in which case *the imagery has now become figurative*. For this reason alone, imagery can be hard to separate from strictly abstract interpretive information.

Finally, Walsh (1988) made the claim that figurativeness requires an initially concrete proverb. This is an interesting claim, but it fails to address the role of context and pragmatic aspects of proverb use in general. Nothing is a proverb until it is used as proverbs are used. Walsh presented abstract proverbs in contextual isolation, a procedure that is likely to produce overly literal interpretations. For example, to use *In war, truth is the first casualty* in domains of domestic, political, or athletic disputes would surely be appropriate, but the isolated proverb is unlikely to arouse such applications. In contrast, concretely stated proverbs clearly are pragmatically deviant. Why would someone talk about real-world things when those things are not part of the discourse? Often enough they are so redundant, deviant, or simplistic that any would-be interpreter is likely to think that there is "something more here." What could anyone do with a statement such as *Policemen catch flies and let hornets go free* except to interpret it nonliterally because policemen do no such things. The statement is semantically and pragmatically weird.

The basic issue is how an utterance is thought about by the language user. Users are unlikely to apply so-called abstract proverbs in any domain other than that conventionally associated with the proverb. When this happens, the proverbs will not act like figurative statements. This does not mean that they do not have figurative potential, only that it may take prompting, illustration, and a special frame of mind to actualize their potential. Concrete statements can be put in contexts that obliterate their figurative potential, whereas abstract statements can be made to yield figurative meanings. It's just that, without relevant context, some concrete statements are more likely to trigger a nonliteral thought mode.

In conclusion, proverbs do not have to be concrete to have figurative potential, and abstractness does not necessarily rule out such potential. Again, that is because figurativeness is a matter of use and mode of thinking, not something that is ineluctably tied to a particular semantic dimension of the linguistic form. Therefore, proverbial or figurative potential cannot be made to depend exclusively on the concreteness of the proverb statement. Concreteness per se is neither necessary nor sufficient for figurative potential.

The DCT provides an interesting addition to the set of theories about proverbs. Proverb imagery is important, and the use of the intended meaning versus expressed meaning distinction adds to the theory. A recent statement about the theory by Paivio (personal communication, Oct. 8, 1996) would have verbal associative processes play a larger role in proverb processing than is evident in Walsh's (1988) study. Yet there are serious complications. The concept of an imagen is somewhat unclear, for example, and logogens are primarily phonetic, not semantic, entities. Perhaps the key issue is that the dual coding approach fails to restrain the functions of the imagery and verbal systems, there being little of which these systems, singly or in associated combination, are not considered to be capable. Language processing is much too complicated to be explicable by using only a few general concepts. Other theorists have been forced to make more fine-grained distinctions, and to include a broader range of concepts, as our discussion of the ECBT and GCMT indicates. Still, the DCT is young and relatively untested. Future elaborations of it will be well worth examining.

Conclusions About the Three Theories

The ECBT and DCT are psychological theories, whereas the GCMT is a linguistically oriented theory. All three theories, however, are designed to handle proverb comprehension. The ECBT and GCMT were extensively compared earlier, because they are the most detailed theories to date. The DCT is new and the least elaborated, so it is harder to compare it with the other two theories. For example, it is not clear how the proverb is defined in the DCT. A proverb cannot be just any concretely worded statement for which there is some potential for a difference between the expressed and intended meaning. The DCT would apparently have the statement be concrete, however. The DCT also makes no statement about the question of whether a proverb utterance initiates problem recognition, as described by the ECBT or proverb recognition, according to the GCMT. Because the DCT uses speech act theory, however, it seems to lean toward the former. The DCT is similar to the ECBT in other respects, although these, again, are inferences on the author's part and not explicit commitments that have come from adherents of the DCT. The ECBT emphasizes both automatic and nonautomatic processing, the use of general rather than specific cognitive mechanisms, the separation of figurative from literal meaning, and a general imprecision in getting figurative meanings and interpretations. The DCT is framed within the context of two general approaches, the dual coding idea and speech act theory, both of which would have it line up with the ECBT rather than the GCMT.

Together, the three theories have identified most of the phenomena and issues regarding proverb comprehension. Stated differently but less optimistically, the theories have provided names for the mental accomplishments of the proverb user. What is missing is a bona fide explanation of these accomplishments. In particular, the daunting problem is that of meaning or mentalese. For proverbs, and for language in general, crucial questions are how meaning is constituted and how it is used by linguistic structures. The content of meaning is not the same as the language in which it gets expressed. Scholars have analyzed meaning for over 2,000 years, and there has been no major breakthrough. We know much more about what it is not than what it is. Many concepts have been tendered for the crown, but there have been no victors. We know what some of the processes are—inference, comparison, and so forth—but we do not know how they do what they do. Furthermore, even if one grants that proverbs are set into correspondence with topics by an analogy or metaphoric mechanism, this does not explain how they work. Use of an analogy or metaphor is an accomplishment, not an explanation of the accomplishment. On a larger scale, a number of empirical pieces are missing from the puzzle (chapter 7 elaborates on this point). The lack of more adequate theories of proverb cognition is partly a reflection of this circumstance but also of the state of the art in cognitive science. The mind-brain has failed to yield its best kept secrets, and we are in the position of those unfortunates who palpate the elephant but collectively cannot get the big picture. Still, there has been significant theoretical advance regarding proverbs in the last decade, and a certain scholarly enthusiasm has come to the fore. There is good reason for optimism.

SUMMARY

Earlier theoretical approaches to proverbs largely stemmed from the cultural view and thus focused on the particular interpretations and social effects of familiar proverbs. These approaches did not address issues of microcognition such as the memory format of a proverb, how figurative meanings are constructed, the mental format for these meanings, and the mental processes behind their application.

Current theories, namely the ECBT, GCMT, and the DCT, have taken a more microcognitive perspective. The ECBT relies on an information processing standpoint that makes proverb comprehension a matter of both rapid, relatively automatic comprehension processes and more effortful solutions to a series of subproblems. Its newest version, ECBT-2, postulates that proverb creation, production, and comprehension rely on generic ideals that are part of a poorly organized but powerful intuitive system. The GCMT couples the cultural view with a particular cognitive linguistic outlook, making proverb comprehension a matter of accessing prestored proverb meanings and applying them by means of a metaphoric mechanism. The DCT is an empiricistic-associationistic position emphasizing that proverbs must be relatively concrete to function as statements whose intended meanings can be different from their literal meanings. Presently, only the ECBT has been used to successfully direct and integrate a large number of empirical findings, and its range has been expanded in the ECBT-2.

Even though all three theories have provided some insights into proverb cognition, they have largely failed to provide detailed accounts of the mental mechanisms used and the mental products generated during the comprehension and use of proverbs. Explication of these matters remains as a task for the future.

5

Under, Inside, and Outside the Proverb

A proverb "knows" that *Variety is the spice of life*. During its lifetime a proverb takes on many identities. It begins as a nascent thought, masquerades as a linguistic form, and then joins a family of related events, real and potential. This chapter traces this evolution in terms of the conceptual forces that motivate proverbs, their internal dynamics, and how they become manifest in illustrations of various kinds. In spatial metaphoric terms we travel under, inside, and outside the proverb. There are important theoretical issues in this topological travel, although they are not as empirically grounded as they might be.

UNDER THE PROVERB

Marking

Occasionally, someone may want to mark the significance of an episode. Societies and individuals have a large array of methods for doing so. Personal methods include remembering, writing, using keepsakes, and telling other people about the episode. Societally, marking includes anniversaries, ceremony, ritual, scripting, monuments, and visual and verbal records of all kinds.

Individuals and societies also may mark something by means of a proverb. A premise that arises from the cognitive ideals hypothesis is that proverbs mark ideals. This suggests, in turn, that the real action for proverbs lurks beneath the surface in the form of these ideals. This being the case, it becomes possible to elucidate in a systematic way how proverbs get created and why they are used on any given occasion.

Proverb Creation

What is happening in the mind of someone who creates a new proverb? The cognitive ideals hypothesis provides the beginnings of an answer. To reiterate, the hypothesis stipulates that an ideal is expressed by means of a particular instantiation, which, in turn, is reflected in the immediate literal schematic logic of the proverb. This logic is the crucial part of the proverb's specific ideal.

To try out this notion the author analyzed most of the proverbs on the list of 160 proverbs described in chapter 4. This analysis amounted to a three-step process: identify the generic source of the proverb; specify how the source is instantiated; and describe the general form of the literal logic of the proverb. These steps are illustrated below for 10 proverbs.

You can't sell the cow and drink the milk.
   Physical principles constrain events.
   Physical containment proscribes separation of thing contained from its container.
   If A produces B, eliminating A precludes retaining B.

A rolling stone gathers no moss.
   Physical principles constrain events.
   Physical movement proscribes substance attachment.
   If A moves it does not accumulate B.

The sweeter the cherry the bigger the pit.
   Parts of the same structure have correlated structures.
   Biological structures are correlated in various ways.
   As A becomes more positive, part B of A becomes more negative.

Crows mourn the dead sheep and then eat them.
   Behavior should be consistent with circumstances.
   Behavior should be ethically consistent.
   A acts positively with respect to B but A also acts negatively with respect to B.

Spilling wine is worse than spilling water.
   Conserve value.
   Some personal possessions are more valuable than others.
   Losing a valuable fluid is worse than losing a less valuable fluid.

He is not a good soldier who fights with his tongue.
   Behavior should be consistent with circumstances.
   People who have prescribed social roles should perform in a way
   that is consistent with those roles.
   If person A is supposed to do B but does C, then A is not a good
   B.

Better be the head of a dog than the tail of a lion.
   Conserve value.
   Higher level biological functions are more valuable than lower
   level biological functions.
   A higher level part of a low-status animal is better than a lower
   level part of a higher status animal.

*If you are going to jump out of a moving car, do it before it is going too
fast.*
   Preserve the self.
   Minimize the exposure of the bodily self to potentially injurious
   physical forces.
   If person A is in B and wants exit from B, which is moving, A
   must exit B before it moves faster.

A knife can't whittle its own handle.
   Physical principles constrain events.
   Inflexible physical objects with function A cannot perform A on
   themselves.
   A does B but it cannot do B to A.

Great weights hang on small wires.
   Physical principles constrain events.
   Heavy objects require correspondingly strong objects to support
   them.
   Heavy A hangs on thin B.

There are some uncertainties in this analysis. First, there are
no algorithms for specifying generic ideals, what their various

instantiations might be, how abstractly these notions should be cast, or how they should be described verbally. The same applies to extricating the logic of the specific ideal. Second, the transformation from generic source to generic instantiation to specific ideal is problematic, even assuming that a proper source has been identified. Surely, generic sources do not have a well-structured logic that is isomorphically mapped into the logic of one of its instantiations. (The construction and verbal description of them here should not obfuscate their probable imprecise and nonverbal character.) Rather, the source ideal acts as an overall framework that guides the creation of an instantiation. The instantiation acts to constrain the specific ideal in more immediate ways, however. There are only so many ways that, for example that the statement, "Some personal possessions are more valuable than others," could be expressed in a specific ideal and still retain the meaning of this generic instantiation. However, the ultimate selection of the surface form of a proverb is due to a variety of factors, including what concepts are salient for a culture or individual.

In conclusion, the process by which proverbs are created involves a number of steps. There is an initial inductive phase during which various experiences are interpreted to have a common meaning. This meaning is judged worthy of preservation because it reflects a generic ideal, so it is marked. This meaning is then translated into a particular verbal statement. To do this, the generic ideal and an instantiation are accessed, and they are verbally expressed in the literal proverb. This process, however, is not well understood. Furthermore, it is possible that some proverbs emerge by a different route, beginning as literal statements that later get used in figurative ways (see chapter 7).

Proverb Production

Hypothetically, the motivation for using proverbs should parallel that for creating them. The speaker's P-task is to interpret a topic so that it is consistent with a generic ideal, to match the ideal to a proverb, and, given a set of felicity conditions, to utter the proverb. By the cognitive ideals hypothesis, therefore, people are greatly concerned with ideals, especially with deviations from them, and wish to set things right by virtue of uttering a proverb. This approach to production is a statement about what people are trying to do in using a proverb, not about the conditions for or manner of their use. The same proverb could be used under different circumstances and in different ways to reach different goals. What remains constant is the betokened ideal.

INSIDE THE PROVERB

Once the proverb has been created and made public we can look inside at its internal dynamics. An a priori question is why proverbs take on the particular form—words and syntax—they do. Another consideration, and part of the mystery and aesthetic of proverbs, comes from the recursive internal mechanism by which they operate. Proverbs feed on themselves, and with some creativeness they also can be transformed to produce new, strange, and sometimes humorous proverbs.

Literal Proverb Content

If proverbs are based on the perfectionism of ideals, how is the goal attained? Why, in other words, do proverbs take the particular lexical and overall sentential form that they do? Practically every factual or fact-like statement could become a proverb. Of this large set, however, only a tiny fraction become proverbs. What distinguishes this fraction from the remainder? Why is it, for example, that the injunction against desiring something other than what we have is expressed as *The grass is always greener on the other side of the fence*, rather than, say, *The next boat always catches more fish*, or as a large number of comparable assertions? Any of these assertions would preserve the basic logic and the pragmatic thrust of "The grass...."

There are several factors that operate to constrain the literal content of a proverb. First, the number of proverbs that are needed is limited. As regards marking, only certain kinds of events will be considered the right kind to mark for proverbial encryption, those that are deemed important, likely to recur, and derivative of a norm, ideal, or standard. Most of the information in semantic memory likely does not meet these requirements and, in addition, is not abstract enough. Furthermore, of the potential set of proverbs, almost all have already been pressed into service in other domains, and to have a statement do double duty would only confuse matters. Why, for example, should the assertion, "Tuesday comes before Wednesday," be used proverbially?

Other selection processes operate to reduce the number. There is a limit to the ways in which a generic ideal can be expressed adequately. Concepts are more transparently expressed in some ways, using certain mechanisms, than others. Proverbs often use familiar poetic devices, for example.

Along these lines, there may be a reason why proverbs are generally stated in concrete terms. Concrete statements are not only a rich source of information, but the real world that they refer to has a more transparent and specifiable logic than abstractly stated words and ideas. That is, the physical constraints inherent in the environment yield a more lucid and compelling intrinsic logic. If the perceptible world were less stable, more chancy and unpredictable, then people would be less willing to use it as a means of grounding their thoughts. Proverbs are typically put in more concrete terms, therefore, because these terms efficiently arouse a transparent schema-based logic. If this line of reasoning is sensible, then what people do by marking with proverbs is to translate the ideal as a mental hypothetical into an analogous concrete reality. In this way, the ideal becomes real. Call this the *grounding hypothesis*.

None of this explains why a proverb uses a particular verbiage, of course. For cultural proverbs there is undoubtedly great pressure to select widely familiar schemas, those that appeal to the most inclusive audience. After all, these proverbs are created to tell the world about their creator's invention. Success in doing so requires common ground. Particular words and domains are therefore more likely to be pressed into service to convey it.

Strange Loops

Proverbs have a strange loop quality. The "strange loop" phrase comes from Hofstadter's (1980) Pulitzer Prize-winning book, *Gödel, Escher, Bach: An Eternal Golden Braid*. The braid in this case involves recursion or self-reference, which can be found in nearly every facet of existence. We laugh when we see a dog chasing its tail. Why? Put your hands up in front of yourself, and rotate them so that the fingers point toward one another. This is a kind of recursion—a hand pointing at a hand. Then there is the time-honored Russian gift of a doll that contains a doll that contains a doll and so on. In language there is self-embedding in which one linguistic construction is placed within another. A simple example is the subordinate clause that most of us learned to recognize in grade school. Take the sentence: The woman who liked to play tennis was a fine mathematician. Here one (deep structure) sentence, "the woman liked to play tennis," is embedded in the larger sentence. This can be done ad infinitum, and it is the main reason why there is no longest sentence in a language. From the language realm we can also cull the classic Epimenides Paradox, also called the Liar's Paradox: "All Cretans are liars," or more simply, "This statement is false."

Hofstadter (1980) delved into the more complicated cases of Gödel, Escher and Bach. Gödel, a mathematician, demonstrated that any mathematical system cannot be both logically consistent and complete. It is either one or the other, but not both. Gödel proved it but had to use self-referential statements to do so. In one of Escher's lithographs, *Hand with Reflecting Globe*, one sees the artist, his hand extended to grasp a globe that is held by the mirror image hand of the artist, who is presumably drawing a picture of himself as reflected by the globe. Similarly, Bach's music contains themes that are repeated, though perhaps in different keys, at different times, in different tempos, by counterpoint, and the like. Quite unusual orders of complexity can be attained in the process. The key idea in all of these examples is quite as Hofstadter put it: A system starts out, moves away, and then comes back to the starting point, but in a strange way.

This is exactly what happens with proverbs. The original literal meaning model is used to help build a figurative meaning model that acts, in turn, to instantiate the literal model. The fact that the two models are so different yet related is part of the proverb aesthetic. The fact that children are unable to appreciate the loopiness of proverbs may be at the heart of their difficulty in understanding them. It is only when an outside agent steps in or additional information is provided that the child can make the connection.

Then there are proverbs about proverbs such as *Wise men make proverbs and fools repeat them*. The very act of saying the proverb puts one in the fool category, if only momentarily. This recursion game is endless because we can now make up proverbs such as *Do not repeat proverbs that would make one a fool*; *Anyone who repeats proverbs that warn against repetition of proverbs is a fool*; and *Refrain from using proverbs that request that proverbs not be repeated*. It is also possible to construct complex proverbs that recursively combine two or more proverbs (e.g., *A stitch in time saves nine but not all stitches are worth a pound of cure*).

In Hofstadter's (1980) treatment of strange loops there is always an "inviolate level," a level that is responsible for the tangled loop level but outside of it. For proverbs, the literal meaning and figurative meaning form a strange loop, or "tangled hierarchy," to use another of Hofstadter's terms. Theoretically, the inviolate level is the set of interpretive processes that move literal and contextual meanings into a figurative meaning. People's accomplishments vis-à-vis proverbs warrant the need to postulate such tacit and powerful mental activities. Much of cognitive science and the cognitive view about proverbs is based on just this premise. Mindwork is carried out quickly, efficiently, and some would claim, hardly ever with conscious access. Thus, we are conscious of the tangled loop of literal and figurative meanings but not of how the mind connects them.

Perverted Proverbs

The human mind seems naturally inclined to seek change. *Old ways are best* but *variety is the spice of life*. Visual art seems to move in cycles from representational to less representational forms and then back again. Proverbs are like art. One can play with them. Doing so inevitably leads to new forms, wacky ones in some cases. While inside the proverb, in other words, we can transform it into new varieties.

Transformations on proverbs vary from very simple linguistic changes to more complex changes that retain the logical scheme of the proverb but insert something new.

Here are some simple linguistic transformations of familiar proverbs:

A stitch in time saves nine?

The grease is got by the squeaky wheel.

A bird in the hand isn't worth two in the bush?

On the other side of the fence the grass is always greener.

There is a silver lining in every cloud.

All of the above transformations have probably been uttered. It is easy to imagine some circumstances in which this would happen. As proverbs that stand on their own, however, these transformations do not quite make it. It is not just that they are distortions of the familiar, but that the emphasis is misplaced.

Here are some more complicated transformations of proverbs:

Different Volks for different folks. (*Different strokes for different folks.*)

One man's sushi is another man's steak. (*One man's meat is another man's poison.*)

Good things still come in small packages. (*Big things come in small packages.*)

Chaste makes waste. (*Haste makes waste.*)

Where there's a will there's a relative. (*Where there's a will there's a way.*)

These transformations change one or two words in the original, still recognizable proverb. Indeed, recognizability is necessary for the proverb to have the intended effect. The first three were invented by advertisers (Mieder & Mieder, 1977). The last two change one word for humorous effect.

Parenthetically, there are wacky paraphrases of proverbs, some of which have been in the public domain for years:

Surveillance should precede saltation. (*Look before you leap.*)

It is fruitless to become lachrymose over precipitately departed lacteal fluid. (*Don't cry over spilt milk.*)

A revolving lithic conglomerate accumulates no congeries of small, green bryophitic plants. (*A rolling stone gathers no moss.*)

These examples reinforce the claim that proverbs are forged by a different set of economic forces than their paraphrases. They are, in addition, grist for a bit of humor.

Even more complicated transformations are possible, however:

Void will be void. (*Boys will be boys.*)

Spare the rod and spoil the drag race. (*Spare the rod and spoil the child.*)

A niche in time is thine. (*A stitch in time saves nine.*)

Time wounds all heels. (*Time heals all wounds.*)

The early nerd gets the curd. (*The early bird gets the worm.*)

Here, the "perverb" maker (from Nierenberg, 1983, for the first three examples; the author for the last two) has used the form and underlying logic of a familiar proverb to create an arguably sensible, new meaning in a new conceptual domain. All of them are plays on words. But they are not especially wacky or pernicious.

Here are some wacky ones:

A watched proverb butters no parsnips. (*A watched pot never boils.*)

A buttered parsnip watches no proverbs either. (A watched proverb butters no parsnips.)

Opporknockety only tunes once. (*Opportunity only knocks once.*)

Ghouls rush in where dead men once were live. (*Fools rush in where wise men fear to tread.*)

People who live in glass houses should not grow Koans. (*People who live in glass houses should not throw stones.*)

These perverbs can be made sensible with some imagination. They are the product of either the professional paremiologist, and so a mere amusement, or, as in the first three cases, the creation of a graffiti aficionado (Nierenberg, 1983). No matter, they are interesting.

Proverb Combinations

All of the previous perverbs tread on a single proverb. It is possible to create perverbs by other means, such as by combining proverbs in various ways. Whole proverbs can be combined, or proverb parts and the rules of grammar can be used to pull off the trick as follows:

A stitch in time is worth a pound of cure. (From *A stitch in time saves nine* and *An ounce of prevention is worth a pound of cure.*)

Look before you cast pearls. (From *Look before you leap* and *Casting pearls before the swine.*)

Haste makes the pot boil. (From *Haste makes waste* and *A watched pot never boils.*)

Once bitten, makes the heart grow fonder. (From *Once bitten, twice shy* and *Absence makes the heart grow fonder.*)

He who hesitates and watches the grass grow greener is lost. (From *He who hesitates is lost* and *The grass is always greener on the other side of the fence.*)

The foregoing are variously sensible. They can be made sensible by ignoring their parent proverbs, but keeping the meaning of these proverbs in mind while trying to get a meaning for the perverb can produce a meaning just as sensible if more complicated. In this case, the author combined proverbs without really thinking about what they might mean. One proverb was just chopped off at a convenient linguistic stopping place and spliced onto a second whose parts would fit in. The fact that we can get meaning from these perverbs is a tribute to the human ability to make sense out of nearly anything, or at least to believe that we have made sense out of it.

Theoretically, there are more principled ways for combining proverbs so that more predictable meanings could occur. For example, the same generic ideals or domains can be sampled. Perhaps the first example, "A stitch...," illustrates this possibility. The two parent proverbs have similar meanings, and these meanings occur in the same order, first an urging to do something now rather than later, and then the value in doing it. Thus, the new perverb is almost as good as its parents. One could also put contradictory proverbs together in the same sentence—*Look before you leap, but he who hesitates is lost*—just to emphasize the inherent tensions in some situation. It would probably be bad counseling, a double bind par excellence, but realistic nevertheless.

This exercise on perverbs merely demonstrates that if one has enough time, it is possible to create a set of totally worthless new proverbs. (Mieder, 1989, provides a larger discussion of proverb parodies, poems, and illustrations of the proverb.) They are nearly worthless as a cultural species, but not as a cognitive species. It would be difficult to use them anew in some social situation with any sort of effect other than amusement. However, overfocusing on the cultural level blinds us to some important information. These perverbs are consistent with the cognitive view's emphasis on the theoretical import of idiosyncratic proverbs. When a perverb is used in public, and some are, the theoretical issues raised are as pressing as they are for any production P-task.

Staying Inside Is Hard

Proverbs are not designed as ends in themselves, with merely internal processes taking place. Internal loops are interesting, but recursion is not the point of proverbs, nor is their transformation into other proverbs. Language has an aboutness to it: We want to use it to talk about things that are outside the language system. Even the strange loop in proverbs has an aboutness because the proverb, as a figurative meaning, is about itself as a literal meaning. Language is not primarily designed to comment on its own occurrence because, if it were, language could never move forward to new topics. Even the repetition of prayers and mantras has a goal beyond mere repetition. So it is with proverbs. We have to move outside their literal membrane to appreciate their vitality. Furthermore, essentially any mental operation that can be performed on a proverb moves the mind away from it to new kinds and layers of information.

OUTSIDE THE PROVERB

Although the things that are or can be made internal to the proverb are enlightening, the external life of the proverb is what makes it famous. Proverbs are part of the public scene because they have idealized meanings that have important social consequences. Meanings are hardly ever created for no reason. People want to do things with meaning. In this section, therefore, we look outside the proverb to all the different ways in which proverbs can make connections to other proverbs and nonproverbs alike. The basic theme is that proverbs extend into a wide conceptual network of meanings, perceptual modalities, and formats. First, we look at the proverb-to-proverb relationship and then at the more important question of how the proverb can be illustrated by interpretations and examples.

Proverb to Proverb

The set of possible relationships among proverbs is of some interest. All sorts of schemes for relating them can be imagined. Some schemes stem from traditional topics such as synonymy and antonymy, but other relationships are possible as well, such as taxonomic, linear, and more complicated categorical links. We can even ask whether there are Adam and Eve proverbs, proverbs that seem to give rise to other proverbs. For example, if the cognitive ideals hypothesis has any validity, then perhaps proverbs that express abstract notions about perfection constitute superordinate proverbs. We here examine the more prosaic of proverb relationships first.

Synonymy.   It has long been noted that many proverbs express similar meanings or synonymy. If there are no meaning mates for a proverb, then some can be made up. Thus, there are proverb duos such as the following:

An ounce of prevention is worth a pound of cure.
A stitch in times saves nine.

The grass is always greener on the other side of the fence.
The loaf in another person's hand is always bigger.

Not every oyster contains a pearl.
Treasure won't be found in every shipwreck.

The squeaky wheel gets the grease.
The loudest baby is fed first.

There is no corn without weeds.
No rose without the thorn. (from Case, 1991)

Triples are also possible, as in these proverbs:

A stitch in time saves nine.
A patch on the tire saves a trip to the garage.
One shingle today saves a roof tomorrow.

Too many cooks spoil the broth.
With seven nurses the child loses an eye.
Two pilots in the boat and it will sink.

A man's tie does not match all his suits.
An actor fills some roles better than others.
In the wrong chord a note may fail. (from Case, 1991)

It is possible, of course, to create long sets of synonymous proverbs, but for what purpose? The author sees two.

First, it could be argued that to the extent that a culture has two or more synonymous proverbs, then according to the cognitive idealshypothesis, the ideal, norm, or standard behind those proverbs may be important in that culture. Numerous scholars have made something like this claim when many different proverbs are found that comment on the same realm of life in a culture, or that characterize something significant about that culture (Obelkevich, 1987) or its people's character (Parades, 1970). The hypothesis that cases of synonymy betoken cultural importance seems no less a shaky one, although the author knows of no data that bears on it. Of course, contradictory proverbs may point toward more salient cultural issues than synonymous ones.

Second, and more theoretically, cases of proverb synonymy cannot be explained by any current theories of meaning. It is easy to handle the syntax of synonymous sentences such as *The squeaky wheel gets the grease* and *The grease is got by the squeaky wheel*. The major vocabulary is retained in both, and the second can be produced by certain so-called linguistic transformations from the first. As shown by the standard example of "The boy hit the ball" and "The ball was hit by the boy." The topic, and therefore the emphasis, is different in these kinds of transformationally related sentences, however. The key problem is that linguistic transformational theory tells us nothing about why the two transformationally related sentences are synonymous, because synonymy is a matter of semantics. Indeed, in older transformational approaches, preservation of meaning was a precondition for the application of a transformational rule.

One can move up a step to more complicated cases of synonymy, such as the converses, "Eve bought the car from George" and "George sold the car to Eve." To account for the synonymy here, one needs to stipulate co-reference, namely that Eve, George, and the car are the same things in the two sentences, but also that buying and selling are related in a higher order schema involving a seller, a thing sold, and a buyer of the thing.

For the synonymous proverb sets given earlier, however, we encounter a serious theoretical challenge. The proverbs in each set are not related by virtue of syntactic or semantic rules. Their synonymy arises from deeper, more substantial conceptual happenings about which very little is understood. Part of the answer may be that the synonymous sentences derive from a common generic ideal. In this sense, synonymous proverbs would arise from a common origin in ways analogous to surface metaphoric expressions arising from Lakoffian conceptual metaphors.

As a personal aside, it was just this kind of consideration that piqued the author's interest in proverbs in the early 1970s. At that time Chomsky's linguistic theory was still on the psychological scene, its heydey having been about 1962 to 1970. It was clear by the late 1960s, however, that this theory could not account for more complex cases of synonymy. That the meaning of proverbs was not somehow a Chomskyan deep structure—something like a basic literal meaning—was also clear. Thus the theoretical problems presented by proverb synonymy, or in general by the kind of conceptual similarity seen in any two or more sentences, simply outstripped the machinery of transformational linguistic theory. In this sense, proverbs present an acid test for any theory of language comprehension.

Antonymy. The other side of the coin is *antonymy*, or more precisely, contradiction. Proverb meanings can be contradictory, something that paremiologists have noted over the centuries. This seems surprising to some people once they come to appreciate the fact. It is a crossing of the personal with the cultural views of proverbs that yields the surprise, however. People apparently believe that proverbs have a particular shared meaning in a culture and that this meaning has a kind of all-purpose truth value. It therefore comes as something as a shock when people discover that there is a proverb, one that may even exist in their own proverb repertoire, that contradicts another proverb. Before proceeding, we examine some contradictory proverbs:

Absence makes the heart grow fonder.
Out of sight, out of mind.

Birds of a feather flock together.
Opposites attract.

Too many cooks spoil the broth.
Many hands make light work.

Look before you leap.
He who hesitates is lost.

Don't count your chickens before they're hatched.
Get the kitty litter before the kittens arrive.

Silence is golden.
The squeaky wheel gets the grease.

Don't beat a dead horse.
Keep your nose to the grindstone.

If you lie down with dogs, you'll get up with them.
If you can't beat 'em, join 'em.

Variety is the spice of life.
Don't change horses in midstream.

A spoonful of tar spoils a barrel of honey.
Roll an apple pie in the dirt and it is still an apple pie.

(These examples were taken from Evans & Berent, 1993; Tiegen, 1986; Yankah, 1984; and the author made some up.)

These pairs vary in contradictoriness. *He who hesitates is lost* and *Look before you leap* are prototypical opposites, with exhortations to "Go!" and to "Wait!" at clear odds. Of course, these are not antonyms in the sense that "open" and "closed" are in stipulating mutually exclusive situations. A window is either open or it is closed, or nearly so. Then there is context, which makes one proverb appropriate and another, potentially inconsistent proverb inappropriate.

Empirical studies suggest that each in a pair of contradictory proverbs can be judged as truthful, even when the original authentic proverb is changed by introducing a "not." For example, *Truth needs no colors* and *Truth needs colors* are clear opposites. (See Furnham, 1987, and Tiegen, 1986, for studies on contradictoriness, and Yankah, 1984, for a discussion of the proverb as a cultural truism and as a contextually sensitive form.)

The key insight here is that, according to the discussion in chapter 1, proverbs are not taken to be synthetic statements whose truth value is to be judged by an empirical test. Proverbs are not statements of the "All TVs have screens" variety, although precisely this kind of statement can be taken as figuratively true in some situations. Neither are they analytic statements or necessarily true on some a priori basis. But they seem like analytic statements and that is part of their attraction. In the words of Cram (1994), "In the case of the proverb...we start out from the assumption that it offers a valid explanatory formula and then seek out appropriate contexts in which to apply it" (p. 90).

We do not seek to falsify proverbs nor, for that matter, do we seek to confirm them. Rather, we are presented with topics that evoke ideas that we attempt to analogize and comment on by means of a proverb. There is a built-in confirmation bias in the use of proverbs and when another proverb is applied to the same topic, it is done to emphasize a different aspect of the topic. One and the same proverb can have a negotiable meaning with respect to the same topic because variable aspects of proverb meaning can hookup in different ways with variable aspects of a topic's meaning. In any event, the figurativeness of proverbs and the fact that they are, as Cram (1994) says, invoked as remnants of the past, protects them from being disconfirmed. Like many folklore genres, they are a privileged form of communication. That people rarely become conscious of the contradictoriness of proverbs and are surprised when this property is pointed out is consistent with this treatment of the proverb.

The existence of contradictory proverbs is also consistent with the cognitive ideals hypothesis. If a proverb is created to express a particular meaning, then it is predictable that its complement either exists in the repertoire of the person who knows it or it has a strong potential to become manifest. This is somewhat like the case of the physicist who claims that particle X exists and therefore, for theoretical reasons, particle anti-X also exists. The author knows of no serious inquiry into the question of whether every familiar cultural level proverb has a contradictory pair in that or another culture, but this would make for an interesting study. Proverbs that went uncontradicted might be considered cultural common denominators.

Symmetry. Because proverbs can be synonymous on the figurative level, *symmetry* is another interesting property that can emerge. Here is the recipe for symmetry: Get two proverbs that are synonymous. Then construct a sentence that is a literally proper instance of one of the proverbs. Do the same for the second, and Presto! The two literally related sentences now become figuratively related to the other proverb. What was literal becomes figurative as seen in this example:

> A *stitch in time saves nine*.
> Karen noticed a small hole in her overcoat, but she didn't stitch it and it got bigger.

> A *patch on the tire saves a trip to the garage*.
> George forgot about putting a patch on the suspicious hole in his tire and wound up with a flat.

The same recipe can be used with contradictory proverbs, as follows:

> *Look before you leap*.
> Pete went to the nearby department store and bought the first computer he looked at and then regretted it.

> *He who hesitates is lost*.
> Mary was very choosy about taking a job and ended up unemployed.

The first instance is consistent with the "be cautious" exhortation of *Look before you leap*, but it is strangely inconsistent with the "go for it" urging behind getting lost through hesitation. The same applies for Mary. The strange part is that the characters in the two instances engage in activities that are consistent with the pragmatic force of the proverb, but the end result of their activities is inconsistent with it. Both instances in this example are figuratively related to both proverbs but in symmetrical ways. The example also demonstrates how proverbs can be shown to be contradictory, but that showing it requires the immediate juxtaposition of the proverbs with specially prepared topics.

Symmetry is not an idle curiosity. For experimentalists, this property can be very handy. For example, one issue in research on figurative language is whether it can be understood only by first understanding it literally. Does some kind of literal meaning have to be constructed before a figurative meaning can occur, or can figurative meaning be obtained in a more direct fashion? This is sometimes called the *stages issue*.

To answer this question, experimenters have to set up conditions so that the material (metaphor, proverb, etc.) in question is likely to be processed in either a literal or nonliteral way. This can be done by using one set of materials and having all of them processed literally, then having a different set processed nonliterally. In some respects this procedure is acceptable, but it has at least one serious potential flaw: The materials are confounded with the experimental condition. That is, set A gets processed literally, whereas set B gets processed nonliterally. If there is a difference in performance between the two conditions, or even if there is no difference, the result could be due to the fact that the experimental condition and the material set are perfectly correlated (confounded). Thus it would be entirely appropriate to ask whether the results were due to the experimental manipulation, the materials, or both.

Symmetry allows the experimenter to unconfound the two factors. The reason is that one and the same input can be made to be processed in two different ways, either literally or figuratively. Because experiments on the stages issue are complex, partly because the materials are complex, perhaps symmetry should be taken very seriously.

Experimental-theoretical questions aside, symmetry is a challenge. It is a linguistic analogue to visual double entendre. One and the same instance is interpreted differently, in this case because it is put in different settings.

Hierarchies and Superproverbs. Proverb to proverb relationships have been discussed in terms of synonymy and antonymy. Other relationships are possible. For example, many kinds of concepts are arranged in hierarchical ways, such as taxonomies. Human beings are mammals that are animals that are living things that are physical things. There are *partonomies* such as eyes, nose, and mouth as parts of the human face. Also, for many categories there are *prototypes*, which are the best examples of the category in the sense that the prototype shares more features with other category members than any other member, and the fewest features with other categories (Rosch, 1978). Other kinds of category relationships are also possible.

Various categorization schemes have been tried with proverbs, as discussed in chapter 1, and the author has proposed a new one. Lamentably, there is a potentially infinite set of ways in which to categorize proverbs. As any expert on the issue of similarity would tell us, it is possible to find a resemblance between any two things in the universe. Of course, some resemblances are more theoretically intriguing than others. For a cognitive scientist the question is whether a categorization scheme provides important information about the mental processes and structures that emerge during proverb comprehension and use. If not, the scheme may yet be important for folklorists, ethnographers, and others whose interests lie outside the realm of immediate mental processing. To the author's knowledge, no proverb classification schemes have emerged with clear implications for proverb microcognition, although schemes based on contrasts and opposition are highly suggestive. To be sure, certain variables are important, such as proverb familiarity, imagery-evoking power, syntactic complexity, and the like, but these are metavariables that apply to all proverbs.

Seemingly, only one empirical study on proverb classification exists. White (1987) asked 17 native speakers of English to write an interpretation for each of 11 common proverbs, to sort them according to their similarity of meaning, and then to rationalize their sorts. A statistical analysis of the sorting indicated that the proverbs fell largely into two groups: those that urged some kind of action to achieve a goal and those that urged a person's acceptance of their situation. "Action" proverbs included *The squeaky wheel gets the grease, Necessity is the mother of invention*; and *Where there's a will there's a way*, whereas the "acceptance" category included *Don't cry over spilt milk*; *You can't have your cake and eat it too*; and *Time heals all wounds*. One proverb, *Rome wasn't built in a day*, did not seem to fit comfortably in either category. The significant finding here is that the more general sorting dimension concerned the basic pragmatics of the proverbs, that is, whether to do something or not. More particular groupings made by the participants depended on the inferences they made about human characters in the proverbs. In general, the results of this study seem to be consistent with the cognitive ideals hypothesis, and especially with the typology of ideal-confirming versus ideal-disconfirming proverbs.

This typology raises the interesting question of whether there could be "super proverbs," proverbs that would capture the essence either of proverbs in general, or at least of the category they might represent. One approach to this question is empirical. We could present people a long list of proverbs that were, for example, ideal-confirming proverbs and have them rank-order the proverbs for this property, and employ a similar procedure for ideal-disconfirming proverbs.

Using this method, a superproverb would be defined as the prototype for its class. We might expect, for example, that *A stitch in time saves nine* would rank very high, not merely because it is familiar, but because it is clear in telling us what to do to save some effort, an important human ideal. This raises interesting corollary questions about why some proverbs do become familiar whereas others become less so or drop out of sight altogether. Does transparency of ideal and of specific logic play a role or are purely cultural factors at work? Could both be involved?

One implication of the cognitive ideals hypothesis is that a proverb would become familiar if it drew on an important common human ideal but also rang true with respect to its more culturally determined specific ideal and logic. Using this approach, we could build our own superproverbs. Hypothetically, these novel proverbs would do well in the ranking procedure just described, a result that would lend some legitimacy to the hypothesis and its attendant typology. For the time being, however, no particular novel supraproverbs come to mind, unless it would be something like *Mend the fence and milk the cows*. This proverb's basic message is that things should be set right, which, according to the cognitive ideals hypothesis, is what all proverbs encourage.

Priming the Proverb.   Cognitive scientists have developed a number of techniques for getting at the ways in which information is stored in long-term memory. For example, we seem to have organized packets of information in memory, somewhat fluid to be sure, but stable enough. The word "bird" is more closely connected to "feather" than it is to "megabyte." Although our memories may sometimes seem like a vast, cluttered warehouse put together by a drunken sailor, the truth is quite the opposite.

Psychologists have developed a number of techniques for probing memory such as free recall, recognition, and using partial stimuli as memory prompts. One technique that has become popular is called *priming*.

To do a priming study, people are presented with one stimulus (the prime) and then a second stimulus (the target) to see if the prime had any influence on the target. As a simple example, suppose we wanted to know whether the word "Monet" would prime the word "Seurat," but not the word "Jackson." We tell our subjects that we will give them a name of a person and we want them to decide as quickly as possible whether a second stimulus (the target) is also a name of a person.

On some trials the target is a made-up name, such as "Frimlo," for which the correct response is "no." Our subjects respond by pressing the "y" (yes) key or the "n" (no) key on a keyboard. We can make the time between presentation of the prime and the target a constant, such as 1 s, or we can vary it. In any event, in our example if the name "Seurat" is related to the name "Monet," which would be expected if the subject was familiar with French impressionist painters, then seeing the name "Monet" should speed up the decision about the name status of "Seurat," but not the name status of "Jackson," an American artist.

The idea then is that response times and response correctness should provide some evidence about how some names are organized in memory. One explanation for the speeded-up response is to say that the prime activated some memories of the Monet concept, and this activation spread to the related concepts in proportion to their degree of relatedness. This is just a more technical way of saying that the prime reminded us of the target. The priming technique with its many variations has turned out to be a useful tool for getting at various properties of memory, such as the degree of automaticity in memory search. Research indicates that people may sometimes be reminded without any awareness of the process (Schacter, 1987).

Using the priming technique, we could do some interesting experiments with proverbs. A basic question about them concerns their familiarity. Yet familiarity has been assessed exclusively through rating tasks. By priming, however, we could give our subjects a fragment of a proverb such as "A stitch in time...," or "A watched pot...," and then, as the target, the complete proverb. The more familiar the proverb, the faster the decision should be. However, unfamiliar proverbs should also elicit fast reaction times, but in connection with a response of "no." The interesting cases would be those proverbs that are somewhat familiar, for which the response would be a "yes," but a slow response relative to the extreme cases of familiarity. The data from this sort of study could then be correlated with the ratings data to get a converging validation of familiarity.

The priming technique could also be used to investigate the automaticity of figurative meaning. To do this, we could make up pairs of synonymous proverbs, in which the proverbs in set A vary in familiarity, and those in set B are newly made and therefore unfamiliar. In this case, we would have pairs of proverbs with similar figurative meanings but different literal meanings. As a control, we could also make up a set of C proverbs that were unrelated in meaning to A.

In the experiment we would first present either B (e.g., *With seven nurses the child loses an eye*) or C (e.g., *A man's tie does not match all his suits*) as the prime, and then A (e.g., *Too many cooks spoil the broth*). The subjects' task would be to decide whether A (the target) had a meaning that was similar to the prime. To the extent that the meaning for the target proverbs was prestored and automatic, the reaction times to the targets should be faster. We could also reverse the procedure and present the original target proverbs first. To the extent that the meanings for these primes could be readily assembled, they should facilitate responding to the B or C targets.

Many variations on this general procedure could be used. Potentially, this kind of study could help adjudicate the automaticity issue that divides the extended conceptual base theory and the great chain metaphor theory. It also has important implications for the stages issue and therefore for the standard pragmatic model. In general, more online procedures such as priming would complement the many offline studies on proverbs.

Proverb to NonProverb: Illustration

The ecologically valid approach to what is outside the proverb involves questions about how it is interpreted and instantiated, not about how one proverb can be related to another. But effective interpretation and instantiation requires the intermediary of figurative meaning. This meaning is an unobserved, hypothetical entity, however. In a word, it is private. Theoretically, this meaning can be made manifest through verbal interpretations, pictures, and examples, which serve as illustrations. The next three sections focus on these illustration forms.

Verbal Interpretations.   We tend to take verbal interpretations for granted as honest, sincere attempts to reflect some state of affairs. If we see a movie with friends and later ask them for an opinion of it, we are likely to believe that they are trying their best to put their thoughts into words. We assume that they abide by basic rules of communication such as trying to be truthful, relevant, sincere, and transparent in what they are communicating. We probably even tacitly assume more basic things, such as that they are capable of being truthful and relevant, and that they have something to be truthful and relevant about!

However, what is this something anyway? It is not the movie. The movie is something that they processed on a number of levels: perceptually, emotionally, intellectually. When we ask them what they thought about the movie, it is not a question about whether they literally looked at the movie or whether their visual and auditory perceptual systems were operating, but what their cognitive-emotional reactions were. Thus when we assume that they are being cooperative when they speak, our assumption is not about the movie, but about what the movie meant to them. They are communicating something about their thoughts.

This translation process is variously successful. It is a common experience that verbalizations can miss the mark. An individual may have little expertise in the domain, and his or her vocabulary or willingness to monitor the verbalization-experience relation may be lacking. Therefore, the distinction between meaning and its illustration is an important one.

Thus it is with proverb interpretations. Very large numbers of people have been asked to provide them: college students who participate in scientific studies, psychiatric patients who are given Gorham's Proverb Test, children who are asked by researchers, and adults who take the Wechsler Adult Intelligence Scale test.

All of these interpretations have been provided under relatively controlled circumstances. Typically, individual proverbs have been presented without the aid of context, although not always. What do people's interpretations actually look like? Hardly ever is a sample provided, so some examples have been reproduced from interpretations by college students who wrote them in the author's research laboratory at the University of Cincinnati. These samples were selected on a quasi-random basis from a much larger set. The proverb is presented first followed by the interpretations, which are presented exactly as they were written:

Spilling wine is worse than spilling water.
   Some things are free and some are not.
   It is better to wreck junk than to wreck something good.
   When something bad happens you should be thankful it wasn't worse.
   While the event was bad it could have been worse.
   Some things are more valuable than others.

The best fish swim near the bottom.
   People always look for what's best for themselves.
   The best things in life are the hardest to reach.
   The best of something is usually unreachable or hidden from view.
   You are less likely to be fooled by someone (or something) if you stay away from them (or it).
   Check all alternatives before making a final decision. You can never be too sure of one thing.

The cow gives good milk but kicks over the pail.
   Initially things are beginning well. However, they turn to bad after a little time.
   The good that one does is often overshadowed by the bad.
   It doesn't matter how good something is as much as if it's done.
   People often have great talents but refuse to share or let those talents benefit others, only themselves.
   Success is nice but there are always downfalls that accomplish it. Be cautious!

Bees have honey in their mouths and stingers in their tails.
   People who have good qualities usually possess bad qualities, too.
   It may look okay from the front but the back is a different story.

Things aren't always what they seem. You better check twice before you bite.
There are two sides to everything, good and bad.
Don't trust a stranger no matter how sincere they seem.

Great weights hang on small wires.
Little people can do great things.
Large problems are solved.
A thing is often stronger and more important than it seems.
Important things are balanced delicately.
Big problems depend on small ones.

The aforementioned five proverbs are all unfamiliar. Most of them were made up specifically for laboratory use. Still, the students who interpreted them knew that they were interpreting proverbs, and they had been given examples of what a proverb was and what a good interpretation looked like. This set of interpretations is rather sobering. Most are acceptable, a few are excellent, and a few are poor in that they seem only distantly related to the proverb. Some proverbs, such as "Bees..." and "The cow...," are relatively easy to comprehend, whereas "Great weights..." has been notoriously difficult to comprehend for college students who trek into our lab. The difficulty is apparently that "great weights" and "small wires" can be decoded in many ways, and "hang" is not always taken to mean "depend," its idiomatic meaning, probably because the entire sentence must first be viewed nonliterally for this meaning to arise.

Whether the interpretations that these students gave were faithful renderings of the meanings that the proverbs arouse is debatable. How could we tell? One way is to do a two-phase experiment. In phase one, give people proverbs and have them write interpretations. In phase two, give them examples (positive instances) of the proverbs' standard meanings, in which the latter is defined in terms of high consensual agreement between experimenter and participants (college students). Also give them examples of proverbs (negative instances) that they were never presented in the first phase. Can the students tell the difference between the positive (correct) examples and the negative (incorrect) examples, and how is this discrimination related to the interpretations? The answer is that students typically perform better than chance in making this discrimination, and their performance is modestly related to the goodness of their interpretations, with correlations ranging from .20 to .65 (Honeck, Riechmann, & Hoffman, 1975; Temple & Honeck, 1992).

If the elicitation of proverb interpretations from supposedly lucid, intelligent college students is fraught with problems, then these problems are exacerbated when the subjects are not a normal adult population. Children's interpretations tend to be very literal (see chapter 6) as are those of schizophrenic individuals who provide bizarre interpretations as well (Andreason, 1977). In fact, the interpretations of patients with schizophrenia are so hard to judge for goodness and, more important, seem to have such low validity and little usefulness in general, that some have called for an end to their use.

For example, Andreason (1977) had 14 to 15 patients diagnosed as schizophrenic, manic, or depressive attempt to interpret 10 proverbs. The interpretations were then given to 24 psychiatrists who rated the proverbs on a 3-point scale for correctness, abstractness, concreteness, bizarreness, and personalization. The diagnostic category of the respondents was unknown to the raters. The results indicated that interrater reliability was quite low overall, and even lower when done by diagnostic category. Depressives could be distinguished from schizophrenics and manics but the latter two categories only weakly. It was concluded that proverb interpretations, "are of little value as an indicator of thought disorder and as an aid to differential diagnosis and they they are therefore of little practical use,...they may be misleading because of their poor reliability, and their widespread use should probably be discontinued" (p. 218).

There are mitigating circumstances. People suffering a form of psychopathology are notoriously difficult to test. They may be taking drugs; their attention is likely to wonder; they may give simple or evasive answers; they may rightly view the testing as sterile, and so on. In reviewing such testing with Gorham's Proverb Test, Mieder (1978) also noted that researchers often assume that there is only one correct, unambiguous interpretation when, in fact, some proverbs routinely get different, equally good interpretations. Mieder stressed an interdisciplinary approach to judging interpretation goodness.

Mieder's critique can be seen to flow from the cultural view. Proverbs need not always be set within some context, however, nor must their cultural origin and function be respected. Sometimes a researcher is interested in people's ability to interpret unfamiliar proverbs or proverbs without supportive context.

These latter goals, which stem from the cognitive view, have motivated a great deal of research on the proverb. Some evidence suggests that so-called field-independent individuals are somewhat better at interpreting proverbs than field-dependent individuals (Cunningham, Ridley, & Campbell, 1987). This is presumably related to the field-independent person's lesser reliance on and need for contextual clues, as well as a greater tolerance for ambiguity. Similarly, students who show a greater tendency toward psychopathological thinking (e.g., delusions, hallucinations, flat affect, attentional problems) are more likely to produce bizarre and idiosyncratic interpretations for unfamiliar proverbs (Allen & Schuldberg, 1989). Proverb familiarity is also known to affect interpretation goodness, although the relationship is weak (Cunningham et al., 1987). Indeed, it is reported that some African-American respondents on Gorham's Proverb Test did not even attempt to interpret some unfamiliar proverbs, although, generally, the more abstract interpretations were slightly correlated with age, educational level, and self-described socioeconomic status (Penn, Jacob, & Brown, 1988). One interesting finding in this study was that if respondents indicated that they knew what proverbs were, they produced significantly more abstract interpretations. Finally, there is also a relationship between the kind of picture someone draws on the Draw-a-Person test and their proverb interpretations: Better interpretations are loosely correlated with better pictures (e.g., more detail, better overall figures; Gustafson & Waehler, 1992).

There are other reasons for soliciting interpretations without a context. Sometimes one simply wants to know what kinds of interpretations people produce, not whether they are correct. When interpretations are judged for goodness, however, they must be judged against some standard. A single individual is not always in the best position to do the judging because he or she might have overlooked valid interpretations and, in fact, may have constructed an idiosyncratic meaning. A more consensual, empirical procedure is required. For example, in experimental research we routinely get college students to generate interpretations and then inspect these for typicality. We call the most

prototypical interpretation the standard and less typical interpretations, nonstandard. A thorny issue in this procedure is what
constitutes the "same" interpretation. If there are 100 interpretations to look at, and 50 seem to be saying the same thing, how
is this decided? There are no hard and fast rules. We have
sometimes taken the standard interpretation written in our own
way and placed it along with nonstandard interpretations, and
then have asked new groups of students to judge which is the best
interpretation of the proverb. This procedure ordinarily produces
90% agreement with the standard interpretation, and therefore
with our version of it. This process is not perfect, but no empirical
procedure is. It is necessary, however, when the goodness of
interpretations is judged, as a means of ruling out personal
biases. The logic of the process is much the same when someone
claims to have a test of intelligence, anxiety, optimism, or whatever.

In conclusion, verbal interpretations illustrate the figurative
meaning of a proverb. If the figurative meaning is well understood, a verbal rendering of it may still miss the mark, although
it is unlikely that someone could write a good interpretation
without a serviceable figurative meaning. Verbal interpretations
are imperfect indicators of figurative understanding, and they
become more imperfect as the intellectual and verbal abilities of
the interpreter are reduced. Characteristics of the proverbs themselves can also affect interpretive goodness such as familiarity
and syntactic complexity, as can the testing situation.

Visual Interpretations.   Proverbs can be illustrated visually as
well as verbally. They can be rendered as oil paintings, cartoons,
wood carvings, and pictures. Almost any visual medium is fair
game.

The most famous realistic visual illustrations are those of the
16th century Dutch artist Pieter Bruegel. (Dundes & Stibbe,
1981, provide an in-depth discussion of Bruegel's work.) His
best-known work is *Netherlandish Proverbs*, an oil painting that
represents over 100 proverbs, the exact number being a matter
of debate (Mieder, 1993a; Sullivan, 1994). Bruegel's apparent
intention was to parody the human situation, man's foibles, folly,
and fickleness. In Bruegel's era, proverbs were quite popular,
being used to inculcate Christian morality as well as a more

humanist viewpoint (Sullivan, 1994). People were considered to be the source of all manner of societal evils, and as Bruegel's age saw man, he was a feckless fellow who went blundering through life forever committing those foolish acts that a succession of pithy proverbs warned him against. He was always to be seen incorrigibly mistaking dung for diamonds, casting roses before swine, covering the well after the calf has fallen in, following blind men into a ditch and trying to squeeze blood out of a turnip. (Foote, 1968, p. 142)

It is also significant that many paintings of the era were made with the intention to get people to spend some time examining them. (This is something I [the author] can attest to because I attached a copy of T. E. Breitenbach's poster, *Proverbidioms*, to my office door, a picture that resembles Bruegel's in many respects. People would sometimes spend 30 to 45 minutes trying to find all the wise sayings there. Of course, they could do this because, as is the case for Bruegel's painting, the artist used partially literal depictions of the proverbs.)

Because many proverbs are stated in concrete ways, it becomes possible to represent their meanings using familiar objects and events as Bruegel did. To represent *A net with a hole in it won't catch any fish* is easy enough. One simply draws a lake scene with a fisherman standing on shore holding a net that obviously has a hole in it, with a fish falling out the bottom of the net. This seems like a straightforward process. But it is not! If someone asked us to draw a picture of the "Net..." proverb, what would we draw? Would your picture be the same as mine? It is not likely. My image for the proverb was motivated by memory of a lake in Wisconsin and other autobiographical details. Different people will draw different pictures, but will anything remain constant? The answer hinges on the concreteness of the proverb and what kind of meaning people draw in the first place. Notice that my lake scene drawing was based on having developed a literal meaning for the proverb. If other people do the same, then it is likely that their drawings will contain a net with a hole in it, fish slipping through the net, and perhaps a person in a particular kind of environment holding onto the net. The details—size, color, exact shape of the net, presence of people, and so forth—may differ, but the key concepts in the proverb will be there. Even so, such concrete illustrations leave out the important intermediary of interpretation: For the drawing to illustrate the proverb the two have to be connected by means of an interpretation.

What if the proverb is less concrete? *A stitch in time saves nine* seems like a drawing-friendly proverb. But how is the "saves nine" element to be drawn, seeing that it involves a change over time in the state of something? Perhaps whatever is being stitched has to be shown in increasingly deteriorated condition as time passes. Maybe two parallel drawings have to be composed: one set of drawings shows the defective item with a tear, then getting stitched, with the scenario ending there; a second set of drawings shows the same defective item not getting stitched and deteriorating over time. Drawings have limitations. Time is often a crucial element in proverbs, and yet time must be conveyed visually in a spatial way if drawings or other noncontinuous media are used, or sequentially across continuous frames if video is used.

If "A stitch..." is somewhat difficult to draw, what happens when more abstract proverbs are used? *Great weights hang on small wires* seems concrete enough, just like "A stitch...." The problem comes in how to represent weights, great, wires, small, and hang, the whole proverb in other words. If we take our job to be that of representing the proverb's literal meaning, tokens will have to be found for all of the major concepts. We start the drawing with a big, gray, steelish ball, draw a thin line under and around the sides of it, and attach the line to a phantom line that runs across the top of the page. The author has asked many people to draw this proverb, and it is edifying to observe all the different ways in which this is accomplished. Some people add stress lines around the line or wire or whatever their token is. Even with all the variability in the drawings one can discern something like common elements, although this is an empirical issue.

At this point one might say, "OK, drawing proverbs is easy enough. There is variability, different tokens for types, and maybe some problems with time, but nothing insurmountable." What needs to be borne in mind to this point, though, is that the proverbs to be drawn were relatively concrete, and our artists were presumably trying to draw something like a realistic representation of them. What happens when we move one step away from the level of the "Great weights..." proverb? Suppose we try *An ounce of prevention is worth a pound of cure*. Perhaps we first draw a young girl getting a vaccination or what looks to be a vaccination, then a frame to the right that shows the same girl with polio but with a large diagonal line going through the entire frame to indicate "not." A second set of drawings may show a picture of a young boy who is not getting a vaccination and in a second frame the same boy walking with a withered leg and a cane. We might also try to draw something more abstract such as a balance scale with a small cube on one side balancing a bigger cube on the other. In another drawing, still using a balance scale, we might put a syringe on one side and an obviously sick person on the other, although this juxtaposition may evoke the idea that getting a shot made someone sick.

Clearly, the literal meaning of a proverb is not so easy to represent. It is made more complex with proverb abstractness and the interactiveness of conceptual elements, that is almost always. Even at the literal level, therefore, the theoretical and practical problems are similar to what they were for verbal interpretations. A meaning is a potential, and it can be illustrated in quite different ways. However, we know that people are able to reliably match pictures of the literal meaning of a proverb with verbal instances of its figurative meaning. Assuming that the pictures represent only one of many possible meanings, it follows that they would have a core meaning that could be used for matching purposes.

Moving from literal visual renderings of the proverb to nonliteral ones, suppose that we now ask people to draw, not the objects and events explicitly mentioned in the proverb, but the abstract meaning of the proverb, and that they do it without using concrete, representational objects. For example, suppose they draw *The cow gives good milk but kicks over the pail*, without drawing cows, milk, or pails.

This is the task we set for a group of college students several years ago. What the students did was interesting and in some instances creative. Figures 5.1 through 5.3 show drawings by two students each for three different proverbs.

There is the temptation to overinterpret these drawings. A more conservative attitude still suggests that something reliable is happening. The researcher's dilemma is that there is no standard way, or even a complex novel way, of coding the drawings. How then are they to be described in a more systematic, formal way?

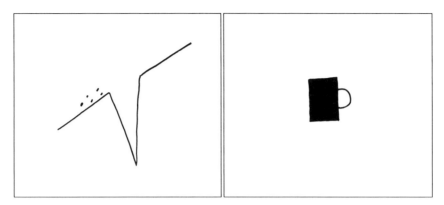

FIG. 5.1.   Abstract drawings of *The cow gives good milk but kicks over the pail.*

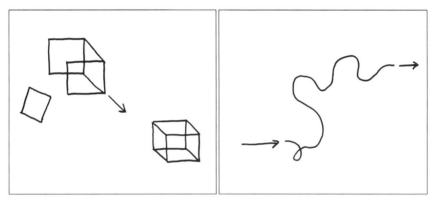

FIG. 5.2.   Abstract drawings of *You can't make an omelette without breaking some eggs.*

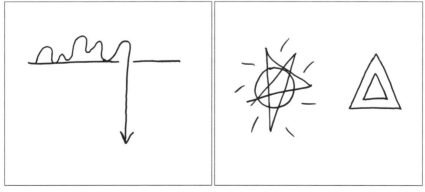

FIG. 5.3.   Abstract drawings of *That which will not be butter must be made into cheese.*

If we know what the proverb is and simultaneously inspect the drawing, it is possible that this joint knowledge creates meanings for the drawing that it does not otherwise have. The real question is whether the drawing could reliably be related to other inputs such as verbal examples or even literalized pictures of the proverbs.

This is the strategy we followed in two different studies. In one, we presented college students some realistic pictures of the literal meaning of some proverbs, along with some abstract drawings of these same proverbs (Honeck, Case, & Firment, 1988). On each of 11 trials, the students saw the realistic picture and two alternative abstract pictures, one of which was drawn to present the figurative meaning of the proverb. The students' task was to select the abstract picture that had the same underlying meaning as the realistic picture. The results indicated that the students could do this matching at a level above chance. Moreover, the better their rationale for their choices, the better they did (92% correct with appropriate rationales and 56% correct with inappropriate ones). We speculated that the students were able to form analogies between the two sets of pictures by using abstract meanings.

A later study demonstrated that abstract pictures can be used to reliably rank a set of verbal instances of the figurative meaning of a proverb (Feldhaus & Honeck, 1989). We could put an abstract picture at the top of a page, then put the instances in random order below it and ask people to rank the instances in terms of how well they illustrate the meaning of the picture. Not only will their rank-orders be consensual, but the orders will correlate well with orders that are generated when either a proverb or a verbal interpretation is used as a standard. Because these several orderings are correlated, the conclusion is inescapable that the proverb, a verbal interpretation of it, pictures of its literal meaning, and pictures of its figurative meaning all tap into the same abstract meaning. Proverbs can be illustrated in a variety of ways, so some kind of core meaning must be at work. This conclusion applies to physiognomically related events as well (e.g., the color yellow and a happy mood; Marks, 1996) and to metaphor (Kennedy, Green, & Vervaeke, 1993).

Verbal Examples. A proverb can be illustrated with verbal instances. This happens when a topic is judged to fit a proverb's figurative meaning. For example, *Once burned, twice shy* is illustrated by "The 3-year-old got bit by her puppy and now she won't go near the cat."

Categories, including proverb categories, have a number of parameters. The first is *range*, the number of different conceptual domains to which the category can be applied. Second, is *width*, the number of different aspects of a domain to which the category can be applied. These admittedly ill-defined variables are continuous, although it is possible to make them orthogonal. Thus, there are proverbs that fit into only one of the four categories created by taking extreme values of the range and the width variables (big and small range combined with big and small width). A big-range-big-width proverb is *A net with a hole in it won't catch any fish*, because its meaning can be applied to practically any domain and potentially to many different aspects within each domain. A big-range-small-width proverb is *Haste makes waste* because although it potentially applies to any domain in which time is important, it is restricted to mappings that involve only the undue speeding up of some process within the domain. A small-range-big-width proverb is *A penny saved is a penny earned* because it applies almost exclusively to money matters but potentially to a large number of different kinds of transactions involving money. A small-range-small-width proverb is *Plan before you paint* because it is probably limited to painting.

This fourfold scheme is purely speculative and has no empirical foundation. However, in laboratory studies, if people are presented a wide range of instances during an initial learning phase, they will do better in recognizing novel positive instances that come from a wide range. If all the instances that someone experiences during learning concern sports, then the chances are reduced that the person will recognize a potentially new instance that concerns politics. Of course, too much variability in the range may prevent the development of a stable category meaning. How instances are presented to learners is a delicate matter and depends on the nature of the category to be learned, the learner's expertise, and what the ultimate goal of the learning is.

The author knows of no studies on the variability of instances within a particular domain, the width variable. One problem is that this variable is hard to define, largely because the learner's expertise must be taken into account. Within their area, experts make different distinctions than do novices. Similarly, children do not appreciate either the same range or width of a proverb as an adult does. Children may initially be overfocused on range. To undo this, they may have to hear the proverb in new domains and get some instruction regarding its application. Some African societies instruct in this process (Finnegan, 1970; Penfield & Duru, 1988), but the details are sketchy.

The major theoretical problem with the fourfold range-width scheme is that a proverb is known by its use. *A penny saved is a penny earned* and *Plan before you paint* could well be applied outside the realms of money and painting. The range variable is therefore defined by the imagination of the proverb user, which is subject to the inherent logical constraints of the proverb. The same applies to the width variable up to a point that hinges on the kinds of principled distinctions that could possibly be made within a domain.

Verbal instances vary in ways other than range and width. One simple variable is length. There are single-sentence instances and book-length instances. Fables and allegories fall in between, along with proverb poems (Mieder, 1993a). Almost any single-sentence instance can be elaborated into a more fleshed-in instance. For example, a single sentence illustration of *Bees have honey in their mouths and stingers in their tails* is "The seemingly playful pup took a chunk out of the boy's arm." This can be blown up to become "The boy had just received his first puppy. He looked so cuddly and playful, he hardly seemed like an animal at all. But when the boy reached down to pet him the, pup took a chunk out of the boy's arm." Obviously, this longer instance could now be reduced back down to sentence size. Fables such as Aesop's could also be reduced. It would be interesting to compare the value of length. One pertinent finding is that summaries can be more valuable than all the original text insofar as memory and level of understanding are concerned (Reder & Anderson, 1980).

Sophistication is another dimension on which instances can vary. The boy and his puppy example for *Bees have honey in their mouths and stingers in their tails* does not match the following example from *Macbeth* (Act 1, Scene 3) provided by a colleague and Shakespeare buff:

> And often times to win us to our harm
> The instruments of darkness tell us truths,

Win us with honest trifles to betray us in
Deepest consequence.

This example, if that is a proper description, is much more abstractly stated than the boy and his pup example. Though nonproverbial in form, it is poetic. One could just as well say that Shakespeare's verse is the unseen proverb, and "bees..." is an example. Perhaps the problem is that the verse is restricted in range to matters of betrayal whereas, ironically, "bees..." has a more inclusive range, as well as a more memorable form, so we might bet that "bees..." would attain proverbial status but not the verse.

The theoretical problems raised by instantiation are vexing. Events may or may not become instances until someone deems them to be. This may happen only when the categorizer has just the right knowledge, complementary beliefs, and the motivation to instantiate. Much miscommunication stems from the different ways in which events get categorized and considered. People who do not share mental theories will differ in the kind and range of instances they consider. These theories are part of the background that informs every sort of communication. Scientific work on the categorization processes involved in proverb usage may help shed some light on all of this.

Visual Examples.   The figurative meaning of proverbs can also be illustrated visually. Part of the intrigue of visual events is that they can take on different kinds and levels of meaning, and proverbs can select these. The events may come with meanings, in which case a proverb can emphasize or deemphasize them. If the events are mentally represented on a lower meaning level, a proverb may be able to push that level higher.

According to Mieder (1993a), "proverb illustrations traditionally represent an attempt to depict basic human problems, usually in a satirical and moralistic manner" (p. 59). To convey a figurative meaning, pictures, woodcuts, and cartoons have understandably had to rely on familiar things to represent familiar proverbs. In some cases, pictures are accompanied by captions or other verbiage. Unfortunately, little is known about the process by which people extract meanings from these visual illustrations. Mieder (1989) presented examples of how proverbs have been illustrated in comics, cartoons, and by other visual means.

Experimental work could help clarify this matter, but little such work has been done. The reasons seem to be largely practical. If graphic work has to be done, then one needs either a good artist or a computer expert who can do very sophisticated graphics. Visual instances almost inevitably are better when a time element is used. Pictures have been used to illustrate the figurative meaning of proverbs for children (Honeck et al., 1978). This worked well enough to get above-chance matching of proverb and picture, but it is clear that better graphics are needed. Finally, adults can use the picture of the literal meaning of a proverb to find a matching verbal instance of the proverb's figurative meaning. For example, a realistic drawing of *The cow gives good milk but kicks over the pail* can be matched to "The young girl gave her mother a doll for Christmas and then played with it" (Honeck, Voegtle, & Sowry, 1981).

With modern video recorders it becomes possible to stage instances of proverbs. This puts the researcher in the position of movie playwright, producer, director, and maybe actor. One comes up with a set of proverbs, then goes about dramatizing them in miniature movies. Experimental control considerations must enter in, of course, with the catch-22 that more ecologically valid instances will inevitably introduce more unwanted variables. This would be time-consuming and labor-intensive research but it is certainly worth a try. Modern recording techniques also could be used profitably in field studies of the proverb.

SUMMARY

Thoughts of perfection motivate the creation and use of a proverb. Perfection is rendered in generic ideals that can be instantiated in ways that help guide the construction of a specific ideal, the proverb itself. Generic ideals are universal, whereas specific ideals can be culturally bound. Because effective communication requires verbal economy, sensibility, and logical coherence, the proverb typically gets put in foreshortened, concrete, schematic terms. This thought-to-language translation process is poorly understood. Nevertheless, because perfection is a motivational state of mind, the proverb is constrained to contain terminology that instructs in the path to perfection, either in an explicit, positive way, or implicitly by pointing to clear deviations from the ideal. The upshot is that both ideal-confirming and ideal-disconfirming proverbs are constructed, both of which often express a duality that guides the interpreter toward the ideal. A variety of factors—the generic ideal, linguistics, culture, schematic logic, and individual preferences—determine the final literal form of the proverb.

A critical aspect of proverbs is that they contain strange loops in that the figurative meaning of the proverb serves to instantiate the proverb's literal meaning. This property allows proverbs to be about themselves. Proverbs also invite playfulness, which can yield novel proverbs by transforming older ones in various ways. Still, it is hard to remain within the conceptual envelope of a proverb. The mind spontaneously produces new proverbial, visual, or verbal illustrations of it. In all cases, however, rational illustration of the proverb in some medium requires the construction of a figurative meaning to mediate the connection.

6

Brain, Development, and Intelligence

꙰ ◆ ꙴ

According to the cultural view, proverbs originate and become common knowledge within societies. On one level that is true. The real work, however, is done by the individual human brain. Marvelous though the brain is, it must on the average become 7 years old before it can appreciate the double entrendre of proverbs, and this only when the conditions that subserve understanding are optimal. Why do children find it difficult to understand proverbs? How are intelligence and proverb understanding related? Brains, children, and intelligence, these are the themes of this chapter.

THE BRAIN

Basic Considerations

The brain is a mighty organ. It composes music, distinguishes between a myriad of faces, tells us to avoid things that taste bad, understands words that enter its portals at the rate of five a second, becomes euphoric at the sight of mountain scenes, and plays chess. That is not bad for something that, in the adult human, weighs a mere 3 pounds, and not bad for something that looks like the creation of a mad artist, with furrows, crevices, and

214

prominences that curl and wander from top to bottom. Closer examination reveals a complicated chemistry as well as electrical processes that zip to and fro. Microscopes show the highways for the electrical waves. The exact number of these highways, or neurons, is unknown, but estimates range from hundreds of billions to a trillion. In the neocortex, the outer bark of the brain, there are as many as 100,000 neurons/mm^3 or about 1/25 in on a side (a millimeter is 1/1000 of a meter).

Neuronal density is only half the story. The real work of the brain is in the connections between the neurons. A neuron may connect (synapse) with hundreds or thousands of other neurons. The connections are fast because nervous impulses travel anywhere from 50 to 125 mph an hour (Kolb & Whishaw, 1990). In a body 4 feet long this means that an impulse traveling at 100 mph goes from head to toe in about .03 s. This rate of transmission is even more stunning when one considers that the nervous impulse is generated by chemical processes, which we naively tend to think of as slow.

In its resting state a neuron is polarized, being electrically negative on the inside and positive on the outside. When the neuron is stimulated, chemical processes take place that repolarize the neuron so that now the outside (the membrane) becomes negative, and this wave of negativity passes along the neuron in a self-sustaining way. Once it gets to the end of the neuron (technically, the terminal of the axon of the neuron), it causes the terminal to secrete a tiny amount of chemical called a neurotransmitter. At least 26 different kinds of neurotransmitters have been identified (Gazzaniga, 1988). The neurotransmitter empties into the synaptic cleft, the space between the sending neuron (the axon) and the receiving neuron (the dendrites or input branches of a neuron), energizing the dendrite so that it too can fire away. A single neuron might be capable of firing as many as a thousand times a second. Thus the mathematics of brain activity are, well, mind boggling, especially when one considers the vast amount of nervous activity that can occur simultaneously.

Although the brain's work is conducted on the microscopic level, it exhibits organization at higher levels, some of which is visible to the naked eye. For example, casual inspection of the brain shows that it has two sides: the left cerebral hemisphere and the right cerebral hemisphere. A big gap called the longitudinal fissure separates the two. The gap is obvious when you look down on the brain. Each side has particular areas, the frontal (front), temporal (side), parietal (top side), and occipital (back) lobes. If you imagine standing over the brain, then putting both your hands into the longitudinal fissure and pushing the two sides apart, you would see a big white band that connects the two sides. This is the corpus callosum, and it is the major conduit between the two.

An obvious question is whether the two sides do different things. More generally, do different parts of the brain do different things? The answer is a modified yes. The brain has different structures that have special functions. That is especially true if we start at the bottom of the brain. Structures there are involved in vital functions such as breathing, arousal, blood pressure control, body temperature, eating, fighting, fleeing, sex, posture and fine motor control, and certain aspects of memory. However, even at the top or cortical level of the brain there is some division of labor, with different modules dedicated to different functions. In the case of proverbs, we are primarily concerned with what happens at the cortical level and especially with the left and right cerebral hemispheres.

Proverb Studies

As early as 1965 there was some evidence that brain damage affected proverb processing. Fogel (1965) used Gorham's Proverb Test, which in this case involved presentation of a four-choice multiple-choice test consisting of 40 proverb test items. He gave it to 100 control patients from the general medical wards in a hospital and to 100 brain-damaged patients with varying symptoms. Although the difference was small, the brain-damaged patients selected the correct abstract interpretation less often. This result was consistent with the already familiar observation that brain damage generally reduces people's ability to process inputs on an abstract level.

The picture was refined by Benton (1968), who also used the multiple-choice portion of Gorham's Proverb Test. Patients with bilateral frontal lobe damage performed more poorly than patients with either unilateral left or right frontal lobe damage. Of the latter categories, those with right side damage performed most poorly, getting about 20 of the 40 items correct, compared to about 26 for those with left side damage.

In general, studies on the effects of right brain damage carried out in the 1960s produced unclear results. The results of various studies suggested right hemispheric involvement in language functions, but methodological difficulties inherent in studies of brain-damaged individuals prevented more precise statements. The exact location and extent of brain damage is often hard to specify because patients may have attentional, motor, or other problems that cloud the measurement of their true abilities. Also, the damaged area may serve more than one function or be so intertwined with other areas that any statement about disability becomes highly tentative.

In the 1970s the language capacity of the right hemisphere became better defined. Research on so-called split-brain patients indicated that the right hemisphere was much more linguistically sophisticated than previously thought, although there was some disagreement about the level of sophistication, which is a continuing debate (Corballis, 1991). These patients had surgery that involved cutting their corpus callosum and, in some cases, parts of other structures that connect the two sides of the brain. The patients had severe cases of epilepsy, and the surgery was designed to prevent the spread and snowballing of seizures from one side to the other, a goal that was met by the surgery.

A unique kind of human resulted from surgery, however. This was revealed by experimental techniques that made it possible to selectively engage just one hemisphere so that it could be made to know something without the knowledge of the other hemisphere. On some occasions the patients were shown very briefly presented visual stimuli in their left visual field (to the left of a visual fixation point). Owing to the way the two eyes are connected with the rest of the brain, these stimuli ended up in the right hemisphere. Of course, for most humans the right brain can not talk, so these patients had to demonstrate that they understood what was presented by touching objects with their left hand (which connects most strongly to the right hemisphere) or by choosing pictures related to the original visual stimulus. They could connect a picture of a knife with that of a fork, for example, or if a picture of a knife had been presented to the left visual field (right hemisphere) they could pick out a fork, sight unseen, from a set of objects presented to the left hand (Gazzaniga, 1970; Sperry, 1974). These and other studies demonstrated that the right hemisphere has some competence in verbal comprehension. In contrast, the right hemisphere was known to be deficient when it comes to syntax and speech sounds, abilities that the left hemisphere is biologically programmed to carry out with great efficiency (Caplan, 1992).

At the same time, evidence became available that the right hemisphere plays a crucial role in the understanding of metaphor. It was demonstrated, for example, that patients with right hemispheric damage had difficulty understanding simple metaphors (e.g., "a heavy heart") when understanding was measured by having patients point to a pictorial representation of the metaphor, although they had less difficulty when an explanation of the metaphor was required (Winner & Gardner, 1977).

In the 1980s the case was more clearly made for right hemispheric involvement in the processing of nonliteral language (for reviews, see Burgess & Chiarello, 1996; Chiarello, 1991; Gardner, Brownell, Wapner, & Michelow, 1983; Molloy, Brownell & Gardner, 1990). People with right hemispheric damage were shown to have difficulty in understanding metaphor, connotative meaning, sarcasm, indirect requests (e.g., "Do you like cards?" as a request to play cards), jokes and humor, and the moral or point of a story. The right hemisphere is especially sensitive to global, emotional, linguistic prosodic, and facial expressive meanings, so it may be more heavily involved than the left hempisphere in creating a discourse model. In this regard, there is good evidence that damage to the right hemisphere produces deficits in getting the macrostructure (gist), generating inferences (especially more complex and effortful ones), and sustaining and shifting attention (Myers, 1993). Myers stated that "deficits in disengaging and shifting attention may have an impact on mental flexibility such that the ability to generate alternate meanings or change initial interpretations is impaired" (p. 292). This sort of impairment would be fatal to proverb comprehension.

Studies in the 1980s with proverbs confirmed this general picture. Hier and Kaplan (1980) gave tests of vocabulary, logicogrammatical comprehension (e.g., "If Jon went to the movie before Lynn, who went last?"), and proverb comprehension to right brain-damaged patients and to normal controls. Each participant was asked to explain the underlying meaning of proverbs from Gorham's Proverb Test. The two groups performed equally on the vocabulary test, but the individuals with brain damage performed more poorly on the other two tests. A minority of the brain-damaged individuals performed like normals on the proverb test. For the individuals with brain damage, performance on the proverbs test correlated .63 with performance on the vocabulary test, and .70 with that on the logicogrammatical test. The authors speculated that the performance of brain damaged individuals might be accounted for in terms of reduced attentional capacities or by problems in visuospatial processing, which may be more unique to the right hemisphere.

Several years later, Van Lancker and Kempler (1987) sought to confirm the hypothesis that there are distinctive hemispheric representations for formulaic and familiar phrases as opposed to novel phrases. They presented 10 concrete nouns, 20 familiar phrases (mainly idioms and some proverbs), and 10 novel sentences to left brain-damaged (LBD), right brain-damaged (RBD), and nonbrain-damaged (NBD) individuals. Four line drawings were presented along with each verbal item, that, for the phrasal-sentential items, were either literally related, related, opposite, or irrelevant in terms of their conceptual connection. The LBD group performed better than the RBD group on the familiar phrases, whereas the RBD group outperformed the LBD group on novel sentences. The authors concluded that right brain damage yields a deficiency in comprehending familiar phrases. That is, in the normal brain, the right side is more heavily implicated in the processing of familiar, wholistic phrases, proverbs included (see Van Lancker, 1990, for a statement of this general tendency).

Dual Semantic Systems

Chiarello (1991) summarized the findings on nonliteral language. She hypothesized that, whereas the left hemisphere carries out basic linguistic functions in a dedicated way, damage to the right hemisphere produces three related kinds of language problems. It fosters an inability to handle language that has alternate meanings, leads to foreclosure and inflexibility in the development of mental models of meaning, and reduces the ability to use background and contextual information in getting mental models of linguistic inputs, especially extended discourse (conversations, text, etc.). For example, right hemispheric damaged patients often fail to (a) notice that a linguistic input has a metaphoric meaning when one is available; (b) get the humor in a joke, apparently because the punchline does not yield the necessary reinterpretation; (c) recognize a metaphoric relationship between a metaphor and a picture, even when a preceding story promotes this connection (Chiarello, 1991).

Chiarello's three hypotheses certainly seem to apply to proverbs. In order to get a figurative meaning an attempt must be made to revise the literal meaning, move on to a new meaning, and enter the global contextual meaning in which the proverb occurs into the equation. Application of the dual semantic systems model to proverbs yields a straightforward prediction. Damage to the right hemisphere leads to problems in interpreting proverbs because, although the literal-propositional aspect of the proverb is constructed by a functional left brain, the right brain is not doing its job of revising, getting new meanings, and integrating context. Thus, proverbs may serve as an acid test of the dual semantic systems hypothesis, at least in a general sense.

The DARTS Model

It seems clear that the right hemisphere plays an important role in proverb processing. Its precise role is unclear, however, athough the dual semantic systems model implies that its core function is to generate meanings different from those of the left brain. In order to be more explicit about this role the DARTS model is offered. In this model the right hemisphere duplicates (D) the literal meaning model constructed by the left hemisphere, assimilates (A) this model to the more general discourse model that it has developed, recognizes (R) that the literal meaning model is inconsistent with and does not match the information in the discourse model, transforms (T) the literal meaning model into a figurative meaning to make it discourse consistent, and stores (S) this meaning.

The duplication process seems to be a necessary first step. The left hemisphere is designed to quickly and efficiently synthesize phonological, syntactic, and basic semantic information. Theoretically, the literal model that results must be sent to the right side where it needs to be copied. It can then be worked on by the situation model that presumably resides in the right brain. This step is logically prerequisite to recognition that there is a problem in that the literal model does not comport with the situation model. The proverb is odd, and the right brain must signal this. Thus, the R process in the DARTS model is designed to reflect the problem-recognition phase that is postulated in the extended conceptual base theory. The next phase, that of literal transformation, is encapsulated by the T process, which is essentially all of those elaborative processes (inferences, associations, etc.) that yield a figurative meaning. This meaning can then be stored.

When a relevant situation model is lacking (i.e., when a proverb is uttered in the absence of a topic), the proverb would presumably still be routed through the brain. The literal meaning model would be copied to the right side; the incongruity with the discourse model would signal that the proverb is odd; so the right brain should begin transforming the literal model. Because there is no topic to guide this transformation process, it should be more difficult and result in less precise, stable, and organized figurative meanings. Of course, because of the strange loopiness of proverbs, the literal meaning model can serve as a context for launching the search for a figurative meaning. Perhaps the left brain would be more involved than usual under this circumstance.

By the DARTS model, damage to the right brain could impair proverb functioning for different reasons: The literal meaning model cannot be copied; it cannot be compared to a discourse model; the problem-recognition process is impaired; figurative meaning construction has been disabled; or perhaps this meaning cannot be stored. For familiar proverbs, potentially all of the DART steps would be bypassed or foreshortened. Moreover, practically all of the research on the neuropsychology of proverbs has relied on familiar proverbs. However, a familiar proverb may no longer be treated as familiar by a damaged right brain, in which case the proverb would have to be processed anew through the various phases, which the right brain cannot now perform. Judged against the DARTS model, therefore, the results from the neuropsychological studies with proverbs are indeterminate regarding the precise right-brain dysfunction.

Pinpointing the dysfunction will require more precision with respect to proverbs, tasks, and brain characteristics. For example, a strong version of the model would preclude figurative understanding of proverbs when there is extensive damage to the right hemisphere. Less extensive damage might allow the individual to get the figurative meaning, but not the point of it, or to negotiate problem recognition but not get a figurative meaning. A damaged left hemisphere may disallow a precise literal meaning model, depending on the syntax of the proverb. However, the right hemisphere may still be able to compute simple syntax, add inferences, including distant ones, and come up with a serviceable literal meaning model good enough to allow construction of a figurative meaning. An individual presenting with this neurological pattern could theoretically still demonstrate this meaning by reliably connecting it to, say, visual instances. By a strong version of the DARTS model, therefore, it is better to have a healthy right than left hemisphere.

In any event, there is some evidence that the right hemisphere often bests the left hemisphere when it comes to highly conventionalized, fixed expressions such as cliches, slang, frozen idioms, expletives, and the like (Van Lancker, 1990). Left hemispheric damage is more likely to leave such expressions intact. Moreover, the prosodic (musical) features of proverbs can be crucial to their understanding, and the right hemisphere is apparently more sensitive to these cues than the left (Hellige, 1993).

Before commenting more generally on issues of the brain and proverb we must first consider some clinical work on the brain and figurative processing.

Clinical Studies

Some tantalizing tidbits about the brain and literalness come from case studies of clinical populations. For example, autistic individuals tend toward literalism in language, perhaps because they lack a theory of mind (Baron-Cohen, Leslie, & Frith, 1985). If intentions cannot be divined, then it will be difficult to figure out that people may mean something other than what they say. Cases of Asperger's syndrome, or higher functioning autism, are also relevant. Sacks (1995) described the case of a college professor who he claimed operated on a largely literal level, being unable to decode the meanings of most forms of figurative language. If there is brain damage in the case of autism, as currently believed by many scholars, it is not clear what it is or where it is in the brain. Children with Williams' Syndrome, a metabolic disorder, manifest intellectual retardation coupled with good grammatical abilities, fair semantic knowledge, and the use of unusual words. They also show abnormally large event-related potentials (brain waves) to semantic anomaly and infrequent meanings (Bellugi, Bihrle, Neville, Doherty, & Jernigan, 1992). Finally, Smith and Tsimpli (1995) reported the case of Christopher, now in his early 30s, who has command of a number of languages, while being otherwise retarded and relatively unable to interpret figurative genres or even to tell a lie.

The implication of these studies and of the experimental work on brain-damaged individuals is that there is an intricate connection between intelligence, figurative language processing, and cerebral asymmetries. Whatever it is about intelligence that figurative language taps into, it would seem to be a more general intellectual ability, and the right cerebral hemisphere is playing an important role in contributing to this intelligence. The last section of this chapter speculates on what this general capability might be.

Remaining Issues

Further research on the neuropsychology of proverbs must jointly address the details of the proverb user, the proverbs, the task, and proverb processing. Regarding the user, if normal populations are used, degree of lateralization of linguistic function varies with sex (males may be more so), age (children less so?), and handedness (left-handers less so) (Hellige, 1993). Of course, when individuals with brain damage are tested, if at all possible, the nature of the damage should be pinpointed, and general cognitive abilities should be assessed.

The specifics of the proverbs must also be considered. We know that proverbs vary on a number of dimensions such as concreteness and familiarity, and that they often use poetic devices. These factors must be considered in relation to the people being tested, the methodology, and the proverb model.

Regarding methodology, experimental details cannot be overlooked. Task variables, experimental design, and measurement factors are critical, their interaction even more. For example, experimental designs that involve repeated testing of participants can induce mental sets to process inputs in a particular way. In studies that use tropes, participants may develop a nonliteral processing set. In the case of proverbs, this may mean that the problem-recognition phase is negotiated on the very first trial.

Finally, full comprehension of proverbs requires that the listener appreciate the speaker's attitude. Suppose we are jealous of a neighbor who recently bought a laptop computer, one with all the bells and whistles, and a friend knows this and our modest means. Our friend might say, *The grass is always greener on the other side of the fence*, as if to say, "Forget it, you can't afford it." Apprehension of such points seems to require a theory of the other person's mind.

This claim also has been made with respect to irony and metaphor (Winner & Gardner, 1993). Irony requires a second-order inference. For example, suppose you and a friend agree that a novel you both read was awful. If your friend says of the novel, "Yes, what a gem," you must infer not only that your friend does not mean what he or she says, and that what your friend says is not a lie or a naive attempt at deception, but also that your friend has a negative attitude about the novel. In other words, you must become a mind reader. This is a complicated situation, and it helps to explain why children understand metaphor before they understand irony, because metaphor does not typically involve second-order inferences (Winner & Gardner, 1993).

The same general considerations may apply to proverbs. The question now arises: Is one cerebral hemisphere better at intuiting other people's beliefs, intentions, and motivations in general? The evidence thus far, though weak, suggests that the right cerebral hemisphere is more heavily implicated, which may help to explain why damage to the area blocks proverb comprehension. In neuropsychological studies, comprehension is almost always assessed through verbal interpretations and verbal processing in general. However, getting the point of a proverb may well contribute to an interpretation. That is, figurative meaning may entail pragmatic meaning as well. A strong implication of the cognitive ideals hypothesis is that even proverbs uttered in isolation make a point by implicating the utterer's intentions vis-à-vis some ideal.

It is interesting to speculate on all of this, and that is all that the author has done, of course. There are a large number of caveats—the brain is a whole; there is some disagreement about the functions of the right hemisphere; it is not always clear whether there is cooperation or competition between the two hemispheres and it is not clear how to describe exactly what the deficits are that the right hemisphere may show or exactly what causes them. The two brains do seem to be doing different things, yet information has to be integrated at some point, so cooperation is likely.

In conclusion, progress in the neuropsychology of proverbs will clearly depend on precision about the brains, proverbs, methodology, neurological models, and proverb models that are used. This theme will reappear as we examine proverb comprehension in children, our next topic.

DEVELOPMENT

The life cycle of a proverb must be considered against the background of cognitive development, the individual's growing competence in understanding and acting. How do children perform with proverbs? This matter was briefly considered in chapter 1, but it is time to consider the empirical work in detail.

Approximately 16 studies on children's understanding of proverbs have been conducted, although not all have been published in journals. No study has examined the developmental emergence of proverb production, for some obvious reasons. It is hard to know when children will spontaneously utter their first proverb. Teaching them a proverb and then examining its use under controlled circumstances violates the question of spontaneous learning and use. However, a field study might be more successful in observing first incidences of proverb use in cultures in which proverbs are held in high esteem.

Fortunately, as for language in general, proverb comprehension is easier to study. Various questions have been raised about proverb comprehension by children, largely from an empirical rather than a theoretical standpoint. To anticipate somewhat, the answers are a bit disconcerting because the development of proverb comprehension has not been linked in any reliable way to general cognitive development, and only weakly to the presence of specific cognitive skills.

Piaget's Clinical Method

Let us begin, however, at the beginning with the groundbreaking work of the noted cognitive developmentalist, Jean Piaget. Piaget began his illustrious career at Bleuler's psychiatric clinic but then moved on to the Binet–Simon Laboratory in Paris (the same Binet whose name is on the older Stanford–Binet test of intelligence). There he was asked by Simon to translate Burt's Test of Reasoning into French, a test that included proverbs. A short time later at the Institut Rousseau, Piaget began the work on proverbs that ultimately led to the publication in 1926 of what was the first thorough examination of children's comprehension of proverbs (Piaget, 1926).

Piaget's test was, in his own words, originally designed for use with children between the ages of 11 and 16. The children were asked to read 10 proverbs, one at a time, and to match the proverb to one of 12 other randomly ordered sentences, 10 of which expressed the basic ideas of the proverbs. Beyond this the children were told only that the initial set of 10 sentences were proverbs, that a proverb is "a sentence that means something," and that they should find a sentence in the second set that "means the same thing" (p. 160). The children were not told that proverbs have a hidden or underlying meaning, nor were they given any examples, practice, or feedback on the test.

This is a typical example of the Piagetian clinical method, in the sense that if the child is going to demonstrate a competence, it is going to happen spontaneously without any guidance from an adult examiner. Moreover, the examiner exercises minimal control over variables that might influence the child's performance. Because there is no attempt to systematically manipulate variables, no experiment is done. Children are merely observed. The emphasis is not so much on particular child performances but on the child's presumed competence as demonstrated on some particular task.

By Piaget's standards, the 9- to 11-year-old children's performance on the proverbs test was dismal. He writes, "In the majority of the cases the children did not understand the proverbs in the least; but they thought they had understood them, and asked for no supplementary explanation of their literal or hidden meaning" (p. 142). Of course, Piaget knew beforehand that the children would not do well, although he examined only the choices/rationales of those who made at least one or two correct matches, because these children presumably understood the task and the instructions. Bear in mind that Piaget was interested in the nature of children's misunderstandings, and not, for example, the statistical trend in performance across age groups.

He certainly found massive misunderstanding. Take the case of Mat, a 10-year-old girl. She connects the proverb, *So often goes the jug to water, that in the end it breaks*, with "As we grow older we grow better." Mat is able to give a reasonable paraphrase of the proverb and a somewhat poorer but still adequate paraphase of the matched sentence. But now she explains that they are connected, "Because the jug is not so hard because it is getting old, because the bigger you grow, the better you are and you grow old" (Piaget, 1926, p. 150). Hane, age 9, matches up *White dust will ne'er come out of sack of coal* with "We must work to live" because "Money is needed to buy coal." Ec, age 9, matches up *The flies buzzing round the horses do not help on the coach* with "It is difficult to correct a fault that has become a habit" because "The flies are always settling on the horses, and they gradually get into the habit and then afterwards it is difficult for them to cure themselves" (p. 157).

Piaget argued that the children were not just saying anything to explain their matches. They were not inventing explanations, as if they really knew that their matches did not make any sense and were randomly coming up with a rationale. The children were committed to their rationales; they believed them. The rationales were often creative but missed the mark because the proverbs' figurative meanings had not been divined. Therefore, the rationales look silly, facile, and chaotic.

Piaget explained the children's behavior by appealing to the concept of *syncretism*. The children get only the literal meaning of the proverb and try to find a match. But there are no literal matches, so the children end up explaining their choices in purely idiosyncratic ways. They fuse two wholistic meanings into a larger meaning, a schema, that lacks the essential ingredient of a principled deeper meaning. The proverb acts as the focus of the schema and serves to assimilate the other sentence. Fantastic creations result.

Here's an analogy for what Piaget may have had in mind. Suppose we are asked to relate the two sentences, "*Fair face, foul heart* and "Hamburgers don't taste good with ice cream on them." We could say, "Well, the hamburger won't taste good, so the person might act like it did and put on a happy face, but really they think the hamburger tastes foul." This connection relates the two sentences, but it seems forced and artificial.

Piaget's subjects were in essentially the same position by virtue of failing to get the proverbs' figurative meanings. Piaget claimed that the tendency toward syncretism in children has its origins in egocentrism, the tendency of children to understand events only from their own perspective. This, coupled with a strong desire to find a reason for everything, yields the children's rationales. In general, Piaget placed syncretic thought midway between autistic or nonlogical thought and logical analysis. In due time, he claimed, the children will become logical thinkers, and this will allow them to perform more ably on the proverbs task. Apparently, Piaget never actually confirmed this prediction in a thoroughgoing fashion.

Later Studies

Piaget's 1926 study and the various considerations it aroused, prefigures all of the later research on the topic. Piaget's task placed a big load on the working memories of the children, although to be fair, scholars in his era did not factor in short-term memory limitations. To perform successfully, Piaget's subjects had to negotiate several subtasks: read a proverb, construct its figurative meaning, remember this meaning, read another set of 12 sentences, get a figurative meaning for each sentence, and select just one that matched the referent proverb's figurative meaning. Either that, or in the absence of a figurative meaning for the proverb before reading the choices, synthesize a common figurative meaning for the proverb and the correct match once it was read. Even with good working memories, the children still had to keep their attention riveted while searching for a nonliteral connection. Moreover, there was no background context against which the children could appreciate the significance of the proverb. The only context was provided by the 12 choices, which functioned more as distractors, and only one of these was correct for any given proverb. We also do not know how well the children could read or, if they actually were good readers, how well they understood the various sentences. There is also the matter of the proverbs themselves. Piaget provided no listing of them, but what is provided suggests that their syntax was not always simple, and their logic was not always easy to decode. In conclusion, it is a fair guess that even adults would experience some difficulty in doing Piaget's task.

Subsequent studies with children were published in 1944, 1959, and not again until 1975. A series of studies appeared in the late 1970s, followed by a smaller number in the 1980s. To the author's knowledge, only one study has been published in the 1990s at this point (mid-1996). The various studies are summarized in Table 6.1.

Proverb Models, Minds, and Tasks

The general pattern of results in these studies can be stated rather simply. Proverb comprehension improves with the provision of context, the child's reading level (where the task requires reading), the concreteness and familiarity of the proverbs, and, of course, age. If a methodology simplifies the proverbs, corollary materials, and the task, it lowers the age at which comprehension can be demonstrated and improves overall performance. Even 7-year-olds can understand some proverbs. For example, if we show children two pictures, one of which demonstrates the figurative meaning of a proverb, and if the proverb is simple (e.g., *Little chops can cut down big trees*), then the children will be able to reliably select the correct picture. This kind of task minimizes the information processing load on the child. The child gets enough time to look at and understand the meaning of the pictures, which function as anchoring contexts for the proverb. This circumstance mimics the real world of proverb use. In general, when children are asked to interpret or explain proverbs without supporting context, comprehension is reduced. Such techniques are not bad or invalid but their results do need to be compared with results obtained when context is present.

In summary, this collection of studies has identified some important variables in children's comprehension of proverbs: task attitude, metalinguistic abilities, information processing load, context, learning ability, and age. The recent study by Nippold and Haq (1996) discovered that proverb comprehension, as measured by a multiple-choice procedure, improved for grades 5, 8, and

TABLE 6.1
Summaries of Developmental Studies on Proverb Comprehension
(in Chronological Order)

Piaget (1926) Children 9 to 11 years old read 10 proverbs and chose a matching interpretation for each from 12 alternatives. Results: Poor performance and poorly rationalized, literal choices. Conclusion: Egocentrism and syncretism.

Watts (1944) Children 11 to 14 years old read 50 proverbs and chose a matching interpretation from 4 alternatives. Results: Slow improvement across ages from 16.0 to 27.1 correct.

Gorham (1956) Grade 5 children through college seniors read 40 proverbs and chose a matching interpretation from 4 alternatives. Results: Steady improvement from 33 to 81% correct.

Richardson and Church (1959) Children 7 to 12 years old, adolescents, and adults interpreted seven common proverbs read to them by the experimenter. Results: Few good interpretations for the 7- to 12-year-old group, largely literal ones for 7- to 8-year-olds, mixed literal and figurative interpretations for later ages, with some poor interpretations by adolescents and adults. Conclusion: Good performance requires an analytic task attitude and a metalinguistic perspective.

Billow (1975) Children 9, 11, and 13 years old interpreted 12 orally presented proverbs and completed a Piagetian task of combining four circles of different colors in different spatial arrangements. Results: Correct interpretations were .40, 2.40, and 5.30 across ages, with a very low correlation (.12) between performance on the two tasks. Conclusion: The posited relationship between the Piagetian stage of formal operations and proverb comprehension was not confirmed. Metaphoric abilities run ahead of proverb abilities.

Cometa and Eson (1978) Grades 1, 3, 4, and 8 children were read four common and three rare proverbs and interpreted them. They were also given various Piagetian tasks. Results: Children (about 1/3) who passed the chemical combinations task gave adequate interpretations on 90% of the trials, but some children who were not formal operational interpreted some proverbs correctly. Conclusion: Formal operational reasoning does not underlie proverb comprehension.

Chambers (1977) This study was a replication and extension of the Honeck et al. (1978) study. Children 9 and 10 years old were put into one of three groups. Group 1, the experimental group, got two tasks: Choose which of two pictures fit the meaning of a simple, novel proverb, and then choose which of two pictures fits the meaning of a one-sentence instance of a proverb, the basis for the correct pictures and the instance. Group 2 performed only the second task, and Group 3 chose which of two proverbs fit the meaning for a one-sentence instance. Results: All groups performed above chance on all tasks, but the experimental group did not perform better than the other two groups on the second task. Conclusion: The results of Honeck et al. (1978) were replicated with a largely working-class cohort. These children could match verbal instances with pictures and with proverbs on a nonliteral basis.

Honeck, Sowry, and Voegtle (1978) Children 7, 8, and 9 years old got 10 trials. On each they looked at two pictures and tried to match one to an orally presented novel proverb. Results: Above-chance performance by age, proverb, and subject, but no differences between age groups. Conclusion: Context, reduced information-processing load, and simple proverbs allow young children to understand some proverbs.

Douglas and Peel (1979) Children in grades 1, 3, 5, 7 were presented six long sentences, the first part an illustative context and the latter part a proverb, and the children explained the proverb. Results: More literal than figurative interpretations at every grade level, but steady increase in the latter.

TABLE 6.1 (continued)

Resnick (1982)   Children in grades 3 to 7 got six tasks: (a) match a brief story to one of four proverbs; (b) match a proverb to one of four concrete analogical instances; (c) select an abstract meaning for a key word in a proverb; (d) match proverbs for similarity of meaning; (e) select the best interpretation for a proverb; (f) solve some analogies with the same 10 proverbs used in the first five tasks. Results: Moderate correlations between performance on the tasks (.51–.71), with general improvement across grades on all tasks (e.g., mean number correct on interpretation selection task was, respectively, 4.32, 4.90, 6.54, 6.42, 7.88). Conclusion: The posited hierarchical model of abilities underlying proverb comprehension was not confirmed, and a two-phase model with fast, automatic cognition followed by slower, reflective cognition may be better.

Gamlin and Tramposch (1982)   Children in grades 3 to 6 read 20 proverbs and, for each, selected two of four alternatives that were the best meaning match, then chose the preferred one of the two. A second proverb task was given which eliminated confusing foils. Results: Correct responses steadily improved across grades on the two tasks: 7.32/11.58, 9.93/13.57, 12.22/13.94, and 16.03/16.90. Good readers outperformed poor readers, and accuracy and preference were correlated. Conclusion: Two developmental trends were present: an earlier ability to get the correct meaning, coupled with a metacognitive ability that promotes a preference for intended and general meaning, and a willingness to suspend the belief that words always refer to certain (literal) categories. Proverbs are not a unique genre for younger children.

Pasamanick (1983)   Children 6 to 9 years old engaged in an open discussion with a small group of peers and the investigator about what some proverbs might mean. Results: Qualitatively, some success is reported in the children's understanding, presumably beyond their performance as indicated by the literature. Conclusion: Social interaction, abstract strategies, and social knowledge play a key role in establishing connections between proverb image, proverb base meaning, and situations. Social interactions close the gap between actual and potential development.

Nippold, Martin, and Erskine (1988)   Children in grades 4, 6, 8, and 10 read 30 proverbs and selected one of four contextual examples for each. A pictorial analogies task was also completed. Results: Percentage correct across grades was 67, 77, 83, and 85, with performance on the two tasks moderately correlated (.41). Conclusion: Performance was much above that previously reported in previous studies due to control of the reading level of the materials and the use of contexts as choices. Proverbs and analogies are based on similar reasoning processes.

Lutzer (1988)   Children in grades 2, 4, and 6, half of whom were learning disabled and half not, heard 12 common proverbs and told what they meant. Results: Less than 1.25 correct for grades 2 and 4. Metaphorically correct responses differed only for the LD and non-LD groups at grade 6 (1.50 vs. 4.73). Conclusion: Metalinguistic competence was lacking in the grade 6 LD students.

Nippold and Haq (1996)   Students in grades 5, 8, and 11 read paragraph-length stories and then a proverb, one of four types of proverb yielded by combining high or low proverb familiarity with high or low proverb concreteness. The students then chose which of four interpretations was appropriate for the proverb, given the story, where only one interpretation was the correct figurative choice and the others were plausible but nonliterally related to the proverb. Results: Percentage correct was 55, 76, and 89 for grades 5, 8, and 11 students, respectively. Grades 8 and 11 performed better on the concrete than the abstract proverbs; grades 5 and 8 performed better on the familiar than the unfamiliar proverbs. In absolute terms, the differences were almost always less than 10%, however. Conclusions: Proverb comprehension improves most rapidly between grades 5 and 8. The familiarity effects suggest that specific experience with proverbs is beneficial, whereas the concreteness effects suggest that proverbs are decoded by analyzing their words rather than by accessing prestored wholistic structures.

11 students as the familiarity and concreteness of the proverbs increased. The positive effects of familiarity were attributed to a proverb-specific language experience phenomenon, whereas the effects of concreteness were viewed as supporting the idea that the words in the proverb are analyzed (i.e., that proverbs cannot be treated as preanalyzed wholistic word-like units). This latter hypothesis received additional support in a study of proverb explanation across the life span. Performance improved dramatically through adolescence, reached asymptote in the 20s, and remained level through the 50s, with significant decline in the 70s (Nippold, Uhden, & Schwarz, in press).

The important question with respect to these variables is why they have the effect they do, and whether a more general theoretical picture of their effect can be painted. In this respect, the studies have been unenlightening, either because they were designed only to assess the effectiveness of particular variables for proverb comprehension or because, when theoretically motivated, no pattern emerged. For example, no consistent reliable correlation between some measure of a general cognitive ability and proverb comprehension has emerged, save for some moderate correlations with performance on analogy tasks. A few studies have examined cognitive stage factors but without much success.

A fuller understanding of children's comprehension of proverbs will require at least three kinds of information. First, a detailed model of proverb comprehension is needed, the situation being no different from what it was when we looked at the neuropsychology of proverbs. Of the three extant theories, only two are at all detailed, the extended conceptual base theory and the great chain metaphor theory, and only the former has been used in developmental research. Second, we need some statement about the cognitive status of the children who are tested and, in particular, the status of their abilities vis-à-vis the cognitive demands of proverb processing as described by a proverb comprehension model. This will require an assessment of specific kinds of knowledge and abilities such as syntactic and lexical decoding skills, inferential skills, ability to use clues to get beyond the literal meaning level (metalinguistic skills), and perhaps other subskills. General tests of cognitive status such as IQ tests or tests to determine a stage of cognitive functioning, may not be of much help unless it can be shown how they directly bear on the processes stipulated in the proverb comprehension model. Finally, the tasks given to children must be defined in terms of how their components relate to both the proverb comprehension model and the child's cognitive status. If, for example, the investigator uses a pure interpretation task, then we must be informed about the demands it makes on the child and what it would take theoretically to generate a reasonable interpretation.

There is no question that the level of proverb comprehension can be manipulated with relative precision. Provide children a context and they do better. Give them a pure interpretation task and they do worse. Why is this so? Looked at from the standpoint of the extended conceptual base theory, context has an effect on every step. It serves as a common cognitive environment for child and investigator, so that any subsequent mental processing will take place against this background. Even the initial step of getting a literal meaning is affected, because this meaning can be context sensitive. Moreover, proverbs are communicationally deviant. Thus, context solves the problem-recognition problem. In effect, an adult researcher is saying to a child participant: This statement is about the things we have just considered, even if it looks like the statement does not fit. An experimenter tells the child that the proverb is about the context, either explicitly or implicitly, so the crucial metalinguistic issue melts away for the child when context is provided. If the child understands the context and any topic it contains, the child is now in a good position to get an abstract meaning for the proverb. However, because the child can only resolve their similarity on an abstract level, then whatever abstract, general understanding the child might have of the topic can be intermingled with the proverb. The topic also serves to constrain the abstract meaning of the proverb so as to get a more particular figurative meaning. Finally, the topic serves to instantiate the figurative meaning of the proverb and to help get the point of it.

What happens when a child is asked to interpret a proverb without context? The child and the adult share no common cognitive environment, or at least none that is helpful for the task at hand. The adult has produced something that has no reference. Thus there are no obvious clues that the statement should be taken nonliterally. The problem-recognition phase is harder to traverse, and if this phase is negotiated somehow, there is no other information to guide the search for a figurative meaning. All the components of the P-task must be negotiated by means of the child's own internal mental resources. It is no wonder that children do poorly when this task variation is used. Even adults do so from time to time. There is nothing wrong with using such tasks. We just have to understand how they articulate with a proverb model and the child's cognitive abilities.

What of general cognitive abilities, the kind that were discussed in chapter 3? It would be propitious if children's understanding of proverbs drew on this set. It does, in fact, because there is a parallel between general cognitive development and the cognitive prerequisites of every phase of proverb understanding. Each phase entails general processes. Getting a literal meaning for a proverb involves a set of specific linguistic processes, but also inferences, associations and imagery. Children younger than age 7 are less likely to make plausible inferences, and their imagery abilities are less well developed. Imagery development is a constructive process that requires a good working memory, yet young children's working memories are still developing. In general, young children's mental representations are somewhat fragile, yet these representations are grist for the figurative mill. Furthermore, children are naive realists. In general, they assume, tacitly, that things are what they seem to be. Circumstances can be arranged in which they do not make this assumption (Flavell, Green, & Flavell, 1986), but appearance generally matches reality for young children.

John Flavell, a cognitive developmentalist, has elaborated Piaget's position on this. Piaget demonstrated that children are egocentric in the sense that they have difficulty taking the perspective of other people (e.g., describing what someone else sees when that person is seated opposite from the child). In his research Flavell and his colleagues concluded that young children have difficulty representing an object in more than one way, and that incongruity of representation is resolved by relying more on one of the representations. For example, a child may describe a glass of milk behind a blue filter as blue while also claiming that the milk would be white if the filter were removed (Flavell, Green & Flavell, 1986). Flavell et al. (1986) theorized that early pretend play underlies the later developing ability to distinguish appearance and reality. In particular, the idea of dual coding that seems to motivate behaviors such as treating sticks as trucks comes to mediate the appearance-reality distinction.

Proverb comprehension involves just such a distinction. Someone has uttered a statement. It seems to be about the things it mentions, but in reality it is not. The child must be able to fuse appearance with reality to solve the problem. More precisely, appearance must be used to forge a deeper reality. Additional considerations apply at the problem-recognition phase as well. To be able to use appearance, the child must have a clue that he or she does not understand. Yet young children are less able to monitor their own comprehension and poorer still at repairing their noncomprehension even when it is detected (Ackerman, 1984). If someone says something to us and we do not understand, we may ask questions, or ask them to say more or to paraphrase what they say. Young children are less likely to do these things because they are less able to detect miscomprehension in the first place.

There are therefore various reasons why children may fail to understand, from simply not knowing about some domain to being unable to construct coherent mental models when there are missing or contradictory pieces of information. A related problem is that young children can be poor at message evaluation. Children may treat ambiguous messages as if they were clear, and they may confuse the status of a speaker, an important consideration with proverbs, with the quality of what the speaker says (Sonenschein, 1988). It is as if children treat the cooperative principle as gospel, that a speaker can only be clear, truthful, informative, and relevant.

Of course, proverbs violate these maxims, most obviously the relevance and informativeness maxims. What children must come to understand is that speakers can intentionally violate these maxims to attain certain communication goals. The child must learn to treat linguistic messages as clues rather than as ends in themselves. Schooling, reading especially, facilitates this process, but so does interaction with and instruction by adults. A society, such as some African societies, that uses proverbs and other modes of indirect oral tradition may give young children a head start in deciphering hidden realities. However, this skill can be promoted through direct instruction, including direct instruction in interpreting and using proverbs (Feichtl, 1988).

Our discussion has emphasized the problem-recognition phase of proverb comprehension because it is crucial. Without problem recognition, which seems to depend on general cognitive abilities such as comprehension monitoring and the appearance-reality distinction, there is no proverb comprehension. It is because context, experience with proverbs, and direct instruction get children past this mental gate that they can move on to fuller proverb comprehension.

But there are additional problems. The child must operate in an abstract realm of meaning. When an instantiating episode is present, the proverb and episode must be mapped in an abstract analogical way. Young children are capable of analogical reasoning. Even 3-year-olds can appreciate the correspondence between a person's foot or belly and where a mountain's foot or belly might be (Gentner, 1977). Where young children, perhaps all of us, encounter problems is in detecting deeper, higher order similarities between things, precisely the kind that are involved in proverb solutions. For example, children in the fourth grade can generally appreciate the analogy in picture:frame::moon:halo, but have trouble with food:body::snow:river, a more dynamic, functional relationship (see Small, 1990, for a discussion). Understanding the relationship between *Bees have honey in their mouths and stingers in their tails* and "This nice, shiny new car goes really fast" presents a similar kind of problem. Not only is the relationship abstract, but its apprehension requires the right sort of inferences, in this case that the car can be dangerous, expensive, and a drain on resources, and that this contrasts with shininess and newness. Young children are less likely to draw these plausible inferences, all of them based on experience.

Finally, children must come to understand that other people have minds, that minds are the kinds of things that can harbor beliefs, intentions, goals, and feelings, and that these things are not always directly expressed in linguistic and nonlinguistic behaviors. In acquiring a language, children go through a series of stages in which they express their own mental states and intentions (Small, 1990). Appreciation of other people's intentions develops at a slower pace. Once again, research by Flavell (1993) is relevant. For example, a 3-year-old is shown a box of candy, but the box turns out to have crayons in it. Three-year-olds are more likely to believe that other people will think that the box will have crayons in it, whereas 5-year-olds are more likely to assume that others will think that it contains candy. Three-year-olds are less able to entertain the thought—really, the double thought—that others could have false beliefs. In general, there is a long developmental progression involved in coming to recognize intentions, deception, illusion, and false beliefs. Such abilities entail a recursive awareness of content, and along with it, a sophisticated working memory system for connecting the pieces of recursion.

In conclusion, a better understanding of children's comprehension of proverbs will require close attention to the proverbs and cognitive requirements of the tasks used, and these in conjunction with a general model of proverb comprehension.

INTELLIGENCE

General Considerations

Our discussion of the brain and development provides a strong underlying theme. The ability to use and understand proverbs draws on a high order of intelligence. Not only is a healthy brain required, but so are a number of subskills, each of which takes years to develop. Use of proverbs by the mentally handicapped is practically unheard of, and despite the surprising cognitive abilities shown by animals, their use of a proverb-like message has never been documented. For example, whatever one's assessment of the accomplishments of apes that have learned to sign (Gardner, Gardner, & Van Cantfort, 1989), there is nothing to suggest that they have a grasp of the proverb principle. In contrast, deaf children and adolescents demonstrate a rudimentary understanding of proverbs and can profit from instruction in the meaning of proverbs (Israelite, Schloss, & Smith, 1986). This occurs despite subnormal linguistic skills. What is happening here?

We can examine the intelligence behind proverbs by using the cultural, formal, and cognitive views. The cultural view makes the proverb an end product of accumulated societal wisdom. In essence, the larger culture has said that some ways of handling these matters are to be preferred over others. The implicit story is that over history the society has dealt with certain kinds of problems. These problems have been approached from different angles, and there is some large-scale consensus about their solution. This solution has been encrypted in a proverb and other cultural symbols as well. Proverbs therefore become a gift from the collective intelligence of one's ancestors. These forebears say, "We have had these kinds of problems before. This is what we have learned of them. We have put our learning into words. Use the words, and they will save you a great deal of pain. You will have new problems to face. Save your energies for those."

What the cultural view leaves unexplained, of course, is how to recognize that one of those old kinds of problems has occurred or that the circumstances of its occurrence may have changed enough to make one think twice about using a proverb. Life, Western life at least, seems too fluid for the automatic application of proverbs. Cultures and the proverbs they engender may provide some general guidelines for solving problems, but they do not and cannot address the details of everyday problems. None of this ,however, detracts from the sociohistoric intelligence that went into their making and dissemination.

The formal view provides a look at the logic, linguistics, and poetry of the proverb. From this perspective, a great deal of intelligence has shaped the proverb, albeit unconsciously. A range of mental mechanisms have gone into making the proverb memorable, handy, and aesthetic, so there is in the tacit workings of the mind, with all its modular conceptual forces brought simultaneously to bear, a remarkable intelligence to the proverbial form. It is hard to see how we could improve on it, even in our most reflective mode.

This brings us to the larger issue of intelligence and how it relates to the cognitive view. First, we look at some facts. Proverbs were used in conjunction with intelligence testing by the German scholars Finckh (1906) and Bühler (1908). Proverbs still appear on some tests of intelligence, such as the comprehension subtest of the Wechsler Adult Intelligence Scale-Revised (WAIS-R) (Matarazzo, 1972), the Wechsler Intelligence Scale for Children-Revised (WISC-R) and the Stanford–Binet (Terman & Merrill, 1973). On these tests, examinees are orally presented proverbs for which they are asked to provide a verbal interpretation.

An interesting statistical conclusion here is that performance on the proverbs subtests typically correlates in the modest to high positive range with full-scale performance. If someone does a good job of interpreting proverbs, they are likely to have racked up a higher IQ score and, conversely, poor performance on the proverbs is linked to lower IQ scores. For example, correlations as high as .75 on the older Stanford–Binet test have been reported (Terman & Merrill, 1973). In general, performance on a proverbs subtest tends to be one of the better subtest predictors of full-scale IQ. This conclusion is muted somewhat by studies with children. For example, Dunn (1981) measured IQ via the WISC-R for 3rd-, 6th-, and 8th-grade students, and also measured proverb comprehension using a multiple choice test. The two measures correlated well for the 8th graders but not for the younger children.

The PLANTE Model

Although proverbs entail intelligence, the details of the relationship are unclear. What follows is a general cognitive framework for thinking about the relationship.

A great deal has been written about intelligence: what it is, whether it takes different forms such as linguistic and musical, how it develops, why it differs among people, and so on. One useful metaphor in thinking about intelligence is *building*, which is linked in turn to the general concept of indirectness, as discussed in chapter 2. This metaphor is taken from a model called PLANTE that has been used to summarize some of the research on mental retardation (Honeck, 1997). The metaphor is an interpretation of the Levels (L) factor in the model, that is the ability to efficiently move information from one stage, phase, or level of processing to another, or to integrate this information in a coherent way. All intelligence involves problem solving, and solutions inevitably entail building on incoming information and packaging it for the next stage of processing.

We first discuss the building or L factor, then take up the other factors in PLANTE.

Even the simplest of situations involve building. For example, if we ask someone to respond as fast as possible when a randomly occurring light comes on, various processes have to run off smoothly. First and foremost our guinea pig must understand the task, which is to do X when Y occurs but not when Y does not occur. Then during the task, processes must take place in the visual system, a system that moves information along in stages from initial transduction of light energy into nervous energy in the retina to successive processing stages back into the brain. Then motor processes must occur, planned and prepared by the person's understanding of the task and initiated at the right time.

The task just described is simple, but building occurs on every psychological level from perception to memory to thought. If there is a breakdown in the building process due to faulty or inadequate information, a deficient information-integrating mechanism, or information overload, problem solution is less likely. This gets reflected in incorrect and prolonged responses.

One way to appreciate the building metaphor is to look at mental retardation. For experimental testing purposes, mental retardation typically gets defined in terms of IQ, with average IQ set at 100. Those who get an IQ score of 70 or less are arbitrarily defined as mentally retarded. A large number of different biological causes of mental retardation have been identified, although in as many as half the cases, no specific biological cause can be found.

Aside from some very rare cases of *savants* (individuals who are lightning calculators or mechanical whizzes), mentally retarded individuals perform more poorly than nonretarded individuals on practically any psychological test. This happens even though the retarded individuals are almost always older than the nonretarded, owing to the experimenter's desire to equate the two groups on mental age, which requires that older retarded individuals be used. (Keep in mind that the formula for IQ is mental age divided by chronological age.) This across-the-board deficit has sometimes been called the "everything deficit" (Detterman, 1979).

These deficits are not surprising. What is interesting is the nature of the deficits. That is, the retarded individual often seems to have trouble building knowledge in any sustained, effective way. Moreover, it happens in every major psychological system, even in perception. For example, if an object suddenly looms in our visual field we quickly detect and become afraid of it. But it is not so for 4-month-old Down syndrome babies who detect the looming object but seem to be less upset about it than nonretarded babies. The retarded babies cry less, freeze up less, and are less likely to show heart rate deceleration, an indicant of a stressor (Cichetti & Sroufe, 1978). It is as if the retarded babies could not use the literal information of the looming object to trigger the next, clearly intelligent response of becoming afraid. Similarly, retarded 5-year-olds who are shown a familiar sequence of events are less likely to be able to predict which event comes next if the sequence is stopped suddenly in the middle (Brooks & Van Haneghan, 1991). That is, the retarded children are less able to use redundant information to integrate and build a larger, coherent chunk of information.

Perhaps the most interesting data on building in the perceptual realm comes from studies indicating that retarded individuals have deficient stereoscopic perception. In these studies individuals are shown random element stereograms. These stereograms look like a snowy TV picture, just lots of random black and white dots. However, when they are viewed stereoscopically with special glasses or equipment, the normal viewer sees a three-dimensional (3-D) figure. Moreover, if the density of the dots is reduced to as low as 1% of the original figure, a nonretarded individual still sees depth. The retarded individual does not. Even under full density viewing conditions the retarded individual apparently does not see forms very well and cannot ably discriminate forms along the Z-axis, that is as the distance of the form from the individual increases (Fox & Oross, 1988).

The perceptual process under consideration seems to be a nonintellectual one, yet retarded individuals show a deficiency. Explanations for the process have appealed to models that invoke stages of perception. Each stage passes information along to the next stage, but retarded individuals have deficient mechanisms at various points, so they cannot build the most intelligent perception (Fox & Oross, 1988).

This pattern repeats itself in studies of the memory, problem solving, and language of the retarded. Consider some results on language because they bear most directly on proverb cognition. Mentally retarded individuals are delayed, relative to normally developing individuals, in their processing of indirect speech acts, in creating new topics in conversations, in building a coherent model of the text they read, and in following the theme of conversations (Abbeduto, 1991).

We have already discussed indirect speech acts, utterances whose underlying pragmatic meaning differs from their conventional linguistic meaning. For example, the teacher who looks at a pupil and says with a smirk on his face, "Are you going to do your homework?" is probably not asking a straightforward question, but issuing a command, "Do your homework!" Indirect speech acts can become very subtle of course. The recipient of an indirect speech act, including proverbs, must take a number of factors into account—the person speaking, the context, prior communication, and so on—to infer the speaker's intended meaning. This requires building or the integration of a number of different pieces of information. Indeed, it is hard to think of linguistic situations, unless they are overlearned and ritualized, in which there is no building. In essentially all of these situations, mentally retarded individuals fail to build stable, wholistic, coherent mental models.

Being able to move between and among levels is a hallmark of intelligence. It may not be obvious when considering perception or attention. It is more evident when language is examined, but social interaction must also be considered. People do not always act in ways that are honest or consistent. They deceive, lie, fool, scheme, play out hidden agendas, and generally manifest behaviors that are not consistent with their more objective, literal-like behavior. Consideration must also be given to the symbolic meanings of ceremony, role-playing, politeness, and other ritualized aspects of social interaction. Much of social life has an "as if" quality to it, a quality that depends on levels, layering, and embeddedness of different kinds of information. In its social manifestations, especially, mental life exhibits sets of tangled hierarchies, and intelligence requires efficient movement within the hierarchies. Mentally retarded individuals are poor builders not only because they have difficulty building such hierarchies, but because they are deficient in corollary skills.

That brings us to the rest of the PLANTE model. These factors subserve the L factor in the model in that they involve mental processes that produce building.

The P factor refers to *processing efficiency*: how fast and accurately information is encoded in, retained by, transferred through, and recovered from a perceptual, memory, or thought system. It also includes the capacity of a system. On most relatively simple information processing tasks, such as those that involve short-term memory, choice reaction-time tasks, and even very brief, fraction-of-a-second (sensory) memory tests, retarded individuals perform less efficiently.

The listener must perform the proverb task (P-task) efficiently without being overwhelmed by discourse information. Listeners generally do not have 10 or even 5 seconds to figure out how a proverb fits into a conversation. The further along the listener gets in the comprehension process, the more the urgency of processing efficiency is compounded. Problems will pop up first at the literal level, then at the figurative and pragmatic levels. These levels are linked and require building.

The A factor in PLANTE refers to *attention*, the ability to select out relevant aspects of a situation, to ignore irrelevant aspects, and to flexibly shift attention when the situation requires it. Once again, mentally retarded individuals are deficient on A-factor abilities. For example, consider the results from some studies on the Stroop Test. On this test, words that refer to colors are printed in an incompatible color. The task is to report the latter (e.g., to say "green" if the word "blue" is printed in green). Most people experience interference on this task because, after all, saying "blue" when we see the word "blue" is an overlearned, automatic response for experienced readers. People get better with practice, but then when they go back to a normal reading task, saying "blue" when the word "blue" occurs presents no problems. The effect of practice on the Stroop Test does not persist, except for retarded individuals. They get better on the Stroop Test, their errors and time to do the test reduce, but when asked to read words in the usual way, they experience interference, sometimes for several months (Ellis & Dulany, 1991; Ellis, Woodley-Zanthos, Dulany, & Palmer, 1989). This has been called *cognitive inertia*, an inability to override automatic responses by more executive level attentional strategies when this is clearly the appropriate and intelligent thing to do.

Brain damage produces similar kinds of inabilities. In particular, damage to the right hemisphere can cause a variety of attention-related problems such as an inability to sustain attention, to stay aroused and alert, to flexibly shift attention, and to focus on relevant aspects of inputs (Myers, 1993). Reduced abilities in any one of these areas can make it harder to detect, integrate, recode, and revise the proper information during discourse processing, proverbs included. An individual who cannot filter out irrelevant information and focus on facial and other expressive cues, including prosodic-emotional ones, all the while being unable to shift attention to the flow of communication, will be unable to get a figurative meaning for or point of a proverb. Young children have difficulty interpreting proverbs, partly because their attentional and working memory capacity is less than it is for adults. They are less skilled in reading expressive cues and less able to rapidly shift their attention from external information to internally generated meanings.

The N factor in PLANTE refers to *novelty*, the ability to apply knowledge in new domains and in general to be flexible in the use of one's knowledge. It is characteristic of retarded individuals that they do not spontaneously transfer their knowledge from one domain to another. Full proverb comprehension requires just this, of course. A statement that applies to only a single conceptual domain is not a proverb. If an individual could understand a proverb only in conjunction with a particular kind of topic, it would seem odd and hardly smart.

The T factor in PLANTE refers to *transformations*, the various mental operations that can be performed on inputs. Given some input, call it A, intelligence requires that something be done with A, such as changing it to B or analyzing it into parts, finding an associate for it, inferring something from it, and so on.

Once again, studies indicate that retarded individuals get stuck at the A level. For example, they are less likely to rehearse words in order to remember them (Blackman & Lin, 1984), less able to identify the ambiguity and therefore the humor in cartoons (Short & Evans, 1990), and more likely to use simple rules to make a judgment (e.g., about balance scale problems) when more complex rules involving several dimensions (e.g., distance from the fulcrum, weight) need to be taken into account (Ferreti & Butterfield, 1989). If the task involves more automatic kinds of behaviors that do not require some kind of conscious mental effort, the mentally retarded individual may perform more like a nonretarded individual. But, clearly, getting around in the world and understanding it often requires elaborative mental mechanisms. Passivity precludes participation in so-called normal living. Such passivity in cases of brain damage has not gone unnoticed. Not only retarded individuals, but right hemisphere-damaged individuals are more likely to stay at the literal propositional level of text (Frederickson & Stemmer, 1993) and be unable to revise this level to get a new model of the text. Indeed, there is some evidence that mentally retarded individuals focus more on the sequential syntactic aspects of linguistic inputs than on the more important semantic aspects (Abbeduto & Nuccio, 1991). There is an intellectual drive to language understanding that requires a sustained ability to repair, revise, and move on, and it is often missing in the linguistic performance of retarded and brain-damaged individuals.

As applied to proverbs, the T factor is present at every stage of processing. In fact, there are no stages without transformations on inputs. In writing a computer program for the P-task, whether creation, production, or comprehension, the need for a variety of transformations would become evident.

Finally, the E factor in PLANTE refers to *expertise*, how much an individual knows about particular domains. Practically by definition, retarded individuals show across-the-board deficits in expertise. Brain damage, however, can be very selective in eradicating knowledge. An individual may be able to recognize familiar faces but not the meanings of facial expressions. As Restak (1994) stated, they may be able to define a word but not read it, define inanimate things such as a chair but not animate things such as a pig, recognize pictures of most cultural artifacts except musical instruments, and ignore things in the left visual field but not the right. Individuals with brain damage may also remember the general meanings of things (e.g., how to play chess) but not their personal experience with these things (e.g., remembering that one played chess an hour ago) (Tulving, 1989).

Clearly, intelligent use of proverbs requires extensive knowledge, both of a domain-specific as well as domain-free kind. Getting the literal meaning for a proverb requires knowing the core meanings of its words and what the causal structure of events is in the domains of those meanings, but also a basic understanding of all the different domains in which a proverb could possibly be applied. Thus although we tend to think of intelligence in terms of quickness and general problem-solving skills, the fact is that a large knowledge base is a prerequisite. Experts on expertise are fond of saying that physicists are not necessarily adept at fixing their cars. In contrast, expertise in understanding proverbs rarely draws on technical forms of expertise but, rather, on more common, everyday, socially shared forms of knowledge. This is the kind of knowledge that intelligence tests attempt to assess, of course, so it is another reason why performance on proverb subtests of general intelligence correlates with overall test scores.

SUMMARY

The brain has evolved so that the left hemisphere makes rapid computations regarding the phonology, syntax and immediate semantics of linguistic inputs. The right hemisphere is far less accomplished in this respect, but it contributes semantic scope and an appreciation of pragmatic points to the process, albeit at a slower pace. There is division of labor but also cooperation between the two hemispheres, so both are necessary for complete proverb comprehension. The DARTS model was proposed to capture what the right hemisphere's contributions might be.

Nevertheless, a healthy brain does not begin to understand proverbs, even under optimal processing conditions, until about 7 years of age. Full explication of the developmental process awaits an adequate integration of proverb theory, methodological particulars, and theories of cognition.

In particular, proverb processing requires a fair degree of intelligence, which seems to be intimately related to an appreciation of indirectness and dependent on having the subskills necessary to build connected layers of information. The PLANTE model was presented as a means of organizing the interrelationship of proverbs, intelligence, indirectness, and mental building.

7

New Horizons

ℬ ◆ ℭ

The prior chapters tell the current story about proverb cognition, but the story is incomplete. There are gaps in our understanding because the database is inadequate, and theorizing has not been detailed or comprehensive enough. Proverbs could also be used in a wider variety of situations. New studies, new theoretical approaches, and new applications are the themes of this chapter. Of course, new studies may require some new ideas, so the material in these two sections is somewhat interchangeable.

NEW STUDIES

There are a number of areas in which basic research is needed. This partly reflects the difficulty of doing certain kinds of research, but it also indicates the lack of a clear theoretical guide.

Production

This text emphasizes proverb comprehension rather than production. The reason is that little is known, from a cognitive standpoint, about the conditions under which proverbs are uttered and, especially, which proverbs are uttered and why. A number of field studies have examined proverb usage, especially in African societies (for reviews see Monye, 1996; Yankah, 1989a). One question is whether and how the data provided by these studies can be translated into basic cognitive scientific constructs. In this regard one hypothesis is momentarily ventured.

Ideally, proverb production should be recorded when it happens, but this would require a great deal of effort, and even more luck. Yankah (1989b) discussed the problems inherent in studying proverb production. He opted for techniques that come closest to natural ecological conditions, including the tape recording of normal conversations. Other techniques, such as asking informants about their use of proverbs and elicitation through imagined situations, are deemed less valid by Yankah. Almost all researchers have used these more direct techniques, however, by somehow arranging for proverb use. For example, Briggs (1985) used tape recordings of conversations in his presence, whereas Penfield and Duru (1988) used hypothetical situations designed to elicit proverb use and commentary thereon. Gokhan (1992) used an ethnological approach involving diaries, interviews, and participant involvement to analyze the conditions under which proverbs were uttered in a town in Turkey. Various social-psychological factors were found to influence proverb use: the purpose in uttering the proverb, the type and familiarity of relationship between speaker and hearer, and the particular proverb topic. Thirteen different cultural rules were identified that were necessary to define three levels of expertise in proverb use, namely, knowing the proverb's meaning, the details of the speaker–hearer relationship, and what behaviors are appropriate in the situation.

This kind of cultural level data is interesting and valuable on its own level, but it can also play a role in theorizing about the microcognition of proverb production. Apparently, mature proverb use entails a number of relatively unconscious felicity conditions, akin perhaps to production rules that are used in some computer based models of memory (Anderson, 1983). These rules are essentially condition–action or if–then kinds of rules. When certain conditions are present, then certain actions can take place: When the light is red, put your foot on the brake, or when the baseball game is tied in the late innings and you have runners on first and second base with no outs, then bunt. The intent of production rules, of course, is to capture certain kinds of knowledge that people have, particularly procedural knowledge. This is knowledge about how to do things, including tying one's shoelaces, adding a column of numbers, and searching for a needle in a haystack. The kind of rules that Briggs (1985), Gokhan (1992) and others claim underlie proverb use might profitably be thought of as production rules. As the data on proverb production suggests, these rules can, with experience, become automatized, compressed, and tacit. The resulting cognitive process is one of complex pattern matching, in which production rules interact with other forms of knowledge, and the whole is integrated in working memory. In conclusion, this is a good example of how data from one view of the proverb can facilitate theorizing that stems from another view.

Indirect evidence about proverb use comes from studies that estimate the size of the cultural proverb stock in long-term memory. Hoffman conducted free recall and recognition studies showing that college students in the United States may have as many as 300 proverbs in long-term memory, with great variability around this number (Hoffman & Honeck, 1987). Unfortunately, this number tells us little about circumstances of use, and when this is taken into account, the number for both actually used (active stock) and recognized (passive stock) proverbs could be much higher. Other techniques have produced varying estimates of familiarity with, though not necessarily use of proverbs (Mieder, 1992, reviews these studies).

Experimental studies of proverb production are not out of the question. Experimental participants could be presented specific topics, then asked to retrieve a known proverb or even to make up one that would fit the topic. Participants could also be asked to play the role of some character in a scene and then supply a proverb at some point in the unfolding plot. Various social-psychological variables could be manipulated to produce a clearer picture of the cognitive matrix that underlies proverb production. Other manipulations could be tried as well, including providing participants a choice of proverbs to be used.

The cognitive ideals hypothesis could frame some of this work. In general, it can be hypothesized that people create and use proverbs when things are not right, that is, when some event is perceived to be inconsistent with some ideal, standard, or norm. Therefore, people should be more inclined to produce a proverb to the extent that the perceived inconsistency is greater. There should be less inclination to produce a proverb when the ideal is met or when no ideal is involved. Both proverb usage and novel proverb creation are implicated here. That is, perceived discrepancies from an ideal should lead, in the case of familiar proverbs, to more frequent usage, but also to the creation of new proverbs.

One approach to studying proverb creation in the laboratory is to model what happens outside the laboratory. The problem with this approach, of course, is that because proverb creation has not been caught in the act, we know very little about the factors responsible for the process. Generations of paremiologists have referred to the process as "the wit of one." In the speaker's proverb task (P-task), originally described in chapter 3, no position was taken regarding the added mental elements that might be necessary when someone creates a proverb. Perhaps the conventional position regarding creation is that someone interprets events from disparate domains to have the same significance and marks this significance by translating it into a proverb. Call this the *common nonliteral meaning* position.

A different position is that proverbs come into being when a quite literal description is used in an uncommon domain. For example, it is easy to imagine someone, a farmer perhaps, using the phrase *Make hay while the sun shines* to summarize his experience in how to get the best hay product. This phrase, which arouses the ideal of optimal timing, might then be used in contexts unrelated to making hay, but that nevertheless involve the same ideal. Call this the *literal description first* position. This position is less demanding on the proverb creator, for two reasons. First, there is no initial need for constructing a deep correspondence between seemingly unrelated events. This process is delayed until the phrase is used proverbially, the generic meaning of the phrase having surely been derived in its original, literal setting. Second, the proverb is ready-made. The creator does not have to generate an appropriate, poetic-like rendition of the deeper understanding. Proverbs may be created in both ways. Clearly, however, the common nonliteral meaning route suggests a more effortful and creative process.

Language production is hard to study experimentally, but it needs to be done. Moreover, there need not be any of the time-worn tensions between experimental and nonexperimental approaches. This would only have a stultifying effect. Progress is much more likely if scholars from different areas cooperate, and proverb production is a promising topic in this regard. From this perspective, Honeck and Welge (in press) provide some interesting results on proverb creation in the laboratory.

Expertise

Expertise is a hot topic (Chi, Glaser, & Farr, 1988; Ericsson & Smith, 1991; Hoffman, 1992). Expertise has even been examined in conjunction with metaphor (Honeck, 1992), though not with proverbs. Although it is clear that there are cultural and subcultural differences in the use and possibly the comprehension of proverbs, little is known about the details of this expertise. Can experts and neophytes be identified in this realm, and if so, what makes for the difference? More basically, what goes into the making of expertise and how can it be identified?

One technique that has been used in developing expert systems is knowledge elicitation (Hoffman, 1992). Therefore, if the reader will indulge me (the author), I would like to relate some early personal impressions about proverbs. I vaguely remember hearing proverbs as a teenager, from whom I am not sure. I remember hearing *A stitch in time save nine* and thinking, "A stitch in time saves nine what?" Insofar as a linguistic theory would automatically place "stitches" in a deep structure for this sentence, my own fumbling effort was not consistent with this practice. The general sense I have of early exposure to proverbs is that they were somewhat alien—odd sorts of things that got said once in a while and took too long to figure out anyway. I also remember hearing *A bird in the hand is worth two in the bush* and failing to get any real click of comprehension. Of course, one has to understand that a bird in the hand is actually worth having, literally. I do not remember getting past this stage. In short, I suspect that my teenage mind took some proverbs much too literally, perhaps because they were pragmatically odd and because the symbolism in some was beyond my reckoning. Schooling might have had something to do with it because education tends to be literalistic and fact oriented. There is nothing wrong with that, but it produces a mindset that makes nonliteral processing more difficult.

There are certain lessons in all this. Efficient proverb processing has a number of prerequisites, mentioned throughout the book and especially in connection with children's processing of proverbs. A key issue is problem recognition. A major developmental factor here is the extent to which a listener has developed communication skills, including the tacit understanding that people do not always mean what they say. Thus, one might expect large individual differences in sensitivity to the possibility of nonliteral speech acts.

The development of proverb expertise is likely to produce several effects beyond better problem-recognition skills. In particular, expertise should increase the size of proverb memory, sensitize people to proverbs as a distinct genre, make people aware of processing mode and mindset, automate proverb processing and usage, make people aware of and consider different kinds of meanings, sensitize people to ambiguity and the need to persist in searching for a meaning, in general, make people more aware of the power of language. Finally, the public use of proverbs is likely to change with expertise. People know what style of language to use in particular circumstances, and because proverbs are not "in" for mainstream U.S. culture, proverb expertise may lead to highly discriminant usage.

Because proverbs in some African societies are more highly valued than in Western European and North American societies, experts are more likely to be found there. In particular, expertise in proverb use is likely to be more widespread. For example, the proverb seems to sample every aspect of culture among the Igbo people of Nigeria, so there are many skilled proverb users. This skill is manifested in the many strategic ways in which proverbs can be used, such as in opening conversations, closing them, softening arguments, and generally enveloping an entire conversation in a more aesthetic way (Nwachukwu-Agbada, 1994). It would be most informative if a theoretical link could be made between proverb expertise and expertise in other domains. This would require more in-depth study of individual proverb users.

From a performance standpoint, expertise in comprehension should yield some predictable effects: faster problem recognition, faster construction of and better figurative meanings, faster ability to recognize and construct examples, and better ability to recognize more distant examples. Expertise in production would imply greater facility in deciding when to use a proverb, how to use it, what proverb to use, and, of course, a larger memory stock of proverbs to select from.

Proverb Dimensions

Proverbs differ on a number of dimensions. Some have been analyzed empirically. Higbee and Millard (1983) obtained ratings on the visual imagery and familiarity for 203 sayings, including some proverbs. The correlation between these two factors was .57. Norms for imagery, concreteness, goodness, and familiarity were also obtained by Benjafield, Frommhold, Keenan, Muckenheim, and Mueller (1993) on 500 proverbs taken from the *Oxford Dictionary of English Proverbs* (Wilson, 1970). The correlations between these dimensions varied from .30 for goodness and concreteness to .65 for imagery and concreteness.

Norms can be quite valuable for researchers who do laboratory work with proverbs. A practical consideration, however, is that many of the proverbs appearing in dictionaries are often unsuitable for research. For example, proverbs frequently are syntactically or semantically deviant, characteristics that often present methodological problems, unless, of course, they are the object of interest. One solution is to develop a corpus of more experiment-friendly proverbs by culling dictionaries or, better yet, composing new proverbs. The new ones would be unfamiliar, of course. If familiarity was of interest, this could be handled by using culturally familiar proverbs or by experimentally varying exposure to the new proverbs and thereby affecting their familiarity. In any event, there is a need for normative data on a more diversified set of proverbs.

In general, there has been little experimental investigation of proverb dimensions other than that of familiarity. Predictably, familiarity speeds comprehension (Case, 1991; Temple, 1993). Penn, Jacob, and Brown (1988) presented Gorham's Proverbs Test to an African-American sample and found that familiarity increased the likelihood of a correct interpretation, although some unfamiliar proverbs were not interpreted at all. Similarly, Cunningham, Ridley, and Campbell (1987) used Gorham's test with college students and found that there was a small positive correlation between self-rated proverb familiarity and interpretive quality, but only when the proverbs were familiar. Mieder (1992) discussed various studies of familiarity in the context of proverb literacy in a culture. In summary, it is clear that proverb familiarity affects several aspects of performance, most notably comprehension speed and quality.

Other proverb dimensions have received less experimental attention. Walsh (1988) investigated proverb concreteness-imagery and concluded that concreteness was necessary for proverbialness (see chapter 4). Honeck (1973) found that more concrete proverbs were remembered better than less concrete ones. Gibbs (1995) reported that people's images for proverbs are consistent and detailed, and that there is less consistency of imagery for proverb definitions and for proverbs that are unfamiliar but synonymous with familiar ones. Gibbs interpreted these findings in terms of the conceptual metaphor concept. There may be more parsimonious interpretations of these and related data, namely that familiarity and concreteness play the major role in yielding imagery and its consistency, or lack thereof.

Although proverb familiarity and concreteness have been investigated to some extent, this is not true of other dimensions. Even proverb comprehensibility has escaped psycholinguistic attention, as have quaintness, aptness, humor, and aesthetics. Some of these less salient dimensions are undoubtedly correlated, but then so too are imagery, comprehensibility, and familiarity. Data on new dimensions might provide some insight into fundamental questions about what makes some proverbs more comprehensible than others and why proverbs are used in specific ways. The frequent use of proverbs in some African societies implicitly attests to their multidimensional character because on any given occasion, some particular dimension may be used for effect. The cognitive ideals hypothesis could be helpful here, in the sense that comprehensible proverbs might be those whose generic ideal is more transparent. Ideals also undoubtedly differ in many ways that would affect the particulars of their usage.

Emotion

Why has so much been written about proverbs? Why do people create them? Why are many fascinated by them, whereas others groan at their mere mention? What accounts for their staying power in religions, cultures and individual lives?

A good part of the answer to these questions is that proverbs arouse a complex of emotions. Emotion is one dimension of proverbs but it deserves a section of its own.

It is hard to think of an emotion that proverbs could not arouse, from humor to awe to disgust. How do they do it? Proverbs arouse meanings at the word, literal sentence, figurative, and pragmatic levels. Any of these levels can arouse emotion, and they typically do so in concert. The social use of proverbs also contributes to their affective impact. After all, proverbs are used in everyday life to make a point, hardly ever a neutral one, about some matter. People express opinions, attitudes, and beliefs with proverbs, and these are affect laden. Then there is the manner in which proverbs are used in conversations and texts, namely as discourse deviant utterances that distance the speaker from the topic.

Norrick (1994b) claimed that proverbs encode emotion by a variety of devices. They arouse dramatic images as in *Don't cut off your nose to spite your face* and *Don't throw out the baby with the bath water*. They use rhetorical devices such as hyperbole, as in *Old soldiers never die* and *Your eyes are bigger than your stomach*. They frequently refer to charged scenarios involving animals that are then projected onto the proverb's topic, for example, *The silent sow gets all the swill* or *Rats desert a sinking ship*. They often use impolite or improper words, as in *Put up or shut up* and *Them as has, gits*. They use unique figures of speech such as paradox in such proverbs as *The longest way is the short way* or *More haste, less speed*. Norrick also pointed out that proverbs may evaluate emotions, making some emotions bad (e.g., anger, pride), some better (e.g., sorrow, grief), and others best (e.g., joy, love).

If there is anything unique about the way in which proverbs arouse emotion, it may lie in the interaction among three factors. First, there is the proverb's frequent use of poetic devices, whether metaphor, alliteration, rhyme, meter, assonance, and so on. The proverb's use of oppositions and contrasts is relevant here as well. Second, if the cognitive ideals hypothesis is on the right track, proverbs tap into universal feelings and emotions because these are intimately tied to the cognitive content of the ideals, which are states of perfection, the way things are or should be. They therefore have strong emotional potential. Thus, proverbs can sound just right, beautiful, and true, making people feel that all is right in the world. In this sense, there is a forceful aesthetic to proverbs. Potentially, ideals-disconfirming proverbs pack more emotional punch than ideals-confirming proverbs. The reason, of course, is that deviation from the ideal is an occasion for strong emotion.

Clearly, for all these effects to happen, the individual must have constructed a figurative meaning that approximates the underlying ideal. Of course, under certain circumstances, this same figurative meaning may well evoke the standard "proverb groan." It is precisely because proverbs remind people of ideas with which they are already familiar that they can evoke a negative emotion or that proverbs as a whole are sometimes reviled. There are proverb haters as well as proverb lovers. In cultures where the elders are more highly regarded, proverbs may take on a more positive connotation, not just because of the message they bear, but also because they promote social bonding with these revered figures. Finally, there is the gnomic, omnitemporal form of the proverb that contributes to a momentary sense of timelessness and universality.

It is interesting to speculate about the emotional power of proverbs as indeed many scholars have. There is, nevertheless, a dearth of strictly empirical work in which large numbers of informants or experimental participants are observed using and comprehending the emotion of proverbs.

Mental Testing and Proverb Interpretations

Proverb interpretations have been used for almost a century to assess sanity, intelligence, thought disorder, brain damage, and basic proverb understanding. Testing in conjunction with intelligence and brain damage is discussed in chapter 6. Testing of individuals diagnosed as schizophrenic began in earnest with Goldstein (1936; Goldstein & Scherer, 1941) and Benjamin (1944), both of whom remarked on the relatively concrete interpretations of these individuals.

Gorham's Proverb Test (Gorham, 1956, 1963) was introduced in the 1950s and has been used rather extensively since that time. The test has two formats, one in which people are asked to write out an interpretation for each of 12 familiar proverbs (this test has three versions with different proverbs for each), and another that uses a multiple-choice format for the same proverbs. In his original paper Gorham (1956) stated that "excellence of expression was not to be scored; only the ability to change the concrete symbols into general concepts or abstractions," and that "rationality of the abstractions was not considered; bizarre or autistic conceptions were given the same value as more usual responses as long as they met the criteria of converting the concrete symbolism of the proverb into concepts" (p. 3). One sees the beginnings of significant problems with this approach for both reliability and validity, issues that have plagued investigators since that time. (Gibbs, 1995, discussed this matter.)

Gorham's Proverbs Test has been used with limited success. Aside from the scoring issue, there are other complications. For example, the test uses only familiar proverbs (e.g., *Where there's a will there's a way*; *Strike while the iron is hot*) although some of the proverbs on the test that were familiar in the 1950s may be much less so now (e.g., *The used key is always bright*; *A stream cannot rise higher than its source*).

In the author's view, nearly 100 years of testing on verbal interpretations of proverbs has not provided a solid foundation for inferences, either about the interpretations themselves or, especially, concerning what the interpretations imply about mental status. The problems run much deeper than the scoring system used and characteristics of the proverbs, and they are not unique to Gorham's Test. There are at least six related reasons for the poor showing of tests that have used verbal interpretations.

First, it seems like a classic case of putting too many eggs in one basket. It is one thing to ask people to interpret proverbs in an experimental context, then use their interpretations to predict later performance, such as recall of the proverbs or the ability to recognize new examples of them. This is a relatively closed system, vis-à-vis validity. It is another matter to use peoples' interpretations to assess the normality of their thinking. Test administrators have simply asked too much of a single test, especially one that uses a single linguistic genre. Even assuming adequate scoring systems and reliable data, there are too many factors that can affect both proverb comprehension and the ability to put this comprehension into words. Meaning and its expression are arguably quite different things. People may have a serviceable understanding but not be able to express it, or they may express it ambiguously, fractiously, or bizarrely, for reasons that have nothing to do with abstraction abilities.

Proverb comprehension itself can be affected by a host of variables: vocabulary, syntactic complexity, semantic logic, and desymbolization requirements, as well as the various dimensions of the proverb discussed previously. Moreover, interpretations are typically sought in the absence of a topic and larger context, so that the various comprehension factors become more important. There is nothing inherently invalid about presenting proverbs in isolation, but when this is done, one must be acutely aware of the factors that could affect comprehension. As the overall thrust of this text implies, it would also be propitious if the test was administered and interpreted with some appreciation of the comprehension P-task. Isolated proverbs place an immense burden on cognitive resources and any one of the P-task subtasks could break down, resulting in poor comprehension or expression. As was the case when discussing comprehension of proverbs by children and by individuals with brain damage, there is the need to have a simultaneous knowledge about proverbs, models of proverb processing, and the test-taker.

These conditions have almost never been met in all the years of testing. In certain respects, mental status testing with proverbs has been a shot in the dark, as if by analogy we could assess someone's general perceptual-motor skills by giving that person a free-throw shooting test in a noncompetitive basketball situation. One could learn a few things about these skills, but the ability to predict performance on other perceptual-motor tasks would be jeopardized. Inferences about a general perceptual-motor ability would surely be suspect. Yet this is essentially what has happened when proverb interpretations have been used to infer mental status.

Second, there have been few studies on the syntactic, semantic, and stylistic details of interpretations (but see Buhofer, 1987). Under this circumstance, and given the problems with Gorham's test, recent investigators have attempted to develop new tests and scoring systems. For example, Brundage (1993) analyzed the interpretations of brain-damaged and non-brain-damaged individuals in terms of adequacy, promptness, and conciseness. Strub and Black (1985) revised the Gorham Proverbs Test and scored interpretations in terms of whether they were semiabstract or abstract, a division that Gibbs (1995) questioned. Testing of individuals diagnosed as schizophrenic has resulted in response categories of bizarre, literal, abstract, and concrete (Krueger, 1978), which can be clinically diagnostic categories, but there are ambiguities in these categories as well.

A third, related problem is that there is little normative data on proverb interpretation, irrespective of the purpose of the proverb test. Without this data it becomes difficult to interpret any performance. This would be like deriving a score from what we presumed to be a test of humor, but having no other scores on the test for comparing it. As Gibbs (1995) put it, "Without some consensual agreement from a large sample of healthy participants, a patient's response cannot be validly assessed as right or wrong, normal or abnormal, much less judged as abstract or concrete" (p. 147). Using this purely empirical approach, we could get a large number of interpretations for a proverb, find the dominant one, and make this the standard against which all others are judged. Goodness would undoubtedly be a multidimensional variable, however, and it would behoove us to ferret out these dimensions. The score for any given interpretation would therefore amount to a profile on these dimensions, not just, say, a single score for abstractness. Using this approach, interpretive goodness becomes a statistical matter, leading to a bell-curve form of reasoning. This is not theoretically satisfying, but it would be an advance over the current state of affairs.

A fourth problem is the lack of an adequate theoretical framework for constructing proverb interpretation tests and for judging interpretation goodness (abstractness, correctness, etc.). For example, we might ask why there is a dominant interpretation and whether it could be predicted. Using the cognitive ideals hypothesis, it might be possible to predict the kind of interpretations that are most likely for a given proverb. In any event, some combination of empirical norming and theoretical perspective would provide a more solid basis for constructing proverb tests, interpreting the data they yield, and justifying inferences based on the data.

Fifth, a variety of factors are involved in testing with proverbs that are present in all forms of testing, but that become highly salient when proverbs are used. There are the usual issues of the testing situation: the relationship between the tester and testee, the purpose of the test, the testee's awareness of this, and the physical and mental state of the testee. However, because proverbs are something like verbal Rorschach tests, yet seem to require a correct interpretation, it would seem prudent to provide testees with some idea of how a correct interpretation looks. Some practice with feedback on pretest proverbs might make the task less ambiguous to the testee. If so, the test's reliability and validity might improve.

Finally, there is the issue of exactly what is being tested when people are asked to interpret proverbs. The major assumption seems to be that proverbs test abstract thinking ability. Generally speaking, that is true insofar as the test scorer gives higher scores to interpretations that are deemed more correct and correctness amounts to having provided an abstractly stated interpretation that captures what the tester deems is the true underlying meaning of the proverb. But as indicated previously, if the test-taker does not know that this sort of response is being solicited, or of what it consists, then the assumption may be wrong. It may be wrong for other reasons as well, because the expressions of people in social contexts, including test-taking contexts, can be shaped by a host of factors. If the testees are in a schizophrenic state, they may not decode the proverb well enough; they may be highly distractible; they may be providing safe, literal answers; they may be overly egocentric and fail to take other people's point of view, and so on (Gibbs, 1995). If test-takers are normal, healthy individuals, they may not be providing samples of their abstract thinking ability, because if familiar proverbs are used, they may be simply "dumping" already known interpretations, or they may feel uncomfortable about the entire testing situation, especially when they receive a proverb that is difficult to interpret.

Still, it is hard to deny that, under optimal circumstances, something like an abstraction ability is being tested. That is not the problem, however. It is rather that so many other things are being tested simultaneously: basic linguistic ability, attention span, working memory abilities, information processing speed, metalinguistic ability, verbal expressive ability, and less strictly cognitive factors such as cooperativeness, industriousness, the desire to do well, and a general willingness to solve verbal puzzles that have no obvious significance or payoff. Under these circum-stances, the urgency of having an appreciation for the complexity of the proverb, of the P-task involved, and a theoretical guide to these matters becomes clear.

In any event, there is room for the construction and use of new kinds of proverb tests, including those that test without requiring verbal interpretations. For example, proverb familiarity could purposely be manipulated and built into a test. Empirically derived norms could be used to develop a multiple-choice test involving examples, with some of these being visual. Another version of the test could require people to explain the connection between a proverb and an instance. A larger proverbs test that incorporated some of these modifications might be a more valid test of abstract thinking than a single test that yields only interpretations.

Neuropsychology is an area in which the foregoing caveats apply. We already know that damage to the right cerebral hemisphere produces problems in interpreting familiar proverbs. New tests could provide more specific information about the nature of the dysfunction and potentially about proverb processing. For example, it would be interesting to know whether right brain-damaged patients could interpret proverbs by means of pictures. However, in assembling a verbal interpretation for proverbs, this interpretation is spoken or written by the left hemisphere, which makes the interpretation of right brain damage more complicated. A task that did not demand a verbal response might therefore provide an interesting comparison with results obtained using the traditional interpretation task. Similar considerations apply to proverb testing with other special populations, and the DARTS model could be used to design studies that pinpoint the precise nature of any right hemispheric dysfunction. The results of such studies could have some therapeutic benefit.

Intelligence, Creativity, and Skill

In this text, proverbs and figurative language have been framed in terms of intelligence, and intelligence in terms of the concept of indirectness. Of course, many scholars have done something like this in using proverbs to help assess intelligence and general mental health. The discussion in the previous section implies that this connection is suspect, however. It actually is if we restrict our discussion of intelligence to performance on extant proverb tests and if we take a limited view of the requirements that underlie proverb cognition.

The use of proverbs in several African societies is sometimes taken as a measure of skill and intelligence. For example, Obeng (1994) found that Akan speakers in Ghana often used proverbs as indirect means of saving face, avoiding crises, and preserving politeness. Because these are considered wise things to do, proverbs take on the same quality. Monye (1987) argued along similar lines in his study of some Igbo people in Nigeria. In particular, he showed how metaphor, simile and wellerism are used in proverbs to avoid boredom, to persuade, and to attain other social goals. Nkara (1992) presented an intriguing study of the use of "Bisisimi" among Teke (Bantu) speakers in the Congo. During certain ceremonies, older males chant proverbs in a kind of war of wits, one that no doubt has implications for the intelligence attributed to the contestants.

These several pieces of data strongly suggest that there is great skill involved in the use of proverbs in some societies. Moreover, the proverb performances in question all appear to involve the use of proverbs in indirect ways to accomplish a variety of personal and social goals. When we look at the larger picture of individual differences and proverbs, the connection of proverbs and intelligence becomes clearer still. That is, proverb use is practically unheard of in children before the age of 10, in the mentally retarded, in autistic individuals, and in individuals with certain forms of brain damage. All of this suggests that in using proverbs to assess intelligence, tests that engage production might be considered along with those on comprehension. The data that stems from the cultural view of proverbs can uniquely inform us about how such tests could be constructed.

Of course, just because common folk regard some proverb usages as intelligent does not mean that they are, nor does the absence of proverb production and understanding in young children, brain-damaged individuals, and other special populations directly implicate intelligence. We have to know what intelligence consists of to make this judgment. But however intelligence is conceived, either as a biological, societal, contextual, or information-processing phenomenon, it is clear that the proverb is implicated at each of these levels. Most certainly, proverb processing entails many mental activities that are typically discussed in conjunction with intelligence: analogy, induction, synthesis, pattern matching, mental flexibility, mental speed, mental transformations, and a storehouse of knowledge. It may be that the intelligence involved in proverbs is limited to verbal intelligence, but it is hard to deny that proverbs partake of it.

However, it is too limiting to restrict the discussion to the proverb–intelligence relationship. Creativity, talent, and social skills are involved as well. Especially, the person who creates a proverb, but also those who use them appropriately, have performed a miniature form of art. Such creativity complements an underlying intelligence. The fact that proverbs entrain intelligence, creativity, and skill no doubt helps to explain their universal fascination and appeal. However, it will take a deep theoretical understanding to piece these three elements together.

NEW THEORETICAL APPROACHES

Our discussion in this text has demonstrated that proverbs draw on many mental resources and activities. A variety of cognitive scientific concepts, areas, and theories have been used to elucidate this activity. Gaps in our theoretical understanding remain, however.

Microcognition and Comprehension

We need to know more about the microprocessing that occurs as people move from initial exposure to a proverb to complete understanding and use. The transition from literal to figurative meaning is a process that takes time, and important cognitive operations take place during that time. Little is known about the details of this process. The same can be said of instantiation. Proverb comprehension has been caught at the points of phase completion, but not during the phases per se. The problem is that processing may be so rapid that it eludes scientific analysis.

There are sets of related ideas that may begin to resolve this issue: semantic network, spreading activation within the network, unconscious priming, connectionism. The premise vis-á-vis semantic networks is that a word-concept is represented in a large semantic matrix of other concepts (Collins & Loftus, 1975). Priming techniques have been used often in conjunction with this framework, providing evidence that some contexts can automatically activate particular meanings. By implication, people have no awareness that a large set of such meanings have been activated. The organization of the semantic tree seems to guide the meaning selection process in subsymbolic ways. (For an original description of the spreading activation model, see Collins & Loftus, 1975, and for an update Chang, 1986.)

The relevance to proverb processing is that literal meanings, although variable for a given proverb, are accessed in relatively unconscious ways, as are the processes that move literal meanings into figurative ones. Perhaps the priming technique could tell us more about the kinds of information, and therefore the kinds of processes, that facilitate or inhibit development of these meanings.

The semantic network notion is related to connectionism, which is essentially the idea that the mind is a brain that creates knowledge by building connections between nodes in a vast network. Inputs (e.g., words) to the network activate some nodes, inhibit others, and over time begin to produce a stable pattern of response across the network. The system's knowledge is in the pattern of connections or, rather, it *is* the pattern of connections. The strength of the knowledge is reflected in the weight of the connections. In fact, connectionist models amount to making networks function as statistical regression machines that compute the optimal relationship between a set of input variables. Thus, connectionism can be viewed as a modern, mathematically sophisticated form of associationism. The power of the approach comes with the realization that networks can be extremely massive (e.g., the brain has been estimated to contain 10^{15} connections; Sejnowski & Churchland, 1989). There is a great deal of parallel processing, and pieces of knowledge can be distributed redundantly across the network. This last property is valuable because, if one piece is inactivated, another may still be functional, a property that distinguishes connectionist models from traditional semantic network models (Haberlandt, 1994).

Connectionistic models have been applied with some success to processes that involve pattern recognition such as recognition of speech sounds and words, and to pattern generation such as learning the linguistic past tense rule. (See Haberlandt, 1994, for an introduction to these ideas.) According to Haberlandt, "Connectionist models are well suited for situations where several conditions must be met at the same time in order to recognize an object or carry out an act" (p. 168). That is, they are suited to situations in which there are multiple constraints that have to be satisfied. This is clearly the case when it comes to proverb production, but it may also apply to comprehension because literal meaning, figurative meaning, and topic have to be pieced together.

Basically the job of the meaning calculator is to come up with a sensible meaning, given the constraints of existing relevant information. Sentences, proverbs included, can arouse a vast number of meanings, only some of which are relevant. Mutual constraints should operate to prevent irrelevant meanings from developing, while facilitating more sensible ones. Part of the problem here is that meaning generation is both bottom-up and top-down. The particular word meanings that get aroused will depend on the overall sentence context. Connectionist models are capable of handling some top-down effects. For example, the facilitative effect of words on letter perception has been treated in connectionist terms (McClelland & Rumelhart, 1981).

According to present knowledge, semantic network and connectionist models have not been applied to proverbs. However, Chandler (1991) used connectionism to describe metaphor comprehension. Here, a metaphor such as "Joan is a peach" would be interpreted by a process that activates the microfeatures associated with Joan (a female human) but inhibits the microfeatures of peach that do not comport with Joan (e.g., has a yellow color). Features of Joan that might have been weakly activated (pleasantness, nice smile) connect with the stronger value of some of these features for peach. Thus, an originally weakly activated feature such as pleasantness gains in strength. Context and background knowledge strengthens or weakens the initial level of activation of particular features. In general, "the microfeatures and microrelationships representing one concept interact with those of another concept through mutual excitation and competition to arrive at an interpretation for the sentence" (Chandler, 1991, p. 253).

These various network-like models look promising for studying proverb microcognition. However, they have shortcomings, some that are general and others that are more specific to inputs such as proverbs. For example, these models can be too flexible and too powerful and thus lead to post hoc predictions; the choice of semantic primitives is exceedingly contentious; context and background knowledge can be hard to incorporate into these models;

and more conscious reflective processes can override associative mechanisms. Unless a proverb is familiar, figurative meaning contruction and getting the point may be effortful and time consuming, and less likely therefore to invoke the mechanisms that underlie these models. The mind is complex, and there is no reason to believe that it could not make shifts from one sort of mode to another, using potentially different kinds of theoretical mechanisms. One pertinent thought here is that neuropsychological studies of metaphor and idiom comprehension have suggested that quick, relatively automatic semantic processes occur, as indicated by the results of priming studies, but also less quick, more effortful, and attention-demanding pragmatic processes (Burgess & Chiarello, 1996). This could be happening with proverbs as well.

In conclusion, there is a great deal of room for insight into the microworkings of proverb comprehension. Existing studies and theories have only touched the surface.

ECBT-2

The two additions to the extended conceptual base theory, the cognitive ideals hypothesis and DARTS, are invoked numerous times throughout this text. Whether these additions will stand the test of theoretical and empirical scrutiny remains to be seen.

For now we briefly pursue an interesting implication of the cognitive ideals hypothesis. This is the notion that generic ideals may not be specifically encoded in semantic or episodic memory, but, rather, in a more tacit, intuitive way. First, consider some generic ideals:

There is an optimal time for something to be accomplished.

Conserve those things that have potential value.

Something that has a positive value has other positive values.

Success in reaching a goal requires flexibility.

For an instrument to perform optimally it must be in working order.

Things are as they appear to be.

A basic characteristic of something remains a constant.

Effects are proportional to their causes.

A part of a whole needs to fit the whole.

Physical principles constrain physical events.

Inspection of these ideals suggests several things. First, they do not look like the kind of information that is directly learned and stored in long-term memory. They look more like abstract, philosophical generalizations based on experience. If we asked people whether they know these things, they would probably say yes, but they would probably also say that they do not know them in the way that they know that robins are birds or that they had a salad for lunch. They would be unlikely to say, "I remember that things are as they appear to be."

Second, these ideals do not manifest an obvious organization. Therefore, the ideals are not good candidates for inclusion in semantic or episodic memory. In fact, it seems inappropriate to describe them as having been stored. They have more the character of unconscious generalizations that developed in conjunction with other memories. They seem like ghost memories. If they need to be put into conscious form, then if anything, they are assembled in an ad hoc fashion, based on some event (e.g., a proverb) that arouses them. The apparent intuitive character of cognitive ideals makes them good candidates for description in connectionistic and similar terms. That is, their unconscious, nonwell-formed, nonrule-based, pattern cohort-seeking, impressionistic character seems to disqualify them as strictly rule-based. At least, this is true when they are first aroused or when there is no need to make them conscious and explicit. (In this sense, the author's grammatically clean linguistic descriptions of them is probably misleading.) Cognitive ideals are involved in reasoning, but perhaps most often a more associatively based reasoning (see Sloman, 1996, for a discussion of associative-versus rule-based reasoning).

Integrating the Views of the Proverb

An underlying theme in our discussion is that there is a need for a rapproachement of the different views of the proverb. The proverb is complex, so its explication will only suffer if scholars do not consider data and theory from all of the various views of the proverb. This text has drawn largely on material from the cultural, formal, and cognitive views. In many cases, it was shown how the cultural view could help the cognitive theorist, as, indeed, it is clear that the formal view has all along. Perhaps the cognitive view can be of help to its scientific partners, and, potentially, much can be learned from the nonscientific views.

Chlosta and Grzybek (1995) called for a rapproachment of empirical and folkloristic paremiology. As these authors use the term, empirical refers to procedures designed to estimate the statistical frequency of proverbs. For example, the authors asked one sample of informants to indicate whether each proverb in a large collection was unknown to them. A second sample of informants was then given the first few words of the proverbs that were not marked as unknown and asked to complete them. In discussing their results, Chlosta and Grzybek pointed out that empirical methods produce data about the distribution and familiarity of proverbs, but the original constitution of the proverb set must rely on folkloristic research. Similarly, the empirical approach can provide more detailed data about proverbs, such as their variant forms.

Although the Chlosta and Grzybek study stems from the cultural view and focuses on specific questions about proverb currency, it represents a step in the right direction. Ultimately, whether our interest is in the religious significance of proverbs, how they can be used for effective counseling, or in poetry, our goal will be best served by looking at the big picture provided by all of the views. One day in the not too distant future one would therefore hope that a single, integrated view would emerge, a grand paremiological synthesis.

Toward an Integrated View of Figurative Language

In a vein similar to that of the preceeding discussion, there is the need to develop a more integrated view of figurative language. Part of the problem is that the various genres ordinarily get discussed using different vocabularies, which makes it harder to detect similarities in their workings. In part, the description of the six different genres provided in chapter 2 was designed to mitigate this problem and help the integration process along. Also, the literature has been biased toward distinguishing the tropes, an appropriate and important activity, but attempts to integrate have been virtually nonexistent (but see Gibbs, 1993; Lakoff, 1987).

In this text, the various tropes have been set within the larger framework of intelligence, and further still within the concept of indirectness. All of the tropes use indirectness to effect a reschematization of some topic. There is a rescaling, recategorization, or if one prefers, a deconstructing of traditional schemas and categories to create a new meaning. The details of this conception, however, need to be worked out.

Cognitive science is just beginning to learn how this can be done. When it comes to language, novel conjunctions of elements have always provided the impetus and testing ground for theorizing. Chomsky's (1957) theory of language was designed to address this issue on the syntactic level, and it will happen for theories of creative conceptual combination. There are efforts along these lines, but it has proved to be a daunting task. It is one thing to characterize syntactic productivity and quite another to explain how meanings get combined in sensible ways. The problem is acute even at the two-word level. For example, a guppy is a typical pet fish, but it is not a typical fish or a typical pet (Osherson & Smith, 1981). How is it then that low salient meanings get combined to produce an appropriate, serviceable, new compound meaning?

There have been various attempts to answer this question. Models have been developed to explain how adjectival and noun prototypes can be combined to produce prototypical combinations (Cohen & Murphy, 1984; Smith & Osherson, 1984). For example, how are the prototypes for "small" and "galaxy" combined to yield "small galaxy?" Smith (1988) argued that in adjective-noun combinations like "red fruit," the adjective concept does three things: (a) It selects the relevant attributes in the noun (i.e., color); (b) it "shifts all votes on that attribute into the value named by the adjective (e.g., 'red')" (p. 37) in which "votes" refers to the importance of the value; and (c) it increases the diagnosticity of the attribute, that is, its ability to predict category membership for any object that has the attribute. Unfortunately, this kind of set theory approach to the problem may be misplaced, as Lakoff (1987) argued, because, for example, a small galaxy does not seem to be the logical intersection of the set of small things and the set of galaxies, nor does a "red fruit" seem to be the intersection of things that are red and things that are fruit. This problem is recognized by theorists in the area, however, and other approaches have emerged (Wisniewski, 1996).

Nevertheless, the creative combinations approach suggests an avenue for treating the various tropes. All tropes combine concepts in seemingly odd ways. They sometimes can be reformulated linguistically so that views about conceptual combinations can be applied. For example, the format for the topic and vehicle can be changed for some simple metaphors, similes, and oxymora. A metaphor such as "Joan is a peach" can be transformed into an adjective-noun combination: "peachy Joan." This seems harmless enough and no different from saying that "red fruit" is equivalent to "the fruit is red." In the case of similes such as, "Her hair is like spaghetti," we change it to "spaghetti-like hair." Oxymora like "military intelligence" do not have to be changed.

Whether and how metonymies, idioms, and proverbs can be transformed in this manner is more problematic. Metonymy is, from one perspective, a form of "isa" metaphor. For example, using the phrase, "the paper-maker," to refer to a lawyer is to say, implicitly that "the lawyer is a paper-maker"; in transformed linguistic terms, "a lawyer paper-maker." For idioms, the connection is harder to put into a new linguistic package. But we can experiment. If Carol tells a story about a friend and this story creates a whole set of new problems, then we might say that "Carol let the cat out of the bag" or that "Carol's telling the story is a case of letting the cat out of the bag." This is also a kind of "isa" relationship.

The same issue arises in conjunction with proverbs. Suppose a business executive, who started at the lowest level in a company, rose to the top with the help of many others, then acted in a haughty way, ignoring the factors that led to his rise. We could describe him by saying, *Frog forgets he had a tail*. Reformulated, it can be expressed as "The executive's attitude about his new status is a case of *Frog forgets he had a tail*." For both idioms and proverbs, a big sentence has been constructed out of two smaller sentences, one of which is the topic and the other the vehicle for the trope in question. Although the conceptual connections between such topics and vehicles is clearly more complicated than that for, say, noun-noun combinations, there is no reason to believe that the theoretical problems are any different.

Whether these transformations do damage to the meaning and aesthetics of the original form is an empirical question. Scholars have readily acknowledged the necessity of treating synonymy in language, but have been less open to its manifestation when it comes to figurative language. That is, there is more willingness to treat as synonymous, "a red fruit" and "the fruit is red," than "peachy Joan" and "Joan is a peach." There would seem to be no advantage to keeping figurative language in a special category vis-à-vis this issue, however. In every case of tropic understanding, and however these cases might be formulated linguistically, some topic is in need of construal by virtue of its juxtaposition with some vehicle. This is not a problem unique to figurative language. As much as possible, the same set of theoretical principles should be applied to seemingly diverse phenomena. Parsimony would demand it; elegance would invite it.

The cognitive ideals hypothesis might also be extended to tropes other than the proverb. It was suggested in chapter 2 that oxymora, or at least some cases of oxymoron, function by shifting meaning away from some norm or ideal, in keeping with the normality subtraction hypothesis. "Military intelligence" makes intelligence less sparkling than its idealized state. Are ideals involved for other tropes? The classic metaphor, "Man is a wolf," partly derives its force from the hidden assumption that people should ascribe to high ethical ideals. Interpreters of this metaphor often nod their heads knowingly, as if to acknowledge frequent deviation from the ideal. This suggests that any theory treating metaphor comprehension as merely feature transfer or even as an act of categorization (e.g., Glucksberg & Keysar, 1993) will not be adequate. People have strong expectations about what is and what should be, and these will play a vital role in how metaphors are interpreted. This is not a question of the traditional notion of semantic selection restriction rules (e.g., that clouds cannot literally gulp the sun), but of people's tacit assumptions and beliefs about the world. This is just the stuff of ideals.

If this analysis of metaphor is sensible, then perhaps it applies to its close cousin, the simile, as well. The analysis seems less apt for idioms and metonymy. These tropes are used for reasons that may not entrain ideals. Idioms, for example, are not only economical, but endearing as well. They are a socially approved form of jargon, used only by and with members of a particular linguistic community. Metonymy operates under much the same conditions for similar purposes. Possibly these purposes are less conducive to the invocation of ideals than is the case for proverbs, metaphor, simile, and oxymoron. However, insofar as idioms and metonymy can be used to elicit appreciation of ideals, as happens when these forms are used in sarcastic or ironic ways, then the cognitive ideals hypothesis may be applicable.

In conclusion, although the development of theories of proverb cognition is an admirable goal, a general theory of figurative language would be much more compelling.

Computer Simulation

Computer simulation efforts might help in this endeavor. The main reason is that simulation requires that processes and structures be made explicit. A second reason is that all of this must be put into an integrated package. The author knows of no attempts to simulate proverb cognition, although there is a small literature on metaphor (Martin, 1992; Russell, 1986), including the connectionist modeling described earlier.

Computer modeling of figurative language presents a problem precisely because this language is odd, given the typical conventions about what sorts of syntactic and semantic elements can be combined. Even when top-down factors such as context and prior discourse are taken into account, when figurative genres are plugged into computer equations, the outputs look ill-formed and weird. There is the apocryphal story of a computer that interpreted *The spirit is willing but the flesh is weak* as "The vodka is good but the meat is tasteless." It is hard enough for computer programs to handle compounds such as "black bird house," let alone proverbs. Any computer program will have to incorporate all of the processes we have discussed in this text, and perhaps more, because not all of the requisite processes have been identified.

In his overview of computer modeling of figurative language, Martin (1996) stated that three kind of approaches have been used: convention-based, reasoning-based, and context-based.

The convention-based approach associates one sort of mental element with another, for example a metaphoric expression (e.g., "This marriage has hit a roadblock") with a presumed underlying metaphoric basis (e.g., "Love is a journey) or an idiom with an already stored meaning.

The reasoning-based approach relies more on compositionality and general cognitive mechanisms such as analogy. To illustrate, for metonymy, spreading activation mechanisms may be used to hook up the metonymic vehicle with its topic, or, analogy might be used to solve a metaphor.

In the context-based approach, prior discourse plays a big role in constraining possible meanings, with a particular instance of figurative language being used only as a part player in fashioning a discourse-level representation.

For proverbs, all three approaches seem to apply. With the cognitive ideals approach, intuitive mental structures underlie a proverb, proverbs are applied to topics by means of an analogy mechanism, and proverbs are merely bit players in proverb performances. Note that these three approaches parallel the three views used to treat figurative language in general (see chapter 2). The semantic view corresponds with the reasoning-based approach, the pragmatic view with the context-based approach, and the conceptualist view with the convention-based approach. The correspondence is not perfect, but it suggests that computer modeling presents the same kinds of issues and can lead to the same kinds of perspectives that have developed in noncomputer-based analyses of figurative language. Because of the precision required in computer modeling, however, this approach offers the potential for genuine advance.

NEW APPLICATIONS

Some practical applications of proverbs were discussed in conjunction with the practical view. Is there room for novel application? So long as people are in situations that call for marking, inevitabilities in other words, we can answer affirmatively.

Education

Proverbs have both important social and cognitive effects. Might these be used advantageously in explicit ways to teach important educational principles?

Proverbs provide valuable lessons in life, so could we borrow the technique of some religions and use proverbs for moral education of a nonsectarian sort? In the United States there is presently a great concern over values, especially the values that children learn, or do not learn. Do children know what it means and why it would be propitious to be honest, fair, scrupulous, unselfish, altruistic, able to forego a small frustration for a larger reward later on, and so forth? Should these values be taught explicitly in educational systems? If the answer is yes, a controversial answer no doubt, then questions of teaching technique would be raised. Proverbs could have a role here. Students could be provided with various vignettes involving cases of, say, honesty or deceit, asked to discuss them, and then provided with ways of remembering the lesson by means of the proverb. With some imagination, the stories could be constructed to be as interesting as Aesop's fables, a time-honored way of getting children to appreciate a moral point. At various intervals, students could be provided with further training. If a way could be found to help foster memory for the proverbs and facilitate their generalization beyond the schoolroom door, then such an enterprise might be worthwhile. Proverbs have been used in this way in therapeutic situations (Rogers, 1989).

Proverbs also provide a more subtle lesson in thinking. They are verbal puzzles that engage conscious components of remembering, reasoning, problem solving, and communicating. They might therefore promote these skills in other domains. Whether direct training in proverb use would promote general, domain-free thinking skills is another matter. The literature on the promotion of thinking skills is diverse but provides only some optimism that proverb training could have desirable effects. It is certainly worth a try, however. At stake are a number of processes and skills that have crucial application outside the realm of language: analogy, metacomprehension, processing mode and level, task directedness, appropriate usage and style, and identification of others' intentions.

Proverbs could teach children abstract thought and reasoning in several ways. First, there is the matter of meaning levels. As for all proverb comprehension, a child must move off the literal level, but with some help from adults. Children therefore learn that what the utterance seems to be about is not what it's actually means, that it is really about the more general significance of the literal meaning. The child must also come to know that the proverb user intends something and is saying it indirectly.

Children are taught ever so subtly but effectively that people have minds, that minds can be tricky, and that things are not always as they seem. In teaching about kinds and levels of meaning, proverbs seem to provide the metalesson that *Appearances can be deceiving*. There also is often the problem, not present for all proverbs, of desymbolizing key words (metaphor, etc.) in the proverb. This is another lesson in decryption.

Second, there is a mental flexibility factor. The child learns that the same utterance can mean different things in different contexts. He or she is taught that the same concrete interpretation may not suffice in all circumstances. In this case, knowledge becomes less inert, more transferable to new situations, and more decontextualized in general. In the jargon, domain-specific knowledge about a form of language becomes more domain-free, opening up the possibility that the child will begin to appreciate this property across the language spectrum.

Finally, the process of mapping proverb, topic, and generic ideal provides implicit instruction in analogical thinking. It is possible, therefore, that direct instruction in the use and comprehension of proverbs could provide valuable lessons in critical thinking.

This is not mere speculation because there is some evidence that proverbs can facilitate critical thinking skills. Bountrogianni (1988) found that 8- to 11-year-old bilingual Canadian-Greek children preferred the moral of proverbs more than did monolingual Canadian children. This could have been due to ethnic factors, but also to the advantage of bilingualism. If more abstract meanings are made more accessible or natural by bilingualism, morals could be preferred simply because they are more abstract. Training in proverbs could well act like bilingualism in getting children to appreciate the message behind the literal input. Feichtl (1988), it will be recalled, found that direct curricular instruction in proverb interpretation facilitated comprehension of other forms of figurative language. Holden and Warshaw (1985) stated that proverbs can be used to improve the reading skills, writing skills, and vocabulary of children with severe hearing loss. Eissing (1989) used proverbs to facilitate children's inferential reading skills. Finally, even though the data is more anecdotal, proverb use in some African societies appears to facilitate the entire thought process (Penfield & Duru, 1988).

Everyday Tasks

In chapter 1, I (the author) used the personal example of *Plan before you paint*, something I constructed after some rather sorry experiences in painting. I have thought of this saying in contexts other than painting, however, so I can now say that it is a personal proverb. There are undoubtedly numerous tasks that people perform—fixing cars, wall papering, practicing a musical instrument, washing clothes, even interpersonal tasks—that are repeated, that produce mistakes, and therefore could benefit from a verbal coding of the right way to do the task. Verbal coding has the happy effect of promoting long-term memory. Short, pithy, proverb or proverb-like phrases fit this bill. There is no data on the prevalence of personal proverbs that have emerged in this way, but it likely is very large.

There is a self-help craze in the United States. People are interested in bettering their situation, whether physical, psychological, or social. Proverbs could play a role in all of this. Less obvious and perhaps less pop culturally salient self-help uses of proverbs involve more intellectual matters such as simply becoming more familiar with the stock of proverbs in American culture. Some authors consider this to be part of cultural literacy. Finally, I would be remiss if I did not mention that simply reading about proverbs, what they are, how they function, and the role they play in the lives of individuals and their culture, could be edifying as well as educational.

In consonance with the emphasis on empirical efforts in this text, it should be emphasized that the effectiveness of the various uses of proverbs should be documented whenever possible. It is one thing to describe the use of proverbs in advertising, drug treatment programs, competency testing, and the like, and quite another to ask whether their use had the desired effect.

SUMMARY

The immense amount of proverb scholarship has been fruitful and enlightening. Empirical, theoretical, and practical gaps remain, however. Little is known about the cognitive foundations of proverb production, pragmatics, expertise, emotion, or about the microcognitive aspects of proverb comprehension. Suggestions are made about these topics, here and in prior chapters. Furthermore, no adequate, empirically tested comprehensive theory of proverb cognition has been forthcoming. Additionally, the various tropes have not been linked theoretically, although they all seem to be a form of indirection, an apparent hallmark of intelligence, and on occasion, of creativity. There is also room for novel practical applications of the proverb, both time-honored ones and new.

Appendix:
Proverb Source Materials

℘ ◆ ℘

The literature on proverb scholarship is voluminous. The Reference section will allow the interested reader to access much of this literature. The additional references that follow will fill in some gaps. In addition, some relevant non-English language sources are provided.

JOURNALS

Proverbium: Bulletin d'information sur les recherches parémiologiques, Nos. 1–25 (1965–1975), 1-1008, Matti Kuusi et al. (Ed.) (Helsinki). Reprint (Vols. 2). Wolfgang Mieder (Ed.). Bern: Peter Lang, 1987.
Proverbium Paratum: Bulletin d'information sur les recherches parémiologiques, 1–4 (1980–1989), 1-460. Vilmos Voigt et al. (Ed.) (Budapest).
Proverbium: Yearbook of International Proverb Scholarship. 1984ff. Wolfgang Mieder et al. (Ed.) (Burlington, VT).

GENERAL SOURCES

Alster, B. (1996). *Proverbs of ancient Sumer: The world's earliest proverb collections* (Vols. 1 & 2). Bethesda, MD: CDL Press.
Canadian Psychology, 1990, *31* (3), pp. 195–217. (Contains a series of articles on the proverb.)
Mieder, W. (1993). *Proverbs are never out of season: Popular wisdom in the modern age*. New York: Oxford University Press. (A reprinted set of essays by Mieder. Also contains numerous sources on bibliographies, proverb journals, collections and quotations of proverbs, and specific studies on proverbs.)
Mieder, W. (Ed.). (1994). *Wise words: Essays on the proverb*. New York: Garland. (An excellent set of reprinted essays by various authors. Also contains

numerous sources on bibliographies, proverb journals, collections and quotations of proverbs, and specific studies on proverbs.)
Mieder, W., & Dundes, A. (1981). *The wisdom of many: Essays on the proverb.* New York: Garland. (Reprinted 1994, Madison, WI: University of Wisconsin Press.)
Whiting, B. J. (1994). *When evensong and morrowsong accord: Three essays on the proverb.* (A collection of Whiting's essays from the 1930s, edited by J. Harris & W. Mieder.)

SOURCES FOR THE VARIOUS VIEWS OF THE PROVERB

Cognitive View

Brattemo, C. (1968). *Studies in metaphoric behavior in patients with psychiatric diagnosis of schizophrenia.* Sundsvall: Boktryckeri Aktiebolaget.
Buhofer, A. (Häcki). (1980). *Der Spracherwerb von phraseologishchen Wortverbindungen: Eine psycholinguistische Untersuchung an schweizerdeutschem Material* [The linguistic learning of phrasal word connections: A psycholinguistic investigation on the basis of Swiss texts]. Frauenfeld: Huber.
Christen, B. (1995). *Die Rolle der rechten Hirnhälfte im Verständnis von Phraseolexemen mit und ohne Kontext* [The role of the right half of the brain in the comprehension of phraseological units with and without context]. Bern: Peter Lang.
Scherer, T. (1982). *Phraseologie im Schulalter: Untersuchung zur Phraseologie deutschscheizerischer Schüler and ihrer Sprachbücher* [Phraseology at the school age: A study of the phraseology of Swiss-German students and their language instruction texts]. Bern: Peter Lang.

Cultural View

Madu, R. O. (1992). *African symbols, proverbs and myths: The hermeneutics of destiny.* New York: Peter Lang.
Mieder, W. (1989). *American proverbs: A study of texts and contexts.* New York: Peter Lang.
Monye, A. A. (1996). *Proverbs in African orature.* Lanham, MD: University Press of America.
Palacios, J. (1996). Proverbs as images of children and childrearing. In C. P. Hwang, M. E. Lamb, & I. E. Sigel (Eds.), *Images of childhood* (pp. 75–98). Mahwah, NJ: Lawrence Erlbaum Associates.

Formal View

Folly, D. W. (1991). *The poetry of African-American proverb usage: A speech act analysis.* Unpublished doctoral dissertation, University of California at Los Angeles.

Grzybek, P. (1984). Zur Psychosemiotik des Sprichworts [On the psychosemiotic aspects of proverbs]. In P. Grzybek & W. Eismann (Eds.), *Semiotische Studien zum Sprichwort [Semiotic studies of proverbs]: Simple forms reconsidered I*. Tübingen: Gunter Narr.

Hasan-Rokem, G. (1982). *Proverbs in Israeli folk narratives: A structural semantic analysis*. Helsinki: Suomalainen Tiedeakatemia.

Litovkina, A. T. (1996). A few aspects of a semiotic approach to proverbs, with special reference to two important American publications. *Semiotica, 108,* 307–380.

Yankah, K. (1989). *The proverb in the context of Akan rhetoric: A theory of proverb praxis*. Bern: Peter Lang.

Literary View

Carnes, P. (1994). The fable and the proverb: Intertexts and reception. In W. Mieder (Ed.), *Wise words: Essays on the proverb* (pp. 467–493.). New York: Garland.

Mieder, W. (1974). The essence of literary proverb studies. *Proverbium, 23,* 888–894.

Mieder, W. (1989). *American proverbs: A study of texts and contexts*. New York: Peter Lang. (see chapter VIII, Proverbs in Prose Literature)

Practical View

Hertler, C. A., Chapman, L. J., & Chapman, J. P. (1978). A scoring manual for literalness in proverb interpretation. *Journal of Consulting and Clinical Psychology, 46,* 551–555.

Kempler, D., Van Lancker, D. R., & Read, S. (1988). Comprehension of proverbs and idioms in Alzheimer patients. *Journal of Alzheimer Disease and Associated Disorders, 2,* 38–49.

Krueger, D. (1978). The differential diagnosis of proverb interpretation. In W. Fann, I. Karacan, A. Pokorny, & R. Williams (Eds.), *Phenomenology and treatment of schizophrenia* (pp. 193–202). New York: Spectrum.

Mieder, W. (1989). *American proverbs: A study of texts and contexts*. New York: Peter Lang. (see chapters XIII, Proverbs in Comics and Cartoons, and XIV, Proverbs in Advertisements)

Religious View

Fontaine, C. R. (1994). Proverb performance in the Hebrew bible. In W. Mieder (Ed.), *Wise words: Essays on the proverb* (pp. 393–414). New York: Garland. (Reprinted from *Journal for the Study of the Old Testament*, 1985, *32,* 87–103.)

Westerman, C. (1995). *Roots of wisdom: The oldest proverbs of Israel and other peoples*. Louisville, KY: Westminster John Knox Press. (English translation

from *Wurzeln der Weisheit* [The roots of wisdom], 1990. Gottingen: Vanden-
hoeck & Ruprecht)

PROVERB BIBLIOGRAPHIES

Mieder, W. (1978). *Proverbs in literature: An international bibliography*. Bern:
Peter Lang.
Mieder, W. (1990). *International proverb scholarship: An annotated bibliog-
raphy. Supplement I (1800–1981)*. New York: Garland.
Mieder, W. (1993). *International proverb scholarship: An annotated bibliog-
raphy. Supplement II (1982–1991)*. New York: Garland.
Mieder, W. (1994). *African proverb scholarship: An annotated bibliography*.
Burlington, VT: Queen City Printers.

PROVERB COLLECTIONS

Mieder, W. (1986). *The Prentice-Hall encyclopedia of world proverbs: A treasury
of wit and wisdom through the ages*. Englewood Cliffs, NJ: Prentice-Hall.
Mieder, W. (1990). *Not by bread alone: Proverbs of the Bible*. Shelburne, VT: The
New England Press.
Mieder, W., Kingsbury, S. A., & Harder, K. B. (Eds.). (1992). *A dictionary of
American proverbs*. New York: Oxford University Press.
Simpson, J. A. (1982). *The concise Oxford dictionary of proverbs*. Oxford: Oxford
University Press.
Whiting, B. J. (1989). *Modern proverbs and proverbial phrases*. Cambridge, MA:
Harvard University Press.

References

ဢ ♦ ℭ

Abbeduto, L. (1991). The development of verbal communication in persons with moderate to mild mental retardation. In N. W. Bray (Ed.), *International review of research in mental retardation* (Vol. 17, pp. 91–115). New York: Academic Press.

Abbeduto, L., & Nuccio, J. B. (1991). Relation between receptive language and cognitive maturity in persons with mental retardation. *American Journal on Mental Retardation, 96*, 143–149.

Abrahams, R. D., & Babcock, B. A. (1994). The literary use of proverbs. In W. Mieder (Ed.), *Wise words: Essays on the proverb* (pp. 415–438). New York: Garland. (Original work published 1977)

Ackerman, B. P. (1984). The effects of storage and processing complexity on comprehension repairs in children and adults. *Journal of Experimental Child Psychology, 37*, 303–334.

Allen, J., & Schuldberg, D. (1989). Positive thought disorder in a hypothetically psychosis-prone population. *Journal of Abnormal Psychology, 98*, 491–494.

Anderson, J. R. (1982). Acquisition of cognitive skill. *Psychological Review, 89*, 369–406.

Anderson, J. R. (1983). *The architecture of cognition*. Cambridge, MA: Harvard University Press.

Andreason, N. C. (1977). Reliability and validity of proverb interpretation to assess mental status. *Comprehensive Psychiatry, 18*, 465–472. (Reprinted in W. Mieder & A. Dundes, Eds., 1981, *The wisdom of many: Essays on the proverb*, pp. 218–229. New York: Garland.)

Arewa, E. O., & Dundes, A. (1964). Proverbs and the ethnography of speaking folklore. *American Anthropologist, 66*, 70–85.

Arora, S. (1984). The perception of proverbiality. *Proverbium: Yearbook of International Proverb Scholarship, 1*, 1–38. (Reprinted in W. Mieder, Ed., 1994, *Wise words: Essays on the proverb*, pp. 3–30. New York: Garland.)

Ashcraft, M. (1994). *Human memory and cognition*. New York: HarperCollins.

Austin, J. L. (1962). *How to do things with words*. Oxford: Oxford University Press.

Ausubel, D. P. (1968). *Educational Psychology: A cognitive view*. New York: Holt, Rinehart & Winston.

Baddeley, A. D., & Hitch, G. J. (1974). Working memory. In G. H. Bower (Ed.), *The psychology of learning and motivation: Advances in research and theory* (Vol. 8, pp. 47–90). New York: Academic Press.

Barkow, J. H., Cosmides, L., & Tooby, J. (1992). *The adapted mind: Evolutionary psychology and the generation of culture*. New York: Oxford University Press.

Barnes, D. R. (1994). Telling it slant: Emily Dickinson and the proverb. In W. Mieder (Ed.), *Wise words: Essays on the proverb* (pp. 439–465). New York: Garland. (Original work published 1979)

Baron-Cohen, S., Leslie, A. M., & Frith, U. (1985). Does the autistic child have a "theory of mind"? *Cognition, 21*, 37–46.

Barsalou, L. (1983). Ad hoc categories. *Memory & Cognition, 11*, 211–227.

Baumgarten, F. (1952). A proverb test for attitude measurement. *Personality psychology, 5*, 249–267. (Reprinted in W. Mieder & A. Dundes Eds., 1981, *The wisdom of many: Essays on the proverb*, pp. 230–241. New York: Garland.)

Beardslee, W. (1970). Use of the proverb in the synoptic gospels. In W. Mieder & A. Dundes (Eds.), *The wisdom of many: Essays on the proverb* (pp. 161–173). New York: Garland.

Bellugi, U., Bihrle, A., Neville, H., Doherty, S., & Jernigan, T. (1992). Language, cognition, and brain organization in a neurodevelopmental disorder. In M. R. Gunnar & C. A. Nelson (Eds.), *The Minnesota symposium on child psychology: Vol. 24. Developmental behavioral neuroscience* (pp. 201–232). Mahwah, NJ: Lawrence Erlbaum Associates.

Benjafield, J., Frommhold, K., Keenan, T., Muckenheim, R. & Mueller, D. (1993). Imagery, concreteness, goodness, and familiarity ratings for 500 proverbs sampled from the *Oxford dictionary of English proverbs*. *Behavior Research Methods, Instruments and Computers, 25*, 27–40.

Benjamin, J. (1944). A method for distinguishing and evaluating formal thinking disorders in schizophrenia. In J. Kasanin (Ed.), *Language and thought in schizophrenia* (pp. 65– 90). Berkeley: University of California Press.

Benton, A. (1968). Differential behavioral effects in frontal lobe disease. *Neuropsychologia, 6*, 53–60.

Billow, R. (1975). A cognitive developmental study of metaphor comprehension. *Developmental Psychology, 11*, 415–423.

Blackman, L. S., & Lin, A. (1984). Generalization training in the educable mentally retarded: Intelligence and educability revisited. In P. H. Brooks, R. Sperber, & C. McCauley (Eds.), *Learning and cognition in the mentally retarded* (pp. 237–263). Hillsdale, NJ: Lawrence Erlbaum Associates.

Blumenthal, A. L. (1970). *Language and psychology: Historical aspects of psycholinguistics*. New York: Wiley.

Bountrogianni, M. (1988). Bilingualism and metaphor comprehension. *European Journal of Psychology of Education, 3*, 53–64.

Bransford, J. D., & Franks, J. J. (1971). The abstraction of linguistic ideas. *Cognitive Psychology, 2*, 331–350.

Briggs, C. L. (1985). The pragmatics of proverb performances in New Mexican Spanish. *American Anthropologist, 87*, 793–810. (Reprinted in W. Mieder, Ed., 1994, *Wise words: Essays on the proverb*, pp. 317–350. New York: Garland.)

Brooks, P. H., & Van Haneghan, J. (1991). An eventful approach to mental retardation. In R. R. Hoffman & D. S. Palermo (Eds.), *Cognition and the symbolic processes: Applied and ecological perspectives* (pp. 457–476). Hillsdale, NJ: Lawrence Erlbaum Associates.

Brown, A. L. (1989). Analogical learning and transfer: What develops? In S. Vosniadou & A. Ortony (Eds.), *Similarity and analogical reasoning* (pp. 369–412). New York: Cambridge University Press.

Brugman, C. M. (1988). *The story of over: Polysemy, semantics, and the structure of the lexicon.* New York: Garland.

Brundage, S. B. (1993). *Comparison of proverb interpretations provided by non-brain-damaged adults, aphasic adults, right-hemisphere-damaged adults, and adults with probable dementia.* Unpublished doctoral dissertation, University of Minnesota, Minneapolis.

Bühler, K. (1908). Über Gedankenerinnerungen [The remembrance of thoughts]. *Archiv für die gesamte Psychologie, 12*, 24–92, 93–123.

Buhofer, A. H. (1987). Alltägliche Verstehens- und Erklärungsstrategien bei Phraseologismen [Common strategies for the comprehension and explanation of phraseological units]. In H. Burger & R. Zett (Eds.), *Aktuelle Probleme der Phraseologie* (pp. 59–77). Bern: Peter Lang.

Burgess, C., & Chiarello, C. (1996). Neurocognitive mechanisms underlying metaphor comprehension and other figurative language. *Metaphor and Symbolic Activity, 11*, 67–84.

Buss, D. M. (1995). Evolutionary psychology: A new paradigm for psychological science. *Psychological Inquiry, 6*, 1–30.

Caplan, D. (1992). *Language: Structure, processing, and disorders.* Cambridge, MA: MIT Press.

Case, T. (1991). *The role of literal and figurative familiarity in proverb comprehension.* Unpublished doctoral dissertation, University of Cincinnati.

Chambers, J. (1977). *Proverb comprehension in children.* Unpublished dissertation, University of Cincinnati, Cincinnati.

Champion, S. G. (1945). *The eleven religions and their proverbial lore.* New York: Dutton.

Chandler, S. R. (1991). Metaphor comprehension: A connectionist approach to implications for the mental lexicon. *Metaphor and Symbolic Activity, 6*, 227–258.

Chang, T. M. (1986). Semantic memory: Facts and models. *Psychological Bulletin, 99*, 199–220.

Chi, M. T. H., Glaser, R., & Farr, M. J. (Eds.) (1988). *The nature of expertise.* Hillsdale: Lawrence Erlbaum Associates.

Chiarello, C. (1991). Interpretation of word meanings by the cerebral hemispheres: One is not enough. In P. J. Schwanenflugel (Ed.), *The psychology of word meanings* (pp. 251–278). Hillsdale: Lawrence Erlbaum Associates.

Chlosta, C., & Grzybek, P. (1995). Empirical and folkloristic paremiology: Two to quarrel or to tango? *Proverbium: Yearbook of International Proverb Scholarship, 12*, 67– 85.

Chomsky, N. (1957). *Syntactic structures*. The Hague: Mouton.

Cichetti, D., & Sroufe, L. A. (1978). An organizational view of affect: Illustration from the study of Down's syndrome infants. In M. Lewis & L. Rosenblum (Eds.), *The development of affect* (pp. 309–350). New York: Plenum.

Cohen, L. J. (1979). The semantics of metaphor. In A. Ortony (Ed.), *Metaphor and thought* (pp. 64–77). New York: Cambridge University Press.

Cohen, L. J., & Murphy, G. L. (1984). Models of concepts. *Cognitive Science, 8*, 27–60.

Collins, A. M., & Loftus, E. F. (1975). A spreading activation theory of semantic processing. *Psychological Review, 82*, 407–428.

Cometa, M. S., & Eson, M. E. (1978). Logical operations and metaphor interpretation: A Piagetian model. *Child Development, 49*, 649–659.

Corballis, M. C. (1991). *The lopsided ape: Evolution of the generative mind*. New York: Oxford University Press.

Cram, D. (1994). The linguistic status of the proverb. In W. Mieder (Ed.), *Wise words: Essays on the proverb* (pp. 73–98). New York: Garland. (Original work published 1983)

Crépeau, P. (1975). La definition du proverbe. [The definition of the proverb] *Fabula, 16*, 285–304.

Cunningham, D. M., Ridley, S. E., & Campbell, A. (1987). Relationship between proverb familiarity and proverb interpretations: Implications for clinical practice. *Psychological Reports, 60*, 895–898.

Dascal, M. (1987). Defending literal meaning. *Cognitive Science, 11*, 259–281.

Detterman, D. K. (1979). Memory in the mentally retarded. In N. R. Ellis (Ed.), *Handbook of mental deficiency* (2nd ed, pp. 727–760). Hillsdale, NJ: Lawrence Erlbaum Associates.

Dorfmueller, M. A., & Honeck, R. P. (1980). Centrality and generativity within a linguistic family: Toward a conceptual base theory of groups. *The Psychological Record, 30*, 95–109.

Douglas, J. D., & Peel, B. (1979). The development of metaphor and proverb translation in children grades one through seven. *Journal of Educational Research, 73*, 116–119.

Dundes, A. (1975). On the structure of the proverb. *Proverbium, 25*, 961–973. (Reprinted in W. Mieder & A. Dundes, Eds., 1981, *The wisdom of many: Essays on the proverb*, pp. 43–64. New York: Garland.)

Dundes, A., & Stibbe, C. A. (1981). *The art of mixing metaphors: A folklorist interpretation of the "Netherlandish Proverbs" by Pieter Brugel the Elder*. Helsinki: Suomalainen Tiedeakatemia.

Dunn, A. C. (1981). *The development and measurement of analogic thought*. Unpublished doctoral dissertation, University of Utah, Salt Lake City.

Durrell, L. (1959). *The black book*. New York: Pocket Books.

Eissing, C. (1989). Proverbs in the classroom. *Reading Teacher, 43*, 188–189.

Ellis, N. R., & Dulany, C. L. (1991). Further evidence for cognitive inertia of persons with mental retardation. *American Journal on Mental Retardation, 95,* 613–621.

Ellis, N. R., Woodley-Zanthos, P., Dulany, C. L., & Palmer, R. L. (1989). Automatic-effortful processing cognitive inertia in persons with mental retardation. *American Journal on Mental Retardation, 93,* 412–423.

Ericsson, K. A., & Smith, J. (Eds.). (1991). *Toward a general theory of expertise: Prospects and limits.* New York: Cambridge University Press.

Evans, R. L., & Berent, I. M. (October, 1993). Dueling proverbs. *Readers Digest,* 107–108.

Fagan, B. M. (1979). *Return to Babylonia.* Boston: Little, Brown.

Feichtl, N. G. C. C. (1988). *Using proverbs to facilitate metaphorical language comprehension: A curriculum study.* Unpublished doctoral dissertation, University of Maryland, College Park.

Feldhaus, R. O., & Honeck, R. P. (1989). The conceptual basis of graded categories. *Journal of Psycholinguistic Research, 18,* 271–288.

Feretti, R. P., & Butterfield, E. C. (1989). Intelligence as a correlate of children's problem solving. *American Journal on Mental Retardation, 93,* 424–433.

Finckh, J. (1906). Zur Frage der Intellingenzprufung [Concerning the question of intelligence tests]. *Centralblatt für Nervenheilkunde und Psychiatrie, 17,* 945–957.

Finnegan, R. (1970). *Oral literature in Africa.* Oxford, England: Clarendon Press.

Flavell, J. H. (1993). Young children's understanding of thinking and consciousness. *Current Directions in Psychological Science, 2,* 40–43.

Flavell, J. H., Green, F. L., & Flavell, E. R. (1986). Development of knowledge about the appearance–reality distinction. *Monographs of the Society for Research in Child Development, 51* (1, Serial No. 212).

Fogel, M. L. (1965). The Proverbs Test in the appraisal of cerebral disease. *The Journal of General Psychology, 72,* 269–275.

Fogelin, R. J. (1988). *Figuratively speaking.* New Haven: Yale University Press.

Fontaine, C. (1984). Brightening up the mindworks: Concepts of instruction in Biblical wisdom and Rinzai Zen. *Religious Education, 79,* 590–600.

Foote, T., and the editors of Time-Life Books. (1968). The world of Bruegel. *Time-Life Books.* New York: Time.

Forrester, M. A. (1995). Tropic implicature and context in the comprehension of idiomatic phrases. *Journal of Psycholinguistic Research, 24,* 1–21.

Fox, R., & Oross, S. (1988). Deficits in stereoscopic depth perception by mildly mentally retarded adults. *American Journal on Mental Retardation, 93,* 232–244.

Frederickson, C. H., & Stemmer, B. (1993). Conceptual processing of discourse by a right hemisphere brain-damaged patient. In H. H. Brownell & Y. Joanette (Eds.), *Narrative discourse in neurologically impaired and normal aging adults* (pp. 239–278). San Diego: Singular Publishing Group.

Furnham, A. F. (1987). The proverbial truth: Contextually reconciling the truthfulness of antonymous proverbs. *Journal of Language and Social Psychology, 6*, 49–59.

Gamlin, P. J., & Tramposch, F. R. (1982). *Proverbial understanding and the development of metaphorical thinking.* Unpublished manuscript, Ontario Institute for Studies in Education, Toronto.

Gardner, H., Brownell, H. H., Wapner, W., & Michelow, D. (1983). Missing the point: The role of the right hemisphere in the processing of complex linguistic materials. In E. Perecman (Ed.), *Cognitive processing in the right hemisphere* (pp. 169–191). New York: Academic Press.

Gardner, R. A., Gardner, B. T., & Van Cantfort, T. E. (Eds). (1989). *Teaching sign language to chimpanzees.* Albany, NY: SUNY Press.

Gazzaniga, M. S. (1970). *The bisected brain.* New York: Appleton.

Gazzaniga, M. S. (1988). *Mind matters: How mind and brain interact to create our conscious lives.* Boston: Houghton-Mifflin.

Gentner, D. (1977). Children's performance on a spatial analogies task. *Child Development, 48*, 1034–1039.

Gentner, D. (1989). The mechanisms of analogical reasoning. In S. Vosniadou & A. Ortony (Eds.), *Similarity and analogical reasoning* (pp. 199–241). New York: Cambridge University Press.

Gibbs, R. W. (1992). Categorization and metaphor understanding. *Psychological Review, 99*, 572–577.

Gibbs, R. W. (1993). Process and products in making sense of tropes. In A. Ortony (Ed.), *Metaphor and thought* (2nd ed., pp. 252–276). New York: Cambridge University Press.

Gibbs, R. W. (1994). *The poetics of mind: Figurative thought, language and understanding.* New York: Cambridge University Press.

Gibbs, R. W. (1995). What proverb understanding reveals about how people think. *Psychological Bulletin, 118*, 133–154.

Gibbs, R. W., Colston, H. L., & Johnson, M. D. (1996). Proverbs and the metaphorical mind. *Metaphor and Symbolic Activity, 11*, 207–216.

Glucksberg, S., Brown, M., & McGlone, M. (1993). Conceptual metaphors are not automatically accessed during idiom comprehension. *Memory & Cognition, 21*, 711–719.

Glucksberg, S., & Keysar, B. (1993). How metaphors work. In A. Ortony (Ed.), *Metaphor and thought* (2nd ed., pp. 401–424). New York: Cambridge University Press.

Gokhan, A. G. (1992). *What have the ancestors said: An ethnography of speaking proverbs in a Turkish community (Izmir).* Unpublished doctoral dissertation, University of Pittsburgh, Pittsburgh.

Goldstein, K. (1936). The significance of mental lobes for mental performances. *Journal of Neurology and Psychopathology, 17*, 27–40.

Goldstein, K., & Scherer, M. (1941). Abstract and concrete behavior: An experimental study with special tests. *Psychological Monographs, 53*, (Whole No. 239).

Goodwin, P. D., & Wenzel, J. W. (1979). Proverbs and practical reasoning: A study in sociologic. *The Quarterly Journal of Speech, 65*, 289–302.

Gordon, E. I. (1959). *Sumerian proverbs: Glimpses of everyday life in ancient Mesopotamia.* Philadelphia: The University Museum, University of Pennsylvania.

Gorham, D. R. (1956). A proverbs test for clinical and experimental use. *Psychological Reports, 1,* 1–12.

Gorham, D. R. (1963). Additional norms and scoring suggestions for the Proverbs Test. *Psychological Reports, 13,* 487–492.

Green, T., & Pepicello, W. (1986). The proverb and riddle as folk enthymemes. *Proverbium: Yearbook of International Proverb Scholarship, 3,* 33–45.

Grice, H. P. (1957). "Meaning." *Philosophical Review, 66,* 377–388.

Grice, H. P. (1975). Logic and conversation. In P. Cole & J. L. Morgan (Eds.), *Syntax and semantics: Vol 3. Speech acts* (pp. 41–58). New York: Academic Press.

Grzybek, P. (1987). Foundations of semiotic proverb study. *Proverbium: Yearbook of International Proverb Scholarship, 4,* 39–85.

Gustafson, J. L., & Waehler, C. A. (1992). Assessing concrete and abstract thinking with the Draw-a-Person technique. *Journal of Personality Assessment, 59,* 439–447.

Haberlandt, K. (1994). *Cognitive psychology.* Needham Heights, MA: Allyn & Bacon.

Haberlandt, K., Berian, C., & Sandson, J. (1980). The episode schema in story processing. *Journal of Verbal Learning and Verbal Behavior, 19,* 635–650.

Hellige, J. B. (1993). *Hemispheric asymmetry: What's right and what's left.* Cambridge, MA: Harvard University Press.

Hier, D. B., & Kaplan, J. (1980). Verbal comprehension deficits after right hemisphere damage. *Applied Psycholinguistics, 1,* 279–294.

Higbee, K., & Millard, R. (1983). Visual imagery and familiarity for 203 sayings. *American Journal of Psychology, 96,* 211–222.

Hoffman, R. R. (Ed.). (1992). *The psychology of expertise: Cognitive research and empirical AI.* New York: Springer-Verlag.

Hoffman, R. R., & Honeck, R. P. (1987). Proverbs, pragmatics, and the ecology of abstract categories. In R. Haskell (Ed.), *Cognition and symbolic structures* (pp. 121–140). Norwood, NJ: Ablex.

Hofstadter, D. R. (1980). *Gödel, Escher, Bach: An eternal golden braid.* New York: Basic Books.

Holden, M., & Warshaw, M. (1985). A bird in the hand and a bird in the bush: Using proverbs to teach skills and comprehension. *English Journal, 74,* 63–67.

Holyoak, K. J. (1985). The pragmatics of analogical transfer. In G. H. Bower (Ed.), *The psychology of learning and motivation* (Vol. 19, pp. 59–87). New York: Academic Press.

Homa, D., & Vosburgh, R. (1976). Category breadth and the abstraction of prototypical information. *Journal of Experimental Psychology: Human Learning and Memory, 2,* 322–330.

Honeck, R. P. (1973). Interpretive versus structural effects on semantic memory. *Journal of Verbal Learning and Verbal Behavior, 10,* 448–455.

Honeck, R. P. (1992). Metaphor, expertise, and a PEST: Comments on the contributions to this special issue. *Metaphor and Symbolic Activity, 7,* 237–252.

Honeck, R. P. (1997). An outsider looks at mental retardation: A moral, a model, and a metaprinciple. In N. Bray (Ed.), *International Review of Research in Mental Retardation* (Vol. 21, pp. 1–31). New York: Academic Press.

Honeck, R. P., Case, T. S., & Firment, M. (1988). Conceptual connections between realistic and abstract pictures. *Bulletin of the Psychonomic Society, 26,* 5–7.

Honeck, R. P., & Firment, M. (1989). Accessing abstract categories. *Bulletin of the Psychonomic Society, 27,* 206–208.

Honeck, R. P., & Kibler, C. T. (1984). The role of imagery, analogy, and instantiation in proverb comprehension. *Journal of Psycholinguistic Research, 13,* 393–414.

Honeck, R. P., & Kibler, C. T. (1985). Representation in cognitive psychological theories of figurative language. In R. Dirven & W. Paprotte' (Eds.), *The ubiquity of metaphor: Metaphor in thought and language* (pp. 381–424). Amsterdam: John Benjamins.

Honeck, R. P., Kibler, C. T., & Firment, M. (1987). Figurative language and psychological views of categorization: Two ships in the night? In R. Haskell (Ed.), *Symbolic structures and cognition* (pp. 103–120). New York: Ablex.

Honeck, R. P., Riechmann, P., & Hoffman, R. R. (1975). Semantic memory for metaphor: The conceptual base hypothesis. *Memory & Cognition, 3,* 409–415.

Honeck, R. P., Sowry, B., & Voegtle, K. (1978). Proverbial understanding in a pictorial context. *Child Development, 49,* 327–331.

Honeck, R. P., Sugar, J., & Kibler, C. T. (1982). Stories, categories, and figurative meaning. *Poetics, 11,* 127–144.

Honeck, R. P., & Temple, J. G. (1994). Proverbs: The Extended Conceptual Base and Great Chain Metaphor Theories. *Metaphor and Symbolic Activity, 9,* 85–112.

Honeck, R. P., & Temple, J. G. (1996). Proverbs and the complete mind. *Metaphor and Symbolic Activity, 11,* 217–232.

Honeck, R. P., Voegtle, K., Dorfmueller, M., & Hoffman, R. (1980). Proverbs, meaning, and group structure. In R. P. Honeck & R. R. Hoffman (Eds.), *Cognition and figurative language* (pp. 127–162). Hillsdale, NJ: Lawrence Erlbaum Associates.

Honeck, R. P., Voegtle, K., & Sowry, B. (1981). Figurative understanding of pictures and sentences. *Journal of Psycholinguistic Research, 10,* 135–153.

Honeck, R. P., & Welge, J. (in press). Proverb creation in the laboratory. *Journal of Psycholinguistic Research.*

Hunt, E., & Agnoli, F. (1991). The Whorfian hypothesis: A cognitive psychology perspective. *Psychological Review, 92,* 377–389.

Hunt, M. (1982). *The universe within: A new science explores the human mind.* New York: Simon & Schuster.

Israelite, N., Schloss, P. J., & Smith, M. A. (1986). Teaching proverb use through a modified table game. *Volta Review, 88,* 195–207.

Jacquette, D. (1994). *Philosophy of mind.* Englewood Cliffs, NJ: Prentice-Hall.

Johnson-Laird, P. N. (1983). *Mental models: Toward a cognitive science of language, inference, and consciousness.* Cambridge, MA: Harvard University Press.

Johnson-Laird, P. N. (1988). *The computer and the mind: An introduction to cognitive science.* Cambridge, MA: Harvard University Press.

Johnson-Laird, P. N., & Byrne, R. (1991). *Deduction.* Mahwah, NJ: Lawrence Erlbaum Associates.

Kahneman, D., Slovic, P., & Tversky, A. (Eds.). (1982). *Judgment under uncertainty: Heuristics and biases.* New York: Cambridge University Press.

Katz, A. N., & Lee, C. L. (1993). The role of authorial intent in determining verbal irony and metaphor. *Metaphor and Symbolic Activity, 8*, 257–280.

Katz, A. N., & Paivio, A. (1975). Imagery variables in concept identification. *Journal of Verbal Learning and Verbal Behavior, 14*, 284–293.

Katz, J. J. (1966). *The philosophy of language.* New York: Harper & Row.

Kennedy, J. M., Green, C. D., & Vervaeke, J. (1993). Metaphoric thought and devices in pictures. *Metaphor and Symbolic Activity, 8*, 243–255.

Keysar, B., & Bly, B. (1995). Intuitions of the transparency of idioms: Can one keep a secret by spilling the beans? *Journal of Memory and Language, 34*, 89–109.

Kibler, C. T. (1985). *On the structure of conceptual categories.* Unpublished doctoral dissertation, University of Cincinnati, Cincinnati.

Kintsch, W. (1988). The role of knowledge in discourse comprehension: A construction-integration model. *Psychological Review, 95*, 163–182.

Kirshenblatt-Gimblett, B. (1973). Toward a theory of proverb meaning. *Proverbium, 22*, pp. 821–827.

Kolb, B., & Whishaw, I. Q. (1990). *Fundamentals of human neuropsychology* (3rd ed.). New York: Norton.

Krikmann, A. (1974). On denotative indefiniteness of proverbs. Tallinn: Academy of Sciences of the Estonian SSR, Institute of Language and Literature. Also in *Proverbium: Yearbook of International Proverb Scholarship, 2*, 58–85.

Krueger, D. (1978). The differential diagnosis of proverb interpretation. In W. Fann, I. Karacan, A. Pokorny, & R. Williams (Eds.), *Phenomenology and treatment of schizophrenia* (pp. 193–202). New York: Spectrum.

Kuusi, M. (1972). *Towards an international-type-system of proverbs.* Helsinki: Suomalainen Tiedeakatemia. (Also in *Proverbium*, 1972, no. 19, 699–736.)

Lakoff, G. (1986a). A figure of thought. *Metaphor and Symbolic Activity, 1*, 215–225.

Lakoff, G. (1986b). The meanings of literal. *Metaphor and Symbolic Activity, 1*, 219–226.

Lakoff, G. (1987). *Women, fire, and dangerous things: What categories reveal about the mind.* Chicago: University of Chicago Press.

Lakoff, G. (1993). The contemporary theory of metaphor. In A. Ortony (Ed.), *Metaphor and thought* (2nd ed., pp. 202–251). New York: Cambridge University Press.

Lakoff, G., & Johnson, M. (1980). *Metaphors we live by.* Chicago: University of Chicago Press.

Lakoff, G., & Turner, M. (1989). *More than cool reason: A field guide for poetic metaphor*. Chicago: University of Chicago Press.

Leahy, T. H. (1987). *A history of psychology: Main currents in psychological thought*. Englewood Cliffs, NJ: Prentice-Hall.

Levin, S. R. (1979). Standard approaches to metaphor and a proposal for literary metaphor. In A. Ortony (Ed.), *Metaphor and thought* (pp. 124–135). New York: Cambridge University Press.

Lieber, M. D. (1984). Analogic ambiguity: A paradox of proverb usgage. *Journal of American Folklore, 97*, 423–441. (Reprinted in Mieder, W., Ed., 1994, *Wise words: Essays on the proverb*, pp. 99–126. New York: Garland.)

Lutzer, V. D. (1988). Comprehension of proverbs by average children and children with learning disabilities. *Journal of Learning Disabilities, 21*, 104–108.

Mac Cormac, E. R. (1985). *A cognitive theory of metaphor.* Cambridge: MIT Press.

Malgady, R. G., & Johnson, M. G. (1980). Measurement of figurative language: Semantic feature models of comprehension and appreciation. In R. P. Honeck & R. R. Hoffman (Eds.), *Cognition and figurative language* (pp. 239–258). Hillsdale, NJ: Lawrence Erlbaum Associates.

Marks, L. (1978). *The unity of the senses: Interrelations among the modalities.* New York: Academic Press.

Marks, L. (1996). On perceptual metaphors. *Metaphor and Symbolic Activity, 11*, 39–66.

Marks, L. E., & Bornstein, M. H. (1987). Sensory similarities: Classes, characteristics, and cognitive consequences. In R. E. Haskell (Ed.), *Cognition and symbolic structures: The psychology of metaphoric transformations* (pp. 49–65). Norwood, NJ: Ablex.

Martin, J. H. (1992). *A computational model of metaphor interpretation*. Cambridge, MA: Academic Press.

Martin, J. H. (1996). Computational approaches to figurative language. *Metaphor and Symbolic Activity, 11*, 85–100.

Matarazzo, J. (1972). *Wechsler's measurement and appraisal of adult intelligence* (5th ed.). Baltimore: Williams & Wilkins.

Matlin, M. W. (1994). *Cognition*. Orlando: Harcourt Brace.

McClelland, J. L., & Rumelhart, D. E. (1981). An interactive activation model of context effects in letter perception: Part 1. An account of basic findings. *Psychological Review, 88*, 375–407.

Mieder, B., & Mieder, W. (1977). Tradition and innovation: Proverbs in advertising. *Journal of Popular Culture, 11*, 308–319. (Reprinted in W. Mieder & A. Dundes, Eds., 1981, *The wisdom of many: Essays on the proverb,* pp. 309–322. New York: Garland.)

Mieder, W. (1978). The use of proverbs in psychological testing. *Journal of the Folklore Institute, 15*, 45–55.

Mieder, W. (1989). *American proverbs: A study of texts and contexts.* New York: Peter Lang.

Mieder, W. (1992). Paremiological minimum and cultural literacy. In S. J. Bonner (Ed.), *Creativity and tradition in folklore: New directions* (pp. 185–203).

Logan, UT: Utah State University Press. (Also in W. Mieder, Ed., 1994, *Wise words: Essays on the proverb*, pp. 297–316. New York: Garland.)

Mieder, W. (1993a). *Proverbs are never out of season*. New York: Oxford University Press.

Mieder, W. (1993b). "The grass is always greener on the other side of the fence": An American proverb of discontent. *Proverbium: Yearbook of International Proverb Scholarship, 10*, 151–184. (Reprinted in W. Mieder, Ed., 1994, *Wise words: Essays on the proverb*, pp. 515–542. New York: Garland.)

Miller, G. A., & Johnson-Laird, P. N. (1976). *Language and perception*. Cambridge, MA: Harvard University Press.

Milner, G. B. (1969). Quadripartite structures. *Proverbium, 14*, 379–383.

Molloy, R., Brownell, H., & Gardner, H. (1990). Discourse comprehension by right-hemispheric stroke patients: Deficits of prediction and revision. In Y. Joanette & H. Brownell (Eds.), *Discourse ability and brain damage: Theoretical and empirical perspectives* (pp. 113–130). New York: Springer-Verlag.

Monye, A. A. (1987). Devices of indirection in Aniocha proverb usage. *Proverbium: Yearbook of International Proverb Scholarship, 4*, 111–126.

Monye, A. A. (1996). *Proverbs in African orature: The Aniocha- Igbo experience*. Lanham, MD: University Press of America.

Moreno, V., & Di Vesta, F. J. (1994). Analogies (adages) as aids for comprehending structural relations in text. *Contemporary Educational Psychology, 19*, 179–198.

Myers, P. S. (1993). Narrative expressive deficits associated with right-hemisphere damage. In H. H. Brownell & Y. Joanette (Eds.), *Narrative discourse in neurologically impaired and normal aging adults* (pp. 279–296). San Diego: Singular Publishing Group.

Naveh-Benjamin, M., & Ayres, T. J. (1986). Digit span, reading rate, and linguistic relativity. *Quarterly Journal of Experimental Psychology, 38*, 739–751.

Nierenberg, J. (1983). Proverbs in graffiti: Taunting traditional wisdom. *Maledicta, 7*, 41–58. (Also in W. Mieder, Ed., 1994, *Wise words: Essays on the proverb*, pp. 543–562. New York: Garland.)

Nippold, M. A., & Haq, F. S. (1996). Proverb comprehension in youth: The role of concreteness and familiarity. *Journal of Speech and Hearing Research, 39*, 166–176.

Nippold, M. A., Martin, S. A., & Erskine, B. J. (1988). Proverb comprehension in context: A developmental study with children and adolescents. *Journal of Speech and Hearing Research, 31*, 19–28.

Nippold, M. A., Uhden, L. D., & Schwarz, I. E. (in press). Proverb explanation through the lifespan: A developmental study of adolescents and adults. *Journal of Speech and Hearing Research*.

Nitsch, K. E. (1977). *Structuring decontextualized forms of knowledge*. Unpublished doctoral dissertation, Vanderbilt University, Nashville, TN.

Nkara, J. P. (1992). "Bisisimi" or the language of the wise. *South African Journal of African Languages, 12*, 144–149.

Norrick, N. R. (1981). Nondirect speech acts and double binds. *Poetics, 10,* 33–47.

Norrick, N. R. (1985). *How proverbs mean: Semantic studies in English proverbs.* New York: Mouton.

Norrick, N. R. (1994a). Proverbial perlocutions: How to do things with proverbs. In W. Mieder (Ed.), *Wise words: Essays on the proverb* (pp. 143–158). (Originally published in *Grazer Linguistische Studien,* 1982, *17–18,* 169–183.)

Norrick, N. R. (1994b). Proverbial emotions: How proverbs encode and evaluate emotion. *Proverbium, 11,* 207–215.

Nwachukwu-Agbada, J. O. J. (1994). The proverb in the Igbo milieu. *Anthropos, 89,* 194–200.

Obelkevich, J. (1987). Proverbs and social history. In P. Burke & R. Porter (Eds.), *The social history of language* (pp. 43–72). Cambridge: Cambridge University Press. (Reprinted in W. Mieder, 1994, Ed., *Wise words: Essays on the proverb,* pp. 211–252. New York: Garland.]

Obeng, S. G. (1994). Verbal indirection in Akan informal discourse. *Journal of Pragmatics, 21,* 37–65.

Oliver, V. S. (1991). *Indeational fluency and proverb comprehension: Comparisons among and between bilingual and monolingual college students.* Unpublished doctoral dissertation, Northern Arizona University, Flagstaff, AZ.

Osgood, C. E. (1960). The cross-cultural generality of visual-verbal synesthetic tendencies. *Behavioral Science, 5,* 146–169.

Osgood, C. E. (1979). *Lectures on language performance.* New York: Springer-Verlag.

Osgood, C. E. (1980). The cognitive dynamics of synesthesia and metaphor. In R. P. Honeck & R. R. Hoffman (Eds.), *Cognition and figurative language* (pp. 203–238). Hillsdale, NJ: Lawrence Erlbaum Associates.

Osherson, D. N., & Smith, E. E. (1981). On the adequacy of prototype theory as a theory of concepts. *Cognition, 9,* 35–58.

Osherson, D. N., Smith, E. E., Wilkie, O., Lopez, A., & Shaffir, E. (1990). Category based induction. *Psychological Review, 97,* 185–200.

Paivio, A. (1978). Comparisons of mental clocks. *Journal of Experimental Psychology: Human Perception and Performance, 4,* 61–71.

Paivio, A. (1986). *Mental representations: A dual-coding approach.* New York: Oxford University Press.

Paivio, A., & Walsh, M. (1993). Psychological processes in metaphor comprehension and memory. In A. Ortony (Ed.), *Metaphor and thought* (2nd ed., pp. 307–328). New York: Cambridge University Press.

Parades, A. (1970). Proverbs and ethnic stereotypes. *Proverbium, 15,* 505–507.

Pasamanick, J. (1983). Talk does cook rice: Proverb abstraction through social interaction. *International Journal for the Sociology of Language, 44,* 5–25.

Penfield, J. (1983). *Communicating with quotes: The Igbo case.* Westport, CT: Greenwood Press.

Penfield, J., & Duru, M. (1988). Proverbs: Metaphors that teach. *Anthropological Quarterly, 61,* 119–128.

Penn, N. E., Jacob, T. C., & Brown, M. (1988). Familiarity with proverbs and performance of a Black population on Gorham's Proverbs Test. *Perceptual and Motor Skills, 66,* 847–854.

Permyakov, G. L. (1970). *From proverb to folk-tale. Notes on the general theory of cliché.* Moscow: Nauka.

Perry, T. A. (1993). *Wisdom literature and the structure of proverbs.* University Park, PA: The Pennsylvania State University Press.

Piaget, J. (1926). *The language and thought of the child.* New York: Harcourt Brace.

Pollio, H. R., Barlow, J. M., Fine, H. J., and Pollio, M. R. (1977). *Psychology and the poetics of growth: Figurative language in psychology, psychotherapy, and education.* Hillsdale, NJ: Lawrence Erlbaum Associates.

Posner, M. I., & Keele, S. W. (1968). On the genesis of abstract ideas. *Journal of Experimental Psychology, 77,* 353–363.

Pratt, J., & Higbee, K. (1983). Use of an imagery mnemonic by the elderly in natural settings. *Human Learning, 2,* 227–235.

Pylyshyn, Z. (1973). What the mind's eye tells the mind's brain: A critique of mental imagery. *Psychological Bulletin, 80,* 1–24.

Reddy, M. J. (1979). The conduit metaphor—A case of frame conflict in our language about language. In A. Ortony (Ed.), *Metaphor and thought* (pp. 284–324). New York: Cambridge University Press.

Reder, L. M., & Anderson, J. R. (1980). A comparison of texts and their summaries: Memorial consequences. *Journal of Verbal Learning and Verbal Behavior, 19,* 12–34.

Reed, S. K. (1974). Structural descriptions and the limitations of visual images. *Memory & Cognition, 2,* 329–336.

Resnick, D. A. (1982). A developmental study of proverb comprehension. *Journal of Psycholinguistic Research, 11,* 521–538.

Restak, R. M. (1994). *The modular brain.* New York: Charles Scribner's Sons.

Richards, I. A. (1936). *The philosophy of rhetoric.* New York: Oxford University Press.

Richardson, C., & Church, J. (1959). A developmental analysis of proverb interpretations. *Journal of Genetic Psychology, 94,* 169–179.

Riechmann, P. F., & Coste, E. L. (1980). Mental imagery and the comprehension of figurative language: Is there a relationship? In R. P. Honeck & R. R. Hoffman (Eds.), *Cognition and figurative language* (pp. 183–200). Hillsdale, NJ: Lawrence Erlbaum Associates.

Roberts, R. M., & Kreuz, R. J. (1994). Why do people use figurative language? *Psychological Science, 5,* 159–163.

Rogers, T. B. (1986). Psychological approaches to proverbs: A treatise on the import of context. *Canadian Folklore, 8,* 87–104. (Reprinted in W. Mieder, Ed., 1994, *Wise words: Essays on the proverb,* pp. 159–182. New York: Garland.)

Rogers, T. B. (1989). The use of slogans, colloquialisms, and proverbs in the treatment of substance addiction: A psychological application of proverbs. *Proverbium, Yearbook of International Proverb Scholarship, 6,* 103–112.

Rogers, T. B. (1990). Proverbs as psychological theories...Or is it the other way around? *Canadian Psychology, 31*, 195–207.

Rosch, E. (1975). Cognitive reference points. *Cognitive Psychology, 7*, 532–547.

Rosch, E. (1978). Principles of categorization. In E. Rosch & B. Lloyd (Eds.), *Cognition and categorization* (pp. 27–48). Hillsdale, NJ: Lawrence Erlbaum Associates.

Russell, S. W. (1986). Information and experience in metaphor: A perspective from computer analysis. *Metaphor and Symbolic Activity, 1*, 227–270.

Sacks, O. (1995). *An anthropologist on Mars: Seven paradoxical tales.* New York: Knopf.

Sapir, E. (1921). *Language.* New York: Harcourt, Brace.

Schacter, D. L. (1987). Implicit memory: History and current status. *Journal of Experimental Psychology: Learning, Memory, Cognition, 13*, 501–518.

Schneider, W., & Shiffrin, R. M. (1977). Controlled and automatic human information processing: I. Detection, search, and attention. *Psychological Review, 84*, 1–66.

Searle, J. (1969). *Speech acts.* New York: Cambridge University Press.

Searle, J. (1979). Metaphor. In A. Ortony (Ed.), *Metaphor and thought* (pp. 92–123). New York: Cambridge University Press.

Searle, J. (1980). Minds, brains, and programs. *The Behavioral and Brain Sciences, 3*, 417–457.

Seitel, P. (1969). Proverbs: A social use of metaphor. *Genre, 2*, 143–161. (Reprinted in W. Mieder & A. Dundes, Ed., 1981, *The wisdom of many: Essays on the proverb*, pp. 122–139. New York: Garland.)

Sejnowski, T. J., & Churchland, P. S. (1989). Brain and cognition. In M. I. Posner (Ed.), *Foundations of cognitive science* (pp. 301–356). Cambridge, MA: MIT Press.

Shen, Y. (1987). On the structure and understanding of poetic oxymoron. *Poetics Today, 8*, 105–122.

Short, E. J., & Evans, S. W. (1990). Individual differences in cognitive and social problem solving skills as a function of intelligence. In N. R. Bray (Ed.), *International Review of Research in Mental Retardation, 16*, pp. 89–121. New York: Academic Press.

Siebers, T. (1992). *Morals and stories.* New York: Columbia University Press.

Silverman-Weinreich, B. (1978). Towards a structural analysis of Yiddish proverbs. *Yivo Annual of Jewish Social Science, 17*, 1–20. (Reprinted in W. Mieder & A. Dundes, Eds., 1981, *The wisdom of many: Essays on the proverb,* pp. 65–85. New York: Garland.)

Simon, M. J. (1987). Use of the Proverbs Test in the assessment of competency to stand trial. *Psychological Reports, 60*, 1166.

Sloman, S. A. (1996). The empirical base for two systems of reasoning. *Psychological Bulletin, 119*, 3–22.

Small, M. Y. (1990). *Cognitive development.* Orlando: Harcourt, Brace.

Smith, E. E. (1988). Concepts and thought. In R. J. Sternberg & E. E. Smith (Eds.), *The psychology of human thought* (pp. 19–49). New York: Cambridge University Press.

Smith, E. E., & Medin, D. L. (1981). *Categories and concepts.* Cambridge, MA: Harvard University Press.

Smith, E. E., & Osherson, D. N. (1984). Conceptual combination with prototype concepts. *Cognitive Science, 8,* 337–361.

Smith, N., & Tsimpli, I. (1995). *The mind of a savant: Language learning and modularity.* Cambridge, MA: Blackwell.

Snodgrass, J. G. (1984). Concepts and their surface representations. *Journal of Verbal Learning and Verbal Behavior, 23,* 3–22.

Sonenschein, S. (1988). The development of referential communication: Speaking to different listeners. *Child Development, 59,* 694–702.

Sperber, D., & Wilson, D. (1986). *Relevance: Communication and cognition.* Cambridge, MA: Harvard University Press.

Sperry, R. W. (1974). Lateral specialization in the surgically separated hemispheres. In F. O. Schmitt & F. G. Worden (Eds.), *The neurosciences: Third study program* (pp. 5–19). Cambridge, MA: MIT Press.

Strub, R., & Black, F. (1985). *The mental status examination in neurology.* Philadelphia: Davis.

Sullivan, M. A. (1994). Bruegel's proverb painting: Renaissance art for a humanist audience. In W. Mieder (Ed.), *Wise words: Essays on the proverb* (pp. 253–296). New York: Garland. (An abbreviated version of the original, which appeared as Bruegel's proverbs: Art and audience in the Northern Renaissance, *The Art Bulletin,* 1991, *73,* 431–466.)

Taylor, A. (1931). *The proverb.* Cambridge, MA: Harvard University Press. (Reprinted twice: Hatboro, PA: Folklore Associates, 1962; Bern: Peter Lang, 1985.)

Temple, J. G. (1993). *You must walk before you can run: The multi-stage model and the primacy of literal meaning.* Unpublished doctoral dissertation, University of Cincinnati, OH.

Temple, J. G., & Honeck, R. P. (1992). Literal versus nonliteral reminders for proverbs. *Bulletin of the Psychonomic Society, 30,* 67–70.

Terman, L. M., & Merrill, M. (1973). *Stanford–Binet intelligence scale: Manual for the third revision Form L-M.* Boston: Houghton-Mifflin.

Tiegen, K. H. (1986). Old truths or fresh insights? A study of students' evaluations of proverbs. *British Journal of Social Psychology, 25,* 43–49.

Tooby, J., & Cosmides, L. (1992). The psychological foundations of culture. In J. H. Barkow, L. Cosmides, & J. Tooby (Eds.), *The adapted mind* (pp. 19–136). New York: Oxford University Press.

Tulving, E. (1985). How many memory systems are there? *American Psychologist, 40,* 385–398.

Tulving, E. (1989, July/August). Remembering and knowing the past. *American Scientist, 77,* 361–367.

Van Lancker, D. R. (1990). The neurology of proverbs. *Behavioral Neurology, 3,* 169–187.

Van Lancker, D. R., & Kempler, D. (1987). Comprehension of familiar phrases by left- but not right-hemisphere patients. *Brain and Language, 32,* 265–277.

Vygotsky, L. S. (1962). *Thought and language.* New York: Wiley. (Original work published 1934.)

Walsh, M. E. (1988). *A dual coding interpretation of proverb comprehension.* Unpublished doctoral dissertation, University of Western Ontario, Londo, Canada.

Watts, A. F. (1944). *The language and development of children.* London: Harrap.

Werner, H. (1955). A psychological analysis of expressive language. In H. Werner (Ed.), *On expressive language.* Worcester, MA: Clark University Press.

Werner, H., & Kaplan, B. (1963). *Symbol formation: An organismic-developmental approach to language and the expression of thought.* New York: Wiley.

Whaley, B. B. (1993). When "Try, try again" turns to "You're beating a dead horse": The rhetorical characteristics of proverbs and their potential for influencing therapeutic change. *Metaphor and Symbolic Activity, 8,* 127–140.

White, G. M. (1987). Proverbs and cultural models: An American psychology of problem solving. In D. Holland & N. Quinn (Eds.), *Cultural models in language and thought* (pp. 151–172). New York: Cambridge University Press.

Whiting, B. J. (1932). The nature of the proverb. *Harvard Studies and Notes in Philology and Literature, 14,* 273–307.

Whorf, B. L. (1956). *Language, thought, and reality: Selected writings of Benjamin Lee Whorf.* (J. B. Carroll, Ed.). Cambridge, MA: MIT Press.

Wickens, D. D., Dalezman, R. E., & Eggemeier, F. T. (1976). Multiple encoding of word attributes in memory. *Memory & Cognition, 4,* 307–310.

Williams, J. G. (1981). *Those who ponder proverbs: Aphoristic thinking and Biblical literature.* Sheffield: Almond Press.

Wilson, F. P. (1970). *The Oxford Dictionary of English Proverbs.* Oxford, England: Clarendon.

Wilson, F. P. (1981). The proverbial wisdom of Shakespeare. In W. Mieder & A. Dundes (Eds.), *The wisdom of many: Essays on the proverb.* New York: Garland. (Excerpt from Wilson, F. P., 1961, *The proverbial wisdom of Shakespeare.* London: Modern Humanities Research Association.)

Winner, E., & Gardner, H. (1977). The comprehension of metaphor in brain damaged patients. *Brain, 100,* 719–727.

Winner, E., & Gardner, H. (1993). Metaphor and irony: Two levels of understanding. In A. Ortony (Ed.), *Metaphor and thought* (2nd ed., pp. 425–443). New York: Cambridge University Press.

Winton, A. P. (1990). *The proverbs of Jesus: Issues of history and rhetoric.* Sheffield: Sheffield Academic Press.

Wisniewski, E. J. (1996). Construal and similarity in conceptual combination. *Journal of Memory and Language, 35,* 434–453.

Yankah, K. (1984). Do proverbs contradict? *Folklore Forum, 17,* 2–19. (Reprinted in W. Mieder, Ed., 1994, *Wise words: Essays on the proverb,* pp. 127–142. New York: Garland.)

Yankah, K. (1989a). *The proverb in the context of Akan rhetoric: A theory of proverb praxis.* Bern: Peter Lang.

Yankah, K. (1989b). Proverbs: Problems and strategies in field research. *Proverbium: Yearbook of International Proverb Scholarship, 6,* 165–176.

Zolkovskij, A. K. (1978). At the intersection of linguistics, paremiology and poetics: On the literary structure of proverbs. *Poetics, 7,* 309–332.

Author Index

A

Abbeduto, L., 241, 245
Abrahams, R. D., 28
Ackerman, B. P., 235
Agnoli, F., 97
Allen, J., 29, 202
Anderson, J. R., 106, 210, 248
Andreason, N. C., 29, 31, 201
Arewa, E. O., 16
Arora, S., 15
Ashcraft, M., 46
Austin, J. L., 17, 52
Ausubel, D. P., 118
Ayres, T. J., 97

B

Babcock, B. A., 28
Baddeley, A. D., 98
Barkow, J. H., 34
Barlow, J. M., 61
Barnes, D. R., 27, 28
Baron-Cohen, S., 222
Barsalou, L., 103
Baumgarten, F., 29
Beardslee, W., 4, 24
Bellugi, U, 223
Benjafield, J., 253
Benjamin, J., 123, 256
Benton, A., 216
Berent, I. M., 190
Berian, C., 118
Bihrle, A., 223
Billow, R., 230
Black, F., 258
Blackman, L. S., 244
Blumenthal, A. L., 61
Bly, B., 73
Bornstein, M. H., 69
Bountrogianni, M., 275
Bransford, J. D., 61
Briggs, C. L., 33, 98, 113, 248
Brooks, P. H., 241

Brown, A. L., 104
Brown, M., 60, 202, 253
Brownell, H. H., 218
Brugman, C. M., 77
Brundage, S. B., 258
Buhler, K., 238
Buhofer, A. H., 258
Burgess, C., 218, 266
Buss, D. M., 34
Butterfield, E. C., 244
Byrne, R., 112

C

Campbell, A., 202, 253
Caplan, D., 218
Case, T., 136, 157, 187, 188, 208
Chambers, J., 230
Champion, S. G., 24
Chandler, S. R., 265
Chang, T. M., 264
Chi, M. T. H., 251
Chiarello, C., 218, 219, 220, 266
Chlosta, C., 268
Chomsky, N., 269
Church, J., 230
Churchland, P. S., 264
Cichetti, D., 240
Cohen, L. J., 49, 269
Collins, A. M., 60, 263, 264
Colston, H. L., 60, 162
Cometa, M. S., 230
Corballis, M. C., 217
Cosmides, L., 34
Coste, E. L., 165, 166, 168
Cram, D., 16, 17, 18, 191
Crepeau, P., 21, 123
Cunningham, D. M., 202, 253

D

Dalezman, R. E., 93
Dascal, M., 65
Detterman, D. K., 240

Subject Index

A

Aphorisms, 13
Appearance–reality distinction, 234–235
Attention, 105–106
    automatic and controlled, 105, 197
    PLANTE model and, 243–244
    proverb subtasks and, 106
    strategies, 106
Autism, 222

B

Brain, 214–225
    basic considerations, 214–216
    clinical studies of damage, 222–223
    proverb studies and, 216–220
    split-brain, 217–218

C

Categorization, 101–105
    classical view, 102
    coverage concept in, 105
    exemplar view, 102
    probabilistic view, 102
    similarity and, 101–103
    theory-based view, 104
    transfer and, 104
Chinese room, 127
Classical categories, 59, 102
Cognitive ideals hypothesis, 137–145, 155–156, 159–161, 176–178, 191, 249, 271–272
    generic ideal, 137–138
    specific ideal, 137–138
Communication, 106–109
    manifest and substantive factors, 107–108
    nonlinear aspects, 107
Compositionality, 49, 80
Computers, 125–127, 248, 265, 272–273

Conceptual base theory, 95–96, 131, 134–136, 165–166, 208
Conceptual combinations, 269–270
Connection problem, 131
Connectionism, 263–266, *see also* Priming
Cooperative principle, 45, 53, 235

D

DARTS model, 220–222
Deduction, *see* Reasoning
Deep cognition thesis, 61
Dual semantic systems, 219, *see also* Brain

E

Egocentrism, 234
Expertise, 245, 251–252
Expressibility thesis, 93

F

Figurative language, 268, *see also* Literal language
Folk theory, 151
Foregrounding, 116

G

Generic-is-specific metaphor, 147–148, 150–151
Gestalt psychology, 55–56
Gorham's Proverb Test, 201, 216, 219, 253, 256–261
Great chain of being, 147–148

I

Idealized cognitive model, 156
Idioms, 16, 71–73
Imageless thought controversy, 169
Imagens, 162